Critical Inquiry and Problem-Solving in Physical Education

Edited by Jan Wright,
Doune Macdonald and
Lisette Burrows

 Routledge
Taylor & Francis Group

LONDON AND NEW YORK

First published 2004
by Routledge
11 New Fetter Lane, London EC4P 4EE

Simultaneously published in the USA and Canada
by Routledge
29 West 35th Street, New York, NY 10001

Routledge is an imprint of the Taylor & Francis Group

© 2004 Jan Wright, Doune MacDonald and Lisette Burrows (eds)

Typeset in Times by Keystroke, Jacaranda Lodge, Wolverhampton
Printed and bound in Great Britain by MPG Books Ltd, Bodmin

British Library Cataloguing in Publication Data
A catalogue record for this book is available from the British Library

Library of Congress Cataloging in Publication Data
A catalog record for this book has been requested

ISBN 0–415–29163–1 (hbk)
ISBN 0–415–29164–X (pbk)

Critical Inquiry and Problem-Solving in Physical Education

Critical inquiry, critical thinking and problem-solving are key concepts in contemporary physical education. But how do physical educators actually do critical inquiry and critical thinking?

Critical Inquiry and Problem-Solving in Physical Education explains the principles and assumptions underpinning these concepts and provides detailed examples of how they can be used in the teaching of physical education for different age groups and in a range of different contexts.

Topics covered include:

- Sport education and critical thinking
- Dance as critical inquiry
- Media analysis
- Understanding cultural perspectives
- Student-led research and curriculum
- Reflective coaching practice

The authors are teachers, teacher educators, policy makers and academics. Each shares a commitment to the notion that school students can do more than learn to move in physical education classes.

Jan Wright is an Associate Professor and Associate Dean of Research at the University of Wollongong, Australia. She has taught in the area of physical education for over 20 years and has been actively involvd in recent syllabus developments in Personal Development, Health and Physical Education undertaken by the New South Wales Department of Education and Training.

Doune Macdonald is an Associate Professor and Coordinator of Pedagogy in the School of Human Movement Studies at the University of Queensland, Australia. Since 1980 she has taught health and physical education in schools and universities in Australia and the UK and been heavily involved in curriculum development at the state and national levels.

Lisette Burrows is a Senior Lecturer in Physical Education Pedagogy at the School of Physical Education, the University of Otago, New Zealand. Since 1989 she has taught health and physical education and been actively involved in national curriculum review and moderation at primary and secondary levels.

Contents

Figures and tables

Figures

Tables

Contributors

Tom Bell is a senior lecturer in the Department of Exercise and Sport Science at Manchester Metropolitan University in England. Since 1991, Tom has been engaged in pedagogical research that has focussed upon teaching and learning issues connected with the development of knowledge and understanding that sports performers require to be successful competitors.

Lisette Burrows is a senior lecturer in curriculum and teaching at the School of Physical Education, University of Otago, New Zealand. She has published articles on gender, disability, developmental discourses in physical education and young people's perspectives on health. She is currently co-editing a text on teaching health and physical education in New Zealand. Her research interests are in two areas: youth understandings of physical activity and health and the social construction of physical education curriculum.

Hayley Fitzgerald is a research associate with the Institute of Youth Sport at Loughborough University. Prior to taking this position she worked for a disability sport organisation co-ordinating a self-advocacy project for people experiencing learning difficulties. As research associate, Hayley manages the evaluation of a range of national development programmes focusing on including young disable people in physical education and sport. She is currently developing a number research approaches that will enhance the involvement and participation in research by young people experiencing learning difficulties.

Michael Gard is a senior lecturer in dance, physical and health education at Charles Sturt University's Bathurst campus. He teaches and writes about the human body, gender and sexuality, the shortcomings of biological determinism in all its forms, and the use and misuse of dance within physical education. He is also working on the biography of a famous Australian ballet dancer. He is currently writing a book, with Jan Wright called *The Obesity Epidemic: Science and Ideology*, to be published by Routledge in 2004.

Trish Glasby is a lecturer in the School of Human Movement Studies, currently seconded to Education Queensland. Previous positions include Head of Department, State Review Officer (Health and Physical Education), The

Queensland Board of Senior Secondary School Studies and Curriculum Project Officer. She has published articles about the cult of the body, health and physical education curriculum and construction of competence within the teacher education practicum

Linda L. Griffin is an associate professor at the University of Massachusetts at Amherst. She has 27 years of experience as a coach, physical educator and teacher educator. She has given numerous presentations and workshops, completed extensive research, published articles and is a co-author of two textbooks focused on a tactical games approach, *Teaching Sport Concepts and Skills: A Tactical Games Approach* and *Sport Foundations for Elementary Physical Education: A Tactical Games Approach.*

Peter Hastie is a professor in the Department of Health and Human Performance at Auburn University. His area of specialty is sport education, having written numerous research papers examining the model. His latest text, *Teaching for Lifetime Physical Activity through Quality High School Physical Education* has been written for those who are preparing to teach in secondary schools. He has also contributed chapters to Silverman and Ennis' latest release of the books *Student Learning in Physical Education: Applying Research to Enhance Instruction.*

Anne Jobling is a senior lecturer in special education and a co-director of the Down Syndrome Research Program at the University of Queensland. She currently manages the Literacy and Technology Course – Hands On (LATCH-ON) which offers continuing education for individuals with an intellectual disability. Her major research interests are in the field of intellectual disabilities covering lifelong aspects of development related to motor development and health, as well as education and self-regulation.

David Kirk is a professor of physical education in the School of Sport and Exercise Sciences at Loughborough University in the UK and an adjunct professor at The University of Queensland, Australia. He has written extensively on physical education curriculum, sociocultural theories of learning in physical activity, and youth sport. Professor Kirk recently won the International Olympic Committee's Samaranch Prize for his services to the physical education and sport profession.

Doune Macdonald is an associate professor in the School of Human Movement Studies, the University of Queensland, where she co-ordinates and teaches in the Health and Physical Education Teacher Education program. In 1998 she won a Prime Ministerial Award for University Teaching for her work in this area. Her current research interests include investigating the experiences of young people and physical activity from a sociocultural perspective, teacher education and teaching standards, curriculum innovation change, and student resiliency. She is also part of a team writing the Australian Junior Sport Framework.

Cliff Mallett, PhD, health and physical education in Queensland schools for over ten years. He then coached track and field for the Australian Institute of Sport and was an Australian team coach at the 1996 Olympic Games. Cliff now lectures in the School of Human Movement Studies at the University of Queensland, where he coordinates a suite of postgraduate programs in sports coaching. His primary research interests are motivation in elite sport and evaluating the effectiveness of coaches.

Dawn Penney is a senior research fellow in the School of Sport and Exercise Sciences, Loughborough University. Since 1990, Dawn has been engaged in critical policy research, focusing upon contemporary developments in physical education. Dawn is co-author with John Evans of *Politics, Policy and Practice in Physical Education* and editor of *Gender and Physical Education. Contemporary Issues and Future Directions*.

Ross H. Sanders has held the Chair of Sports Science, at the University of Edinburgh since January 2000. He is the previous president of the International Society of Biomechancis in Sports (1999–2001) and founder and inaugural editor of the international scientific journal *Sports Biomechanics*. Professor Sanders was also the founder and editor of the Coach Information Service website (www.sportscoach-sci.com). He is a member of the British Olympic Association Performance Analysis Steering Group and has been involved with analysis of sports performance and dissemination of information to sports practitioners throughout career.

Deborah A. Sheehy is an assistant professor at Springfield College. She received her undergraduate degree from Union University in Jackson, TN, master's degree from the University of Memphis, and her EdD in physical education teacher education from the University of Massachusetts, Amherst. She has 13 years' experience as a physical educator and teacher educator. Dr. Sheehy is a member of both the American Alliance for Health, Physical Education, Recreation, and Dance (AAHPERD) and the American Educational Research Association (AERA).

Jan Wright is currently associate dean (research) in the Faculty of Education at the University of Wollongong. She is co-author of *Becoming a Physical Education Teacher* and has published widely in the area of gender, sport and physical education. Her most recent research draws on a feminist post-structuralist approach to explore the place and meaning of physical activity in the lives of young people. She is currently working with Michael Gard on *The Obesity Epidemic: Science and Ideology*, to be published by Routledge in 2004.

Acknowledgements

The PlaySMART programme has been developed by staff at Manchester Metropolitan University, under the leadership of Tom Bell. The support and involvement of staff at Wright Robinson Sports College and of the East Manchester Education Action Zone in this development is greatly appreciated. Project director Tom Bell can be contacted at: Department of Exercise and Sport Science, Crewe and Alsager Faculty, Manchester Metropolitan University, Hassall Road, Alsager, Stoke-on-Trent ST7 2HL, U.K. T.Bell@mmu.ac.uk

Sections of Chapter 9, 'Rich tasks, rich learning? Working with integration from a physical education perspective', are drawn from a paper by the author published in *Discourse* 2003.

Part I

Locating critical inquiry and problem-solving in physical education

Chapter 1

Critical inquiry and problem-solving in physical education

Jan Wright

Schooling for new times

Whether they agree that we are now in a period of postmodernity, late modernity or high modernity (Kirk 1997), social commentators do agree that we live in times characterised by profound social and cultural changes which are recognisable globally, but reach into the everyday lives of the individual. The nature of these changes is in large part attributed to enormous advances in technology which have allowed for the rapid processing and transmission of information within and across countries and cultures. On one hand, the greater accessibility of information from a larger range of sources has exposed different points of view and thus provided more space for the challenging of taken-for-granted truths. At the same time, however, the ubiquitous presence of television and other forms of electronic media has provided a context in which populations can be persuaded to particular points of view, which include ways of understanding health and the values and meanings associated with physical activity and sport.

For individuals, the information explosion, rapid changes in values across and between generations and social groups, and exposure to a wide range of values, produces a world in which knowledge is less certain and in which identities are no longer experienced as fixed and constant (Fernandez-Balboa 1997). These uncertainties extend to work, health, livelihoods, relationships and so on. Living in such times has effects on how young people think about and do schooling. In Britain, Furlong and Cartmel (1997) have linked these changes to the concept of the risk society (Beck 1992), in which traditional and institutional forms of social and economic relationships have become fragmented and individuals bear the responsibility and cost of shaping their lives. Rather than follow a predetermined linear trajectory, young people are now called on to balance their multiple involvements in study, employment, relationships and leisure; they are active in constructing their own lives. Wyn and Dwyer (1999) and others (Du Bois-Reymond 1998) call this a 'choice biography', emphasising the extent to which young people are making choices and following complex life patterns, rather than experiencing their pathways through youth as linear or preset.

The shifts in young people's life circumstances, and in their responses to these, which have been noted in the youth studies research, have significant implications for the provision of education programs and curricula that meet young people's needs. In the area of physical education, as in many other areas of education, there is a need to rethink the nature, type and content of a curriculum that has undergone little change since the advent of mass schooling in the 1950s. If schools ignore the contexts in which students live and their experiences, knowledge, capacities and concerns, they run the risk of being increasingly irrelevant for many young people.

Young people in western countries today also live in pluralist societies formed by the increased migration of peoples from a multitude of countries and cultures. Boundaries between cultures both within and across countries are more permeable; the mixing of cultures is not seamless, but produces struggles which are inextricably linked with both structural power and the power of particular discourses or meanings to define how particular cultural groups might be thought about and acted upon. According to Carson (Carson and Friedman 1995: ix), taking up the challenge of living in such pluralist societies requires an active engagement with the 'diverse ethnic, racial and national issues' which they present. In this context, The New London Group argue for a new notion of citizenship. Speaking primarily, but not only, of literacy, the group argues for a 'civic pluralism',

> where differences are actively recognised, where these differences are negotiated in such a way that they complement each other, and where people have the chance to expand their cultural and linguistic repertoires so that they can access a broad range of cultural and institutional resources.
>
> (The New London Group 1996: 69)

This may seem beyond the remit of physical education. However, physical education cannot and should not pretend that it can remain isolated from the social and cultural world from which children and teachers, nor from the broader social context which both shapes and is shaped by what happens in the name of education. Burrows' chapter in this book provides the example of how physical education has been radically reviewed to incorporate the world view of the Maori people in New Zealand. This model challenges other governments and physical educators to think radically about the role physical education plays in both reproducing and challenging the power of the dominant ways of thinking about and doing physical education.

Education in a postmodern world

Tom Bentley a social policy analyst and director of DEMOS, UK (2002), points to four key 'structural and cultural changes' of the last two decades which have affected and will continue to affect education. The first and last of these are particularly relevant to teaching and learning in school contexts:

- an economic shift towards service-based and knowledge-intensive industries;
- the creation of societies and communities characterised by social diversity, fluidity and networks where 'traditional forms of authority and social identity' exert less influence;
- major demographic changes and changes in the kinds of working lives that young people of today can expect, as compared to those of their parents; and
- advances in information and communication technologies (ICTs).

(Bentley 2002: 2)

According to Bentley (2002: 2), service-based and knowledge-intensive industries depend on innovation and creativity which, in turn, require workers who have 'a new set of generic skills and qualities, centred on teamwork, communication and the ability to manage one's own learning, alongside specialist and technical knowledge'. Like many other writers (e.g. Hinkson 1991; Kenway and Bullen 2001), Bentley also argues that ICTs will have a profound impact on the nature of teaching and learning. As learners have greater access to proliferating information channels and sources, 'alternative ways to sort, combine and evaluate knowledge in a sea of information' are required (Bentley 2002: 2).

The New London Group (1996) warns, however, that schools should not simply be about producing compliant docile workers. While not underestimating the necessity for schools to provide students with the opportunities to develop the skills necessary for access to new forms of work, the group (1996: 67) argues that schools should also provide the means for critical engagement – that is, 'the capacity to speak up, to negotiate, and to be able to critically engage with the conditions of their working lives'. As Thomson and Comber (2002) point out, many curriculum and policy documents do include goals and outcomes pointing to social learning, active citizenship and student participation. The full realisation of these outcomes for all students, however, has often been constrained by the competing agendas of accountability, performance management and standardised testing. This is not to say that opportunities do not exist in school education for active student participation and the inclusion of students traditionally locked out from responsibility, decision-making and relevant learning. Thomson and Comber describe a number of approaches, and point to the potential of health education and health promotion as sites which are specifically given an imprimatur to 'engage' students, to work with meaningful knowledge, to value their contributions and to engage in advocacy. Other characteristics of the approaches they describe, which are relevant to this book, are 'the importance of working in groups, (and) engaging in cooperative work on team-based action oriented curriculum' (Thomson and Comber 2002: 2).

It is clear from the arguments above that it is the responsibility of schooling to assist the student in developing skills and qualities and particular forms of learning practices, that will enable them to participate in a changing workplace, where specialist and technical knowledge will be rapidly superseded, and to participate in a changing and complex social world, where they will be constantly confronted with enormous amounts of information which may be contradictory and confusing. What are the generic skills they will require to do this and how are they acquired? In the literature there are frequently repeated references to 'deep learning', 'access to deeper, more enduring forms of understanding', 'the need to sort, combine and evaluate knowledge', 'the ability to manage one's own learning', 'communication and teamwork' (Bentley 2002), rich conversations that built on children's life world experiences and 'funds of knowledge' (Thomson 2002), the ability to critically engage with social meanings and so on.

Implicit in all of these concepts is an understanding that learning is not simply about the transmission of a relatively fixed body of knowledge, but about meanings as constructed through the activities of learners as they engage/interact with their environment. A second assumption is that the process of learning and knowing is more important than particular facts or even technical skills, since knowledge is not fixed and specialist skills may rapidly be come out of date. A third assumption is that to be active participants in a world characterised by social and cultural diversity people need to be able to critically engage with that world – with socially produced knowledge, with workplace expectations, and from the point of view of the authors of this book, with the values and social practices associated with physical activity and physical culture (Kirk 1997). They also need to be able to deal with the uncertainty of conflicting and changing knowledge and to make sense of such knowledge so that they can make choices about how they will act.

Defining terms

We would argue that critical thinking, critical inquiry and problem-solving together with related concepts such as critical reflection and critical engagement are some of the main abilities/capacities needed by young people in these 'new times'. The meanings ascribed to each of these terms in the academic literature and in general use in education contexts are not always shared by those who use them and in some cases are the subject of considerable debate. Critical thinking and critical inquiry, in particular, seems to be used almost interchangeably by two rather different groups. There are, however, discernable differences between those who tend to espouse the development of critical thinking as one of the main responsibilities of schooling and those who use the term 'critical' or 'social inquiry'.

Proponents of 'critical thinking' tend to draw on a philosophical tradition of 'logical reasoning' where attention is directed to problem-solving, reasoning and higher order thinking skills. According to McPeck (1981: 7), for example, critical thinking involves a 'judicious use of scepticism'. He suggests that '(l)earning to think critically is in large measure learning to know when to question something, and what sorts of questions to ask'. Critical thinking can engage a social dimension. For Rudinow and Barry (1994) and Brookfield (1987), for example, it involves 'unsettling deeply held beliefs' through the examination of one's own and others' beliefs, through challenging assumptions and claims to universal truths. Rudinow and Barry (1994: 20) argue that 'critical thinking is necessary if we are to make sense of what we hear and read, gain insight into the information and claims that bombard us, make discussions more illuminating, and develop and evaluate our positions on issues'. The emphasis, however, remains on the process, that is the teaching and learning of thinking skills, rather than on what kind of knowledge is questioned. In the context of physical education, Daniel and Bergman-Drewe (1998) argue that critical thinking can be learned through the teaching of games, specifically where a movement education approach is adopted. They also suggest that critical thinking can contribute to improved performance and to the acquisition of the 'practical knowledge' which is at the core of physical education. In this volume, the work of Bell and Penney provides an example of how the tenets of critical thinking have been used in the development of the PlaySMART programme in the UK.

In contrast to a focus on specific skills of reasoning, but still with an interest in students as enquirers, is another approach to critical inquiry which draws on critical and social theory for its rationale. Proponents of this approach are primarily interested in assisting students to examine and challenge the status quo, the dominant constructions of reality and the power relations that produce inequalities, in ways that can lead to advocacy and community action. This approach has influenced the most recent developments in physical education syllabuses in Australia and New Zealand. The syllabuses for both junior and senior secondary students in these countries have an explicit commitment to a 'socio-cultural' perspective, achieved through engaging students in critical inquiry. The various interpretations available around the term 'critical inquiry', however, have left considerable space for the way in which 'socio-cultural' is interpreted in practice. In this volume, the chapters by Burrows and Gard draw on this approach to explore how different forms of movement can challenge both traditional ways of thinking about, and of doing physical activity. They also propose that physical activity, as a site for the production of knowledge and social values, can be a fruitful context in and through which to examine those values and to recognise the means of their production. This theme is taken further in Wright's chapter where media sports texts are examined for the ways in which they can both (re)produce and challenge dominant social and cultural constructions of race, gender and generation.

Related to both of these approaches to critical thinking and critical inquiry and in some ways underpinning them, is an approach to teaching and learning in physical education that draws directly and explicitly on learning theory, and most notably the various forms of constructivist learning theory. For those drawing on constructivism, there is usually a specific interest in one or more of the following concepts: 'problem-solving', 'reflection', 'critical reflection', 'student-centred learning' and/or 'critical engagement'. Specific attention is paid to how students make meaning, how they construct knowledge and how this can best be 'scaffolded'. This approach is discussed in detail by Macdonald in Chapter 2 of this volume. Many of the authors in the volume (for example, Fitzgerald and Jobling, Griffin and Sheehy, Hastie, Mallett) draw specifically on a constructivist framework to explain their purpose and the specific strategies they engage to assist students' learning.

In the context of physical education

As Thomson (2002) and others point out (Tinning *et al.* 2001), schooling is about developing particular kinds of citizens, both explicitly – for instance, the 'active citizenship' described in many policy and educational documents and implicitly – individuals who conform to social values and contribute to society. Physical education has historically legitimised its existence because of its contribution to this enterprise and as the notion of the 'citizen' has changed, so too has physical education (Tinning *et al.* 2001). For instance, in Victorian England physical training was instituted in elementary schools to produce a healthy and docile workforce (Kirk 1999). In the twentieth century, physical education in the English-speaking world has continued to be concerned with the health of young people, but in practice until recently has primarily been a site where the learning of physical skills and knowledge about games, dance, gymnastics has taken place. Its concern has been the development of physical competence and/or the necessity of physical activity/exercise to good health. While this clearly remains a central concern of physical education, there are increasing calls for a physical education which is responsive to contemporary societies and cultures and a physical education that is also able to address broader cross-curriculum goals (in the UK) or curriculum frameworks (in Australia), and which is able to make a contribution to imperatives generated by these new times.

In addition, those areas of social life which are the concern of physical education are themselves radically changing. As the nature of work changes so does the nature of leisure. The forms and practice of sport and physical activity are increasingly influenced by commodification and consumerism and the shift away from team sports to individual recreational activities pursued in many different ways. It is argued (Tinning and Fitzclarence 1992) that if physical education ignores these changes it will become increasingly irrelevant not only to children and young people, but to those making decisions about what should be included in the curriculum and what not.

What contributions does physical education have, then, in the making of citizens in new times? Tinning and Fitzclarence and others (for example, Fernandez-Balboa 1997; Kirk 1997; Laker 2002), argue for a new approach to physical education which takes account of new times and the experiences and interests of young people who live in worlds often vastly different from those who have framed traditional forms of physical education. Kirk (1997: 58), for instance, argues that physical education programmes must 'start to both reflect and contribute more directly to popular physical culture'. He challenges the dominance of team sports sport in physical education and argues for radical changes to ways of thinking about the organisation of physical education, the kinds of physical activities that count and forms of pedagogy employed. He goes on to argue that together with new ways of engaging students in physical activity, physical education should also assist students in becoming critical of the practices associated with popular physical culture. He quotes George Sage to exemplify such an approach:

> Critical social thought applied to sport is not critical simply in the sense of expressing disapproval of contemporary sport forms and practices; instead its intent is to emphasize that the role of sport scientists needs to be expanded beyond understanding, predicting and controlling to consider the ways in which the social formations of sport can be improved, made more democratic, socially just and humane.
>
> (Sage 1992, quoted in Kirk 1997: 59)

Over the last 5 years or so, syllabus writers have not been unresponsive to the challenges posed by changing social and cultural contexts. In the remaking of physical education syllabuses in the late 1990s and 2000s syllabus 'goals', 'statements' and 'standards' have usually included references to the concepts of understanding diversity, problem-solving, critical thinking and critical inquiry. There has been a shift of emphasis to the student as learner, not only of particular forms of physical practices (e.g. motor skills), but as one who can engage in problem-solving, collaborative learning and perhaps to a lesser extent critical inquiry. There has been an expectation that physical education will also contribute to the wider educational goals of providing opportunities for students to learn how to engage with knowledge – that is, that physical education will engage students in activities which require critical thinking, critical inquiry, problem-solving and collaboration with others in the process of learning.

However, the ways in which these concepts have been taken up differ considerably both between and within countries and have very much depended on local political, economic and cultural circumstances. For instance, in the UK, the policy document *Sport: Raising the Game* was produced by the Department of National Heritage (which no longer exists) in a context where concerns about the apparent decline in participation and the lack of success of UK athletes in international competition generated a set of imperatives which saw a focus on sport resurrected in syllabus documents. In Australia and New Zealand, the integration of health education with physical education has produced a different set of expectations that influence what it is possible and not possible to do in physical education. In the USA, the absence of national curriculum makes it difficult to talk about commonalities in practices across states, although the National Standards for Physical Education (NASPE 1995) provides some guidance on current understandings of the physically educated individual from the North American position.

Despite these different contexts, there has, however been a discernible shift in most physical education syllabuses over recent years. This shift seems to reflect two key influences on curriculum planning and the kinds of practices that can constitute the physical education lesson. The first influence can be understood as an increasing emphasis on the social or the socio-cultural aspects of physical education; the second the influence of cognitive theories of learning which have come to dominate learning theory in education more widely. Neither of these are new; in particular a socio-cultural perspective has been argued for by those espousing a critical pedagogical position in physical education for some time (e.g. Crum 1993; McKay *et al.* 1990; Wright 1996). What has changed is that these approaches have moved into the mainstream of physical education and been incorporated formally into curriculum aims and goals and into ways of teaching physical education.

In Australia and New Zealand, a socio-cultural perspective now underpins most syllabuses particularly in the senior years. This has been particularly promoted and facilitated by the joining of health or health education with physical education (HPE). The socio-cultural perspective has been interpreted in a number of ways, none of which are mutually exclusive, ranging from a knowledge of social determinants (e.g. participation in physical activity) to advocacy for social justice as promoted in the Ottawa Charter. In Australia and New Zealand the integration of HPE has also meant that physical education for junior as well as senior students may include classroom-based lessons where students explicitly learn about physical activity, exercise and sport. In both the UK and Australia, national curriculum goals and curriculum frameworks which describe the goals or aims of schooling more widely have also provided an impetus for different ways of writing syllabuses and in the UK spaces for subverting physical education syllabuses (Penney and Evans 1999). For instance, the learning outcomes of the Queensland years 1 to 10 syllabus (Queensland School Curriculum Council 1999) are designed to assist students become lifelong learners. The kind of attributes articulated in this document link closely with those described above in relation to critical thinking, critical inquiry and problem-solving. They are specified as follows:

- a knowledgeable person with deep understanding (decision-making)
- a complex thinker (solve problems, make judgments about accuracy of information, engage in what later defined as elements of critical inquiry)
- a creative person (problem-solving – 'explore options and consequences of their choices . . . think laterally'
- an active investigator ('pose problems, develop hypotheses, initiate and answer questions')
- an effective communicator (. . . use individual and group performances to express ideas)
- a participant in an interdependent world

- a reflective and self-directed learner (can critically reflect on ways in which socio-cultural factors . . . ; critically evaluate assumptions and viewpoints and give reasons to justify conclusion and assertion . . .).

(Queensland School Curriculum Council 1999: 2–3)

The contribution of the Health and Physical Eduction Key Learning Area (HPE KLA) is specified in relation to each of these attributes. One example will provide an indication of how these are elaborated in relation to the learning opportunities designated for years 1–10 HPE.

Reflective and self-directed learner

Learners critically reflect on ways in which sociocultural factors shape personal identity, relationships and participation in physical activity, and consider ways to manage these influences. Learners investigating issues of health, physical activity and personal development reflect on:

- what they have learned;
- how they have learned;
- how they can transfer what they have learned to new situations;
- the impact of their actions on themselves, others and the environment.

They critically evaluate assumptions and viewpoints, and give reasons to justify conclusions and assertions. They plan, monitor the effectiveness of their plans, and use these conclusions as a basis for further action towards the promotion of health and personal development and participation in physical activity.

(Queensland School Curriculum Council 1999: 3)

In the UK and USA, physical education remains quite separate from health education and at least for most of high school, physical activity remains the primary medium for learning in, through and about the physical (Kirk 1997). Social justice perspectives are more likely to be incorporated into notions of appropriate behaviour towards others and sensitivity to difference and diversity. For instance, the document *Moving into the Future: A Guide for Content and Assessment* produced by the National Association of Sport and Physical Education (NASPE 1995) includes in its content standards competencies which relate to the social and interpersonal, as well as to movement and motor skills. For instance, numbers 5–7 of the competencies of a physically educated person are as follows:

5. Demonstrates responsible personal and social behavior in physical activity settings
6. Demonstrates understanding and respect for differences among people in physical activity settings.
7. Understands that physical activity provides opportunities for enjoyment, challenge, self-expression, and social interaction.

(NASPE 1995: 1)

The influential American physical educator Darryl Siedentop was more specific concerning the contribution physical education can make and should make to living in contemporary societies. He argued that students need to be 'involved critically in the sport, fitness and leisure cultures of their nations' (in Tinning 2002: 338) and that physical education teachers need to produce activity-enhancing environments to facilitate the development of physically educated citizens:

- To be adaptable and live with uncertainty;
- An interest in the meaning of activity to young people;
- Skills in working with people across institutional boundaries;
- To be competent leaders;
- To know how to engage children and youth in critical ways with the subject matter.

(Tinning 2002: 388)

In the UK, the emphasis on social justice issues is also less obvious until the senior years. However, physical education in the UK has a long tradition of learning through movement and the most recent iterations of this tradition are approaches such as teaching games for understanding (TGfU) and games sense (Thorpe 1984; and see Griffin, Chapter 2 in this book). At the same time these are underpinned by a notion of equity and social justice – so much so that there has been something of a backlash from traditional sport advocates who see such approaches as undermining and diluting the competitive team sport ethos and the capacity of the UK to compete in international competition. Nevertheless the UK *A-Level Physical Education* (Kirk *et al*. 2002) does provide space for a more critical examination of physical activity. It is underpinned by four principles: interaction of knowledge, making knowledge personal, equity and inclusion, and synopsis. These each provide opportunities for a critically reflective approach to physical education.

For instance, in relation to the principle, 'equity and inclusion', students are advised that it is about valuing and celebrating 'diversity and difference between societies and cultures in relation to sporting interests, traditions and behaviours' (Kirk *et al*. 2002: 11). Applying the principle of 'making knowledge personal' involves:

- discovering the links between what you already know or can do and the new information and challenges that you encounter;
- working out which pieces of information within a whole range of new knowledge you should attend to;
- becoming more aware of how you learn and being better able to learn from experience; seeing the relationships between the local, national and global contexts in which you live; and
- learning through critical reflection on your experience and the experiences of others.

(Kirk *et al*. 2002: 10)

Penney and Evans (1999) suggest that the national curriculum crosscurricular competencies also provide space for ways of doing physical education which go beyond the apparently limited scope of the sport-dominated national curriculum in physical education. They draw on Mawer (1995) to argue that to meet the national curriculum objectives 'a variety of teaching styes and strategies' are required. In relation to physical education this would mean 'addressing the development of "decision-making, problem-solving and person and social skills"'; this would in turn require that students take greater responsibility for their own learning and teachers take on 'a more facilitatory and mentoring role' (Penney and Evans 1999: 133).

Critical inquiry and problem-solving in practice

The following chapters in this volume are designed to locate specific examples of critical inquiry and problem-solving in physical education in their theoretical contexts. As has already been pointed out there is no one way of understanding the concepts of critical inquiry and problem-solving and no attempt has·been made in this collection to privilege one interpretation above any other. Rather, what has been important is that the frameworks on which each author draws are made explicit at the beginning of each chapter. Part I of the book is completed by Macdonald's chapter on learning in physical education which discusses in detail the pedagogical frameworks that underpin many of the following chapters.

In Part II of the volume, the chapters are primarily, although not only, concerned with the practice of physical education as it directly involves students engaging in physical activity. In some school systems, this will parallel physical education in the early and middle years of secondary schooling, in others it will have relevance across all years and we would argue to physical education as it is practised in tertiary education contexts. The first of the chapters in this section are concerned with the way students can be engaged in problem-solving through physical activity. For Griffin and Sheehy this is through teaching games for understanding, for Hastie, through the medium of sport education, and for Bell and Penney through the PlaySMART programme. Gard also examines the potential for dance as a site for problem-solving, but goes further to ask how dance might also be a site for challenging dominant social and cultural meanings. The chapters by Fitzgerald and Jobling and Macdonald both look to the possibilities of student-centred learning and in Macdonald's chapter the potential of physical education contexts for the implementation of an integrated approach to curriculum and pedagogy. Burrows uses the example of Maori models of health and physical education to examine the potential of physical education to incorporate and explore diverse cultural perspectives.

Part III reflects recent developments in physical education, particularly in senior secondary contexts, whereby physical activity has come to be understood as a personal and social practice about which information can be collected and examined for a range of educational purposes. This section of the book provides a number of examples of how this might happen, ranging from those which focus on possibilities of learning particular forms of knowledge within the field using a critical inquiry/problem-solving approach (see, for example, the chapters by Mallett and by Sanders) to those which question the knowledge and social relations associated with sport and physical activity (i.e. the chapters by Gard and by Wright). As a final example of practice, Glasby and Macdonald's chapter raises the issue of what forms of relations between teachers and students are needed if problem-solving and critical inquiry are to take place effectively. They argue for a negotiated curriculum where students are actively involved in decision-making about what they do and how they do it.

In the final chapter, Kirk locates the earlier chapters historically and in relation to contemporary social theory in education. He argues the need for such an approach, but points out the challenges which face those who would be innovative in the ways proposed by authors in this book. Each of the writers, however, demonstrate through their examples of their own involvement in secondary and tertiary physical education contexts that it is possible to think and do physical education differently and we invite readers to think themselves into the possibilities provided here to create enjoyable and challenging physical education experiences for their students.

References

Beck, U. (1992) *Risk Society: Towards a New Modernity*, London: Sage.
Bentley, T. (2002) 'What learning needs, towards educational transformation: a challenge of nations, communities and learners', A keynote paper presented at the Curriculum Corporation Conference, 27 May, Canberra, Australia.
Brookfield, S.D. (1987) *Developing Critical Thinkers: Challenging Adults to Explore Alternative Ways of Thinking and Acting*, London: Open University Press.
Carson, D. and Friedman, L.D. (1995) *Shared Differences: Multicultural Media and Practical Pedagogy*, Urbana and Chicago: University of Illinois Press.
Crum, B. (1993) 'Conventional thought and practice in physical education: problems of teaching and implications for change', *Quest* 45: 339–56.
Daniel, M.-F. and Bergman-Drewe, S. (1998) 'Higher-order thinking, philosophy, and teacher education in physical education', *Quest* 50(1): 33–58.
Du Bois-Reymond, M. (1998) 'I don't want to commit myself yet: young people's life concepts', *Journal of Youth Studies* 1: 63–79.
Fernandez-Balboa, J.-M. (ed.) (1997) *Critical Postmodernism in Human Movement, Physical Education and Sport*, Albany: SUNY Press.
Furlong, A. and Cartmel, F. (1997) *Young People and Social Change*, Buckingham, UK: Open University Press.
Hinkson, J. (1991) *Postmodernity: State and Education*, Geelong, Australia: Deakin University Press.
Kenway, J. and Bullen, E. (2001) *Consuming Children: Education–Entertainment–Advertising*, Buckingham, UK: Open University Press.
Kirk, D. (1997) 'Schooling bodies for new times: the reform of school physical education

in high modernity', in J.-M. Fernandez-Balboa (ed.) *Critical Aspects in Human Movement: Rethinking the Profession in the Postmodern Era*, Albany: SUNY Press.

—— (1999) 'Embodying the school/schooling bodies: physical education as disciplinary technology', in C. Symes and D. Meadmore (eds) *The Extra-Ordinary School: Parergonality and Pedagogy*, New York: Peter Lang.

Kirk, D., Penney, D., Burgess-Limerick, R., Gorely, T. and Maynard, C. (2002) *A-Level Physical Education: The Reflective Performer*, Champaign, IL: Human Kinetics.

Laker, A. (2002) *Beyond the Boundaries of Physical Education*, London: Routledge Falmer.

Mawer, M. (1995) *The Effective Teaching of Physical Education*, London: Longman.

McKay, J., Gore, J. and Kirk, D. (1990) 'Beyond the limits of technocratic physical education', *Quest* 42(1): 52–75.

McPeck, J. (1981) *Critical Thinking and Education*, Oxford: Martin Robertson.

National Association of Sport and Physical Education (NASPE) (1995) *Moving Into the Future: National PE Standards: A Guide to Content and Assessment*, Boston, MA: McGraw-Hill Education.

Penney, D. and Evans, J. (1999) *Politics, Policy and Practice in Physical Education*, London: (E & FN Spon) Routledge.

Queensland School Curriculum Council (1999) *Health and Physical Education: Years 1 to 10 Syllabus*, Brisbane: Queensland Publishing Services.

Rudinow, J. and Barry, V.E. (1994) *An Invitation to Critical Thinking*, Florida: Harcourt Brace.

The New London Group (1996) 'A pedagogy of multiliteracies: designing social futures', *Harvard Educational Review* 66(1): 60–92.

Thomson, P. (2002) 'Going to ground: stories of work, play and educational change', paper presented at the Curriculum Corporation Conference, 27 May, Canberra, Australia.

Thomson, P. and Comber, B. (2002) 'Options within the regulation and containment of student 'voice' and/or students researching and acting for change: Australian experiences', paper presented at the Annual Meeting of the American Educational Research Association
http://www.unisa.edu.au/csipic/publications/publications_Thomson3.html
(last accessed 24 January 2003).

Thorpe, R.D., Bunker, D.J. and Almond, L. (1984) 'A change in the focus of teaching games', in M. Pieron and G. Graham (eds) *Sport Pedagogy: Olympics Scientific Proceedings*, vol. 6, Champaign, IL: Human Kinetics.

Tinning R. (2002) 'Engaging Siedentopian perspectives on content knowledge in physical education', *Journal of Teaching in Physical Education* 21(4): 378–91.

Tinning, R., and Fitzclarence, L. (1992) 'Postmodern youth culture and the crisis in Australian high school physical education', *Quest* 44: 287–303.

Tinning, R., Macdonald, D., Wright, J. and Hickey, C. (2001) *Becoming a Physical Education Teacher*, Sydney: Prentice Hall.

Wright, J. (1996) 'Mapping the discourses in physical education', *Journal of Curriculum Studies* 28(3): 331–51.

Wyn, J. and Dwyer, P. (1999) 'New directions in research on youth in transition', *Journal of Youth Science* 2(1): 5–21.

Wyn, J. and White, R. (1997) *Rethinking Youth*, Sydney: Allen & Unwin.

Chapter 2

Understanding learning in physical education

Doune Macdonald

Introduction

> All teaching methodologies have their roots in particular learning theories.
>
> (Rink 2001: 112)

Our exploration of contemporary learning theories and their relationship to inquiry-based pedagogical strategies in health and physical education is largely informed by constructivist theories of learning that emphasise the active role of the student in building or constructing their own understanding and performance. Definitions of learning vary, and their foci shift from, for example, learning as acquired behaviours to learning as knowledge. Shared by many perspectives on learning are assumptions that learning stems from experience, is a relatively permanent change, and provides a new potential to behave differently (Tarpy 1997). While the language and frameworks for understanding learning are open to multiple interpretations and debate, depending upon the disciplinary perspective from which learning is approached (e.g. psychology, sociology, motor control, education, anthropolgy, cultural studies), this chapter will discuss behaviourist and information processing theories of learning as a prelude to social constructivism.

Social constructivists, or social learning theorists, focus upon the student's construction of knowledge in a social context (families, peer groups, school), with the individual making personal meaning from socially shared perceptions.

> The process of knowledge construction comes about as learners become encultured into the knowledge and symbols of their society. This view moves away from the position that children learn best when they self-discover to a position that advocates collaborative inquiry through which individuals appropriate information in terms of their own understanding of, and involvement in, the activity.
>
> (McInerney and McInerney 2002: 4)

Given constructivists consider that knowledge is not 'out there' to be acquired, this learning theory has implications for not only what is learned, but also how it is to be learned (Rink 1999). There is an assumption that where there is a focus on the use and transfer of problem-solving skills with students as 'the prime movers in the learning process, . . . content is more meaningful, is learned more easily, and pupil motivation is consequently high' (Mawer 1999: 91). Clearly, there are implications with this approach for teachers' work and how they position themselves within the teaching–learning process, as well as school structures and resources.

Rovegno and Kirk (1995) outline the long tradition of social constructivist practices in physical education from the work of Rudolf Laban with movement education in the 1960s to its diminishing influence throughout the 1980s and onwards. A text, edited by Silverman and Ennis in 1996, entitled *Student Learning in Physical Education*, indicates that the learning theories and issues that came to dominate physical education from the 1970s had a strong emphasis on information processing underpinned by the proliferation of the biophysical movement sciences. Subsequently, Kirk and Macdonald (1998) have argued that the legacies of constructivism should be revisited by policy-makers and teachers in health and physical education given the social and educational imperatives for critical and inquiry-based learning as outlined in Chapter 1.

The following sections will briefly outline key ideas of behaviourist and information-processing theories of learning in order to provide a platform to compare and contrast the subsequent elaboration of social constructivist principles. It should, however, be noted that there is a place within inquiry-based pedagogies to draw upon these learning theories and their associated practices (Renshaw 2002). The chapter then turns to two other key issues for contemporary learning in physical education, the impact of information and communication technologies, and the construction of supportive environments for learning. Each section is cross-referenced to subsequent chapters that springboard from aspects of learning theories and bring the associated, inquiry-based pedagogies to life.

Behaviourism

Behaviourism emphasises the external environment in shaping students' behaviours in contrast to social constructivists who value the interaction between the learner and their social context. Behaviourists argue that human learning is determined primarily by the environment and has 'grown out of the tradition that knowledge of the natural world derived from the senses can lead to rational thought and understanding' (Christensen 2001: 17). It contrasts earlier theories of intelligence and learning potential being innate and hereditary. Underpinning behaviourism are two forms of conditioning: classical where a particular stimuli (e.g. a PE teacher's tendency to admonish the slower runners in a class) produces a conditioned response (e.g. students feel sick on PE days), and instrumental or operant where if the behaviour is rewarded (e.g. PE teacher praises a student for volunteering an answer in class) then the behaviour will increase (e.g. student chooses to answer more questions). Therefore, this theory suggests that teachers need to reward and reinforce appropriate behaviours with a view to shaping learning.

Researchers such as Pavlov, Thorndike and Skinner have been associated with the development of behavioural concepts such as reinforcement, punishment and programmed instruction. In turn, these concepts have become teaching strategies that underpin direct instruction which is a highly structured approach to teaching characterised by teacher presentation and modelling, and student practice with feedback (McInerney and McInerney 2002). With direct instruction as a behavioural strategy, teachers typically direct the learning process by:

- selecting what unit is to be taught and when;
- developing explicit steps to learning such as game skills, preceding mini-games, through to strategies and then whole game play;
- ensuring mastery at each stage of the prescribed learning through ongoing assessment;
- providing specific corrective feedback in line with preconceptions of expertise;
- providing adequate and systematic practice.

Worldwide, educators have argued that while direct instruction may be useful for some learners, some forms of learning, and some content, it does not articulate with educational priorities that seek to develop new citizens with new knowledge and skills for new times (Department of Education, Science and Training 2003). Rink (2001) argues that in recent times, physical education has seen a resurgence of the teaching methods 'wars' with direct instruction criticised for its teacher-centred, transmission-oriented and cognitively less demanding tasks. Even those who criticise social constructivism (e.g. Phillips 1995) see value in learning approaches that stress the active role students play in constructing knowledge, the social and developmental nature of learning, the social organisation of knowledge, and that multiple learnings may occur at any one time (Kirk and Macdonald 1998).

Information processing and the role of knowledge in thinking and learning

Information-processing theory argues that the learner actively selects, organises and integrates incoming knowledge and experience with existing knowledge to create new knowledge and understanding. Proponents of this theory criticise behaviourism as positioning the child 'as the passive recipient of environmental forces which were determined either by random events or deliberate manipulation by powerful adults' (Christensen 2001: 25) and giving the teacher undue systematic control over the environment. Information-processing theorists seek to explain the human capacity to understand, solve problems and learn through cognitive research derived from psychological traditions.

Information-processing therefore attempts to 'look inside' the minds of learners to explain the process of learning. It is not only concerned with mental inputs and outputs, but also 'how the learner selects, organises and integrates incoming experience with existing knowledge, and the functioning of meta-mental processes in this' (McInerney and McInerney 2002: 74). In seeking to enhance effective learning, the information processing model has addressed questions of memory (encoding, attention and retrieval), the significance of meaningful information and prior knowledge, and strategies to help learning (e.g. chunking, self-questioning, coding and classifying, concept mapping). The information-processing model has helped physical educators focus on the learner and how their learning can be best managed in terms of, for example: how much can the learner absorb in a discussion on strategies, how should practice be arranged to refine a serve, or how can the Crebb's cycle be scaffolded?

Much of this research has been informed by distinctions between novice and expert performers that suggest:

- performance and problem-solving of complex tasks is enhanced by rich, domain-specific knowledge
- domain-specific knowledge is more meaningful if it is stored, not as isolated pieces of information, but as larger chunks of inter-related ideas and concepts
- expert problem-solvers think about what the problem means and draw on underlying principles
- performance and problem-solving draw on both declarative knowledge (knowledge of facts, theories and objects) and procedural knowledge (skills and procedures that a learner knows how to perform).

(Abernethy *et al.* 1994)

Gagne *et al.* (1993: 232) conclude from their research that 'experts see patterns missed by novices, use these patterns to develop conceptual representations of problems, and use these representations to quickly assess and execute domain-specific skills and strategies'.

The role of teachers in this approach is to assist students to recognise, identify, describe and ultimately learn expert behaviours associated with procedural (how) and declarative (what) knowledge. The student is active in terms of their consent and effort, and the existing knowledge that they bring to learning, and the teacher is active in structuring learning experiences, providing meaningful feedback, modelling and explanations, still using somewhat direct instructional techniques (Rink 2001). Thus, learning is a dynamic and individual process that occurs through the teacher coming to understand the knowledge base of individual learners and expanding upon this through the development of facts, theories, skills, procedures and strategies.

The dimension of active learning within information processing has been represented as: 'I see – I forget, I hear – I remember, I do – I understand' (Cotton

1995: 110). Active learning maintains students' interest and arousal through: increased attention; more effective long-term memory through a sense of personal ownership of the new knowledge; increased student responsibility; the teacher meeting individual needs through a facilitation process; and the student being encouraged to learn how to learn. As explained by Rink (2001), student motivation is a key to engagement within this learning theory in that higher levels of motivation should lead to higher levels of processing. Physical educators who structure their units around problems or challenges such as how to throw a javelin further or increase stability in a dismount must take care in matching the problem to the learner. Some other considerations are the amount of additional time it takes, for example, to decide upon the actions to be taken, act, debrief and reflect. Scharle and Szabo (2000) describe successful learners as those who accept that their own efforts are crucial in the learning process, are willing to co-operate with the teacher and other learners, consciously seek learning opportunities, and monitor their own progress. Clearly intrinsic motivation is a prerequisite for taking responsibility for learning as is self-confidence and skills in cooperation, group decision-making, delegation and cohesion.

Knowledge about one's own declarative and procedural knowledge, metacognitive knowledge, has been a significant feature of the information processing approach to learning (Dunlosky 1998). Metacognitive knowledge develops through interactions between a student's past experience, interactions with peers and teachers, and input from the environment, and serves to remind the learner of how they learn. For example, in physical education asking students to keep a record of the steps they took in their creation of an aerobics routine or how they have come to understand the body's energy systems heightens awareness of their personal learning processes. Too often in physical education, students can focus upon performance and lose sight of the purpose of the task or the learning processes that underpin its refinement (Luke and Hardy 1999). Dunlosky (1998: 377) claims that, '(h)aving students provide explanations for what they are doing when solving a problem can enhance their performance'. Metacognition may be closely aligned to reflection and self-directed learning, concepts that will be developed further in Chapters 4 and 11 in this volume.

Attention to learning or cognitive styles has also derived from the information processing model. Riding (2002) describes cognitive style as a student's preferred and habitual way of organising and representing information. He approaches cognitive styles in two basic ways: whether a learner prefers to take a whole view or see things in parts and whether they are outgoing and verbal or prefer to reflect inwardly. Within an information-processing paradigm, it is understood that people learn best 'when the structure of the material and its mode of presentation matches their cognitive style' (Riding 2002: ix).

Social constructivism and socio-cultural view of learning

Social constructivist theories of learning provide ways of understanding and justifying the place and potential of student-centred approaches to teaching and learning, such as critical thinking, critical inquiry and problem-based learning. As already explained, central issues in constructivist views are that:

*   learning is an active process that is controlled by the learner rather than the teacher;
*   as a result of task engagement a learner builds their unique mental representations;
*   mental structures are shaped by personal perceptions and information processing; and
*   students' knowledge and constructs are considered as legitimate.

There have been criticisms that these views of learning can dismiss the role of the teacher and celebrate the isolated individual's knowledge rather than that of intellectual communities.

> The idea that students' learning is not just a matter of building new knowledge structures, but is part of a process of developing the concepts and under-standings that a community of thinkers share, resolves the problem of isolated, subjective and relative knowledge.
>
> (Christensen 2001: 68)

This thinking is reflected in social constructivism, and has been associated with other terms, such as the sociocultural model of learning, situated learning and situated cognition. It recognises that, if knowledge is constructed in and by societies, and that, if learning is essentially social in nature, then the 'teacher's role becomes one of negotiation and provision of guidance through shared social experience' (Christensen 2001: 69). Social constructivism, therefore, offers physical education a 'matchmaking' role 'by bringing together learning and community' (Renshaw 2002: 3). Therefore, when practised the learning process involves individual and group work, and learning within and beyond the school community using new and varied approaches (e.g. increased use of technology, community-based projects). The foci of learning question the taken-for-granted 'truths' of teachers, texts and sedimented practices (see Chapter 12 on the use of technology in physical education) and generate new ways to view the world.

Much of the work in socially-shared cognition is based upon the Russian psychologist's Lev Vygotsky's (1896–1934) interest in complex human thought, communication and language, together with more recent input from anthropol-ogy and cultural studies (Renshaw 2002). Vygotsky argued the learning process was an appropriation of culturally relevant behaviour. Within Vygotsky's social constructivist perspective, learning is the transformation of basic, biologically determined processes into higher psychological functions through socialisation and education. The tools in this process are pens, paper, computers, videocameras, etc., that provide the means with which to act upon the world and thereby facilitate the extension of knowledge (McInerney and McInerney 2002). Tools are recruited within particular social structures (e.g. school, family, community groups, sports clubs) and in conjunction with 'language' systems (e.g. numerical counting, musical notations, movement patterns, strategic play). As individuals participate in the collective culture with their peers, learning takes the form of:

> a process through which we become one with the collective through carrying out personal activity in collaboration with other people. . . . [C]ognitive development is not so much the unfolding of mental schemes within the individual as the unfolding of cognitive understandings of social beings within social contexts.
>
> (McInerney and McInerney 2002: 45)

From this perspective, students interact with teachers, peers and parents to mediate learning and, where possible, self-manage their learning. A teacher's task can be to scaffold suggested directions, questions, or resources in a way that offers guidance towards a clear goal or outcome. This commitment raises important questions about the physical education teacher's readiness to have students moving along multiple learning pathways, requiring the support of a breadth of resources, or achieving different 'ends'. It may also challenge how students see themselves as learners in that learning is no longer private, individual, prescribed and ends-oriented with content that is accepted as 'truth'. Experience has suggested that teachers need to recognise the pitfalls in these new roles and move towards inquiry-based approaches cautiously (see, for example, Chapter 9 on 'rich tasks').

As will be outlined in Chapter 5, cooperative learning, initially developed by Johnson and Johnson (1975), is a pedagogical strategy that arose from social constructivist theories and underpins many inquiry-based pedagogies. Key features of cooperative learning are the formation of heterogenous groups where members work towards and are assessed upon a group goal. For optimal cooperative learning, teachers and students need to work at establishing clear goals, cooperative strategies and scaffolded tasks suited to the ability and interests of the group. Physical education clearly lends itself to cooperative learning in performance tasks, such as dance routines or team games and their theoretical underpinnings (e.g. how can we challenge and change the gender relations in our dance performance? How can our team better match players to positions?). What should be valued in these contexts is not just that the students are working in groups, but that the groups are learning how to collaborate in, for example, identifying their learning trajectories, allocating roles and responsibilities, peer tutoring, criticising each others' work and resolving conflicts.

Dewey (1916) was concerned with 'what' was learned, as well as how learning was organised. In the context of critical inquiry, his interest in the 'what' was learned raises questions about who chooses the content, why is it chosen, and how is it engaged with by learners. Dewey championed the educational strategy of long-term projects in which students undertook activities and solved problems that were relevant and meaningful to their lives, although perhaps not always so relevant to the demands of the broader, adult community. The focus of learning is, therefore, a larger and more meaningful 'chunk' compared to the small step-by-step increments proposed by behaviourists (Rink 2001). The environment and the teacher help to guide the student or group of students to identify their own problem, task or project. Through such student-centred education, Dewey argued that as students gain experience in projects that are meaningful to them, they should interrogate 'facts', consider the social and political consequences of knowledge, and find new ways of coming to know (see, for example, Chapter 12 in this volume). To assist the critique of knowledge, Dewey argued that using metaphors (e.g. the body as a machine) helps students to see phenomena (e.g. the body) in a new light (Prawat 2002). Dewey therefore foresaw teachers playing very much a facilitatory or bridging role, whereas Vygotsky argued that the teacher should be more proactive in the management and direction of learning (i.e. build the environment that will lead to learning).

The environment/learning interface has been further explored in theories of 'situated learning' (Lave and Wenger 1991) which, as forms of constructivism, also attempt to shift attention from individualistic, 'in-the-head', approaches to learning to a focus on the social settings that construct and constitute learning. Situated learning offers critical inquiry in physical education ways to think about the relevance of knowledge (e.g. does this activity reflect that which is valued in the wider community?), pathways to expertise (e.g. how do professionals in this physical activity field develop their expertise?) and professional enculturation (e.g. what identities does this activity require that I adopt or resist?). Key concepts in Lave and Wenger's (1991) theory of situated learning are:

* learning occurs in communities of practice;
* the learner and the community are engaged in authentic and meaningful tasks;
* early in the learning process the learner is peripheral to that community;
* learning is mediated by the learner's identity and their relative power within the community;
* different learners gain differential access to the community's resources.

Kirk and Macdonald (1998) have proposed that the teaching games for understanding (e.g. Bunker and Thorpe 1983; Grehaigne and Godbout 1995) and sport education (e.g. Siedentop 1994) models of physical education can be better understood and further developed as inquiry-based pedagogies through the lens of situated learning theory. They argue that a situated learning approach leads physical educators to value the richness of games and sport, shifting their attention from skills and drills, to learning experiences that are more student-centred and community-focused (see, for example, Chapters 3 and 5).

The place of technology in learning

The concepts of learning through technology and learning about technology are currently having an important impact on health and physical education curricula and pedagogies. Technologies have the capacity to transform learning relationships and potentially support more innovative gathering, analysing and expression of content (Starko 2001), ranging from conducting complex inquiries into a physical performance (see Chapter 12) to providing access to and critique of media representations of sport (see Chapters 8 and 14). Used judiciously, technologies can assist students, for example, access a breadth of information that provides other ways of understanding an issue, efficiently store, access and analyse personal data or reflections, and/or produce creative representations of their ideas. However, the introduction of technologies needs to be scaffolded as with any new teaching practice.

Plomp *et al.* (1997) outline three stages in the introduction of new technologies. The first is the substitution phase where the same practices (content, pedagogy) occur using new technologies such as would occur where teachers might give students a research task in which the internet is used to access information. The transition phase follows where new practice begins to appear and well-established practices are questioned. Using video cameras to provide data for self- and peer analysis, rather than a reliance only on verbal feedback could exemplify this stage. The third, transformation phase is where technology enables new practices and some old ones appear as obsolete. In some schools and universities, 'attending classes' is optional if not obsolete as students move through tasks using, for example, emailing to outside experts, discussions in on-line chat rooms, downloading web-based resources and videostreaming images of their performances to their teachers. These stages suggest a range of ways that technologies will come to underpin inquiry-based learning across health and physical education contexts. The following chapters will be somewhat indicative of where health and physical education practices are along this ever-changing continuum.

Computer and associated information and communication technologies potentially provide a medium for learning consistent with active participation within a community of learners who construct knowledge jointly.

> A powerful computer environment needs to provide the tools for empowering learners to engage in cognitive struggle with a new learning situation, allowing them to take control of their own learning, reflecting on their thinking and on the consequences of the choices they make – all of which are factors in developing metacognition.
>
> (McInerney and McInerney 2002: 163–4)

More specifically, the inclusion of technologies in health and physical education has the potential to support active participation in the learning process through:

- enhancing the productivity of the learner through access to word processing, spreadsheets, data bases, etc.;
- empowering the learner to construct their own knowledge of a topic and thereby diminish teacher authority;
- developing intellectual and co-operative partnerships amongst groups of students; and
- catering to classroom diversity in learning styles, rates and interests.

Technologies can also impact upon the content of the health and physical education learning process through:

- extending and enriching the school-based experiences through, for example, multimedia, simulations, digital camera/computer interfaces;
- encouraging higher-order thinking skills and creativity through open-ended exploration;
- situating cognitive inquiry through tasks that are meaningful to the students.
                    (Derived from ACDE 2001; Laferriere *et al*. 2001;
                                    McInerney and McInerney 2002)

If supported with the appropriate pedagogical strategies as indicated above, Johnson and Johnson (1996) conclude from their research that computer-assisted, cooperative inquiry promotes higher quantity and quality of daily achievement, greater mastery of factual information, greater ability to apply or challenge factual information, and greater success in problem-solving.

In concert with these opportunities are cautions from the perspectives of quality learning and critical inquiry. On-line tasks need to be supported by structured search procedures and communication strategies and underpinned by prerequisite knowledge and skills to confidently use the technologies, rather than an abandoning of the student to impersonal or inflexible e-learning. Measures should also be taken to ensure that the rapid scanning and collating of information does not undermine original and in-depth thinking. Further, critical questions need to be asked, such as who has produced this technology/information and whose interests does it serve.

Supportive learning environments

Different learning theories generate different emphases as to what constitutes a supportive environment for students. For behaviourists a supportive environment might mean the security of a well-ordered classroom with high teacher praise. In contrast, social constructivists would value a democratic and cooperative learning environment. Darling-Hammond (1997: 105) argues that '(s)ecuring greater student learning will ultimately depend on our developing more skilful teaching and more supportive schooling'. The work of the Gatehouse Project in Australia is helpful in empirically identifying some key elements of a supportive learning environment at the school level. Through longitudinal work in school change processes, the project has identified that learning is optimised when it is underpinned by:

- security – members of a school community need to feel safe, both physically safe and safe to be and express themselves
- communication – staff and students have strategies for building social connectedness
- positive regard – full participation in school activities that is valued and acknowledged.

(Glover *et al.* 1998)

Proponents of critical inquiry have expectations that a learning environment not only embraces positive and inclusive school/classroom climate and structures, but also has a strong agenda for social change. Darling-Hammond in her 1997 text *The Right to Learn* takes a critical perspective on the environment that underpins meaningful learning and articulates it as:

- active in-depth learning
- emphasis on authentic performance
- attention to development
- appreciation for diversity
- opportunities for collaborative learning
- collective perspectives across the school
- structures for caring
- support for democratic learning
- connections to family and community.

At the classroom level the Queensland School Reform Longitudinal Project (QSRLP), developed from the USA authentic pedagogy project (Newmann and Associates 1996), studied over 1000 classes and identified twenty 'productive pedagogies'. These clustered around intellectual quality, connectedness, supportive classroom environment and the recognition of difference (Lingard *et al.* 2000; QSRLP 1999). The findings have extended our understanding of supportive classroom environments by emphasising the centrality of students' decision-making with respect to what and how tasks might be undertaken, self-regulated co-operative behaviours, the social support required for students to take risks in their learning and the importance of quality performance criteria (http://education. qld.gov.au/corporate/newbasics). As highlighted in several of the chapters (see, for example, Chapters 7, 13 and 14), inquiry-based pedagogies are frequently concerned with student decision-making and challenging the status quo and we argue that inquiry-based learning needs to go hand-in-hand with a supportive learning environment that both supports and extends the learner.

More specifically a health and physical education program that supports critical inquiry at the classroom level, and in doing so contributes to a positive school environment, would include explicit attention to and addressing of diversity, social justice and the maintenance of a supportive environment (Australian Education Council 1994). Diversity considerations account for social, cultural, biological and economic factors that can shape students' performances, body image, physical activity preferences and participation patterns, health opportunities, etc. Social justice ties directly to the questions of critical inquiry as a lens for understanding structures and practices that create disadvantage in access to health, physical activity and recognition of performances. A physically and socially supportive environment promotes health and physical activity safely, sensitively and co-operatively. These principles for a positive learning environment are particularly important in the context of health and physical education in which many of the questions addressed relate to personal beliefs, customs, opportunities and attitudes that can vary widely among learners (New Zealand Ministry of Education 1999).

Conclusion

Internationally, there is talk of new learning in a context in which knowledge is highly situated, rapidly changing, and diverse. Good learners in the new times outlined in Chapter 1 will be:

- assisted and self-directed;
- flexible;
- collaborative;
- good teachers;
- good communicators;
- of open sensibility;
- intelligent in more than one way;
- broadly knowledgeable.

(Australian Council of Deans of Education 2001: 87–8)

While theories of learning outlined earlier in this chapter all have contributed, in differing ways and to differing extents, to the pedagogies that can shape critical inquiry, the social constructivist view is particularly important to current notions of new learning (Rink 2001).

Recently, there has been scepticism as to whether any one learning theory or perspective can capture the complexity of learning (Mowrer and Klein 2001; Rink 2001). For example, in the conclusion of a monograph on learners' domain-specific knowledge, Rink and Griffin suggest that information processing and situated learning:

should not be viewed as separate entities as they so often have been (i.e. information processing that deals only with stored memory and situated learning that examines knowledge in action), but rather that the interplay between individuals and the environment is important.

(Rink and Griffin 2001: 405)

In closing, we should reiterate that while some of the language and frameworks of learning theories are contested, the ideas within can provide useful backdrops to the innovative, inquiry-based approaches to teaching and learning elaborated in the chapters to follow.

References

Abernethy, B., Burgess-Limerick, R.J. and Parks, S. (1994) 'Contrasting approaches to the study of motor expertise', *Quest* 46: 186–98.

Australian Council of Deans of Education. (2001) *New Learning: A Charter for Australian Education*, Canberra: Australian Council of Deans of Education.

Australian Education Council (1994) *A Statement on Health and Physical Education for Australian Schools*, Melbourne: Curriculum Corporation.

Bunker, D. and Thorpe, R. (1983) 'A model for the teaching of games in secondary schools', *Bulletin of Physical Education* 19(1): 5–8.

Cotton, J. (1995) *The Theory of Learning*, London: Kogan Page.

Christensen, C. (2001) *Transforming Classrooms: Educational Psychology for Teaching and Learning*, Flaxton, QLD: Post Pressed.

Darling-Hammond, L. (1997) *The Right to Learn*, San Francisco: Jossey-Bass.

Department of Education, Science and Training. (2003) *Discussion Paper: Young People, Schools and Innovation: Towards an Action Plan for the School Sector*, Canberra: DEST.

Dewey, J. (1916) *Democracy and Education*, New York: Free Press.

Dunlosky, J. (1998) 'Linking metacognitive theory to education', in D. Hacker, J. Dunlosky and C. Graesser (eds) *Metacognition in Educational Theory and Practice*, Mahwah, NJ: Lawrence Erlbaum.

Gagne, E., Yekovich, C. and Yekovich, F. (1993) *Cognitive Psychology of School Learning*, New York: Harper Collins.

Glover, S., Burns, J., Butler, H. and Patton, G. (1998) 'Social environments and the emotional wellbeing of young people', *Family Matters* 49: 11–16.

Grehaigne, J.-F. and Godbout, P. (1995) 'Tactical knowledge in team sports from a constructivist and cognitivist perspective', *Quest* 47(4): 490–505.

Johnson, D. and Johnson, R. (1975) *Learning Together and Alone: Cooperation, Competition and Individualization*, Englewood Cliffs, NJ: Prentice Hall.

—— (1996) 'Cooperation and the use of communication technology', in D. Jonassen (ed.) *Handbook of Research for Educational Communications and Technology*, New York: Macmillan.

Kirk, D. and Macdonald, D. (1998) 'Situated learning in physical education', *Journal of Teaching in Physical Education* 17(3): 376–87.

Laferriere, T., Bracewell, R. and Breuleux, A. (2001) *The Emerging Contribution of*

Online Resources and Tools to K-12 Classroom Learning and Teaching: An Update. Final report submitted to SchoolNet/Rescol.
http://www.tact.fse.ulaval.ca/ang/html/review01.html (16 July 2002).

Lave, J. and Wenger, E. (1991) *Situated Learning: Legitimate Peripheral Participation*, New York: Cambridge University Press.

Lingard, R., Mills, M. and Hayes, D. (2000) 'Teachers, school reform and social justice: challenging research and practice', *Australian Educational Researcher* 27(3): 93–109.

Luke, I. and Hardy, C. (1999) 'Pupils' metacognition and learning', in C. Hardy and M. Mawer (ed.) *Learning and Teaching in Physical Education*, London: Falmer Press.

McInerney, D. and McInerney, V. (2002) *Educational Psychology: Constructing Learning*, Sydney: Pearson.

Mawer, C. (1999) 'Teaching styles and teaching approaches in physical education: research developments', in C. Hardy and M. Mawer (eds) *Learning and Teaching in Physical Education*, London: Falmer Press.

Mowrer, R. and Klein, S. (2001) 'The transitive nature of contemporary learning theory', in R. Mowrer and S. Klein (eds) *Handbook of Contemporary Learning Theories*, Mahwah, NJ: Lawrence Erlbaum.

Newmann, F. and Associates (1996) *Authentic Achievement: Restructuring Schools for Intellectual Quality*, San Francisco: Jossey Bass.

New Zealand Ministry of Education (1999) *Health and Physical Education in the New Zealand Curriculum*, Wellington: Learning Media.

Phillips, D.C. (1995) 'The good, the bad and the ugly: the many faces of contructivism', *Educational Researcher* 24(7): 5–12.

Plomp, T., Brummelhuis, A. and Pelgrum, W. (1997) 'Nouvelles approches de l'ensiegnements, de l'apprentissages et de l'utilisation des technologies de l'information et de la communication dans l'education', *Perspectives* 27(3): 457–75.

Prawat, R. (2002) 'Dewey and Vygotsky viewed through the rear view mirror – and dimly at that', *Educational Researcher* 31(5): 16–20.

Queensland School Reform Longitudinal Study (1999) *Report of the Queensland School Reform Longitudinal Study*, Brisbane: Education Queensland.

Renshaw, P. (2002) 'Learning and community', *The Australian Educational Researcher* 29(2): 1–13.

Riding, R. (2002) *School Learning and Cognitive Style*, London: David Fulton Publishers.

Rink, J. (2001) 'Investigating the assumptions of pedagogy', *Journal of Teaching in Physical Education* 20: 112–28.

Rink, J. and Griffin, L. (2001) 'The understanding and development of learners' domain-specific knowledge: concluding remarks', *Journal of Teaching in Physical Education* 20(4): 402–6.

Rovegno, I. and Kirk, D. (1995) 'Articulations and silences in socially critical work on physical education: toward a broader agenda', *Quest* 47(4): 447–74.

Scharle, A. and Szabo, A. (2000) *Autonomy: A Guide to Developing Learner Responsibility*, Cambridge: Cambridge University Press.

Siedentop, D. (1994) *Sport Education*, Champaign, IL: Human Kinetics.

Silverman, S. and Ennis, C. (1996) *Student Learning in Physical Education*, Champaign, IL: Human Kinetics.

Starko, A. (2001) *Creativity in the Classroom*, Mahwah, NJ: Lawrence Erlbaum.

Tarpy, R. (1997) *Contemporary Learning Theory and Research*, New York: McGraw-Hill.

Part II

Critical inquiry and problem-solving in the middle years of schooling

Chapter 3

Using the tactical games model to develop problem-solvers in physical education

Linda L. Griffin and Deborah A. Sheehy

Introduction

Sport-related games, a predominant component of most school physical education curricula, have the potential to help students develop their problem-solving skills, as well as offering them an opportunity to collaborate with others in the learning process. Advocating that sport-related games can be a medium for the development of 'thinking' skills is not new (see, for example, Mauldon and Redfern 1969, when the same principles were advocated for under the rubric of movement education). However, until there was a wider acceptance that the role of physical education extended beyond the physical aspects of education to intellectual, social and moral aspects, little explicit attention was paid to this potential. This is not to say that many syllabuses and programmes did not make claim to these outcomes; they were, however, expected to be developed as part of a student's exposure to games, rather than through intentional planning and teaching aimed at developing the ability to solve problems and make decisions in collaboration with peers.

The approach to sport-related games described in this chapter is based on the assumption that games can provide contexts for students' learning that goes beyond technical skill knowledge, to include the capacity to problem-solve and collaborate through their roles as games players. Games are understood as dynamic situations which constantly present new or different information to participants, which in turn demands the capacity to make decisions in social situations (Griffin *et al*. 1997; Thorpe *et al*. 1984).

In this chapter, we will look at the ways in which the tactical games model, which builds on the original work of the Teaching Games for Understanding model (TGfU) (Thorpe *et al*. 1984), can provide an organising structure to help teachers develop games teaching that promotes more reflective and self-directed learners. Following this approach, the use of games as content in physical education moves beyond the learning and applying of technical skills (the psychomotor domain) towards an increased emphasis on cognitive development, as well as the social aspects of sport. Thus, a broader view of what constitutes a learner's performance, that is, one which moves away from game play analysis only, toward a more holistic view of the learner, becomes possible (Holt *et al*. 2002).

In this chapter, we will describe the theoretical underpinnings of Teaching Games for Understanding (TGfU) and the tactical games models, discuss the origins of and research on the models, outline the key assumptions of the tactical games model, present a conceptual framework and the pedagogical principles for teaching problem-solving and collaboration using the tactical games model, and provide an example of the conceptual framework in action.

The theory of teaching games for understanding and the tactical games model

To improve the quality of the learning experiences presented in sport and physical education settings, professional practice needs to be positioned within a relevant theoretical frame (Kirk and MacPhail 2002; Launder 2001; Rink 1996). Early writings on games teaching by Mauldon and Redfern (1969) res-onate with a constructivist perspective which places students in the centre of the teaching and learning process, that is, where students 'construct' their knowledge from a strong subject–environment interaction (Grehaigne and Godbout 1995). Specifically, we are talking about an approach which focuses on the student actively selecting, organising and integrating incoming knowledge and experience with prior knowledge to create new knowledge and understanding (McInerney and McInerney 2002). From a related perspective, research drawing on information processing theory indicates that knowledge structures internally represent the outside world, these knowledge structures are complex, and they can be changed under various conditions over time (Dodds *et al.* 2001). Knowledge is held to be primarily domain-specific with declarative, procedural, conditional and strategic components. Individual learners may simultaneously be highly knowledgeable about some domains and far less knowledgeable about others, even within a broad field, such as physical education. In addition, individuals in the same class will differ in their knowledge structures. Information-processing theory and research demonstrate some of the complexities of instructional environments that teachers must resolve to best facilitate student learning.

Origins of, and research on, TGfU and a tactical games model

Several educators, including Maulden and Redfern (1969) and Wade (1970) developed an approach to games teaching which puts the player (the students) at the centre of the learning process. During the 1970s and early 1980s Thorpe *et al.* built upon this notion and eventually developed the Teaching Games for Understanding (TGfU) model and the games classification framework (Bunker and Thorpe 1982; Thorpe 1989; Thorpe *et al.* 1984).

Bunker and Thorpe (1982) proposed TGfU as a shift from a content-based approach in the context of highly structured lessons, focusing on the development of techniques, to a more student-based approach which links tactics and skills in a game context. They believed that games provide problem-solving challenges for participants and they identified a range of common tactical challenges presented by 'families' of games. They suggested that by reducing the technical demands of the game through appropriate modifications, participants are able to develop an understanding of the tactical aspects of the game and then build on this under-standing and through technical or tactical practice progress towards the advanced game.

The original TGfU model presented by Bunker and Thorpe (1982) described a six-stage model for developing decision-making and improved performance in game situations. Stage one introduces the game, which in most cases is modified to meet the developmental level of the learner. Stage two encourages students to begin learning the need for rules, even if modified, to shape the game. Stage three presents students with tactical problems to help them increase their tactical awareness. Stage four presents students with questions and challenges to encourage them to explore their ability to solve the tactical problem (the decision-making process) presented by the modified game. Students are asked what to do (tactical awareness) and how to do it (appropriate response selection and skill execution). Stage five begins to link tactical knowledge with skill and movement practice. Stage six is the performance measure leading toward the development of competent and proficient games players.

The tactical games model (Griffin et al. 1997), derived from TGfU, advocates similar principles and includes a variety of levels of tactical complexity, as well as a more authentic framework for assessing game performance. Griffin et al. (1997) proposed a simplified three-stage model which focuses on the essential lesson components of the model, namely modified game play, development of tactical awareness and decision-making through questioning and development of skill (see Figure 3.1).

Recent research on games teaching has focused on the merits and impact of a technical versus a tactical focus to games instruction. This orientation has attempted to compare the tactical game first approach with the traditional technique first approach (Allison and Thorpe 1997; Mitchell et al. 1995; Rink 1996; Turner

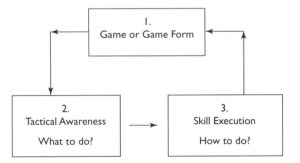

Figure 3.1 Three-stage tactical games model (Griffin et al. 1997)

and Martinek 1992). While some of the findings indicate increased level of enjoyment, motivation and tactical understanding of players in the tactical based environment, the results have been inconclusive about the superiority of either teaching approach. A major assumption in this type of research is that either a tactical or a technical approach is better for developing competent game players. This assumption indicated a limited understanding of the complexity, diversity and demands of games and creates an unnecessary dichotomy. It also highlights a misconception of the TGfU model with regard to the importance of both technique and tactics in competent game play (Kirk and MacPhail 2002; Rink *et al*. 1996). Despite the conceptual and research developments associated with the TGfU model, there remains a void in the articulation of usable strategies that can guide and integrate theory with professional practice (Chandler 1996).

Recently, researchers have offered possible ways to guide our thinking and research on games teaching and learning. Kirk and MacPhail (2002) modified and extended the original TGfU model by drawing on a situated learning perspective. Situated learning theory is interested in the relationships among the various physical, social and cultural dimensions of the context of learning (Lave and Wenger 1991). The situated learning TGfU model, therefore, advocates a need for explicit attention to the learner's perspective, game concepts, strategic thinking, cue recognition, technique selection and skill development. It is interested in the coming together of tactics and technique, and the notion of situated performance as legitimate peripheral participation in games (Kirk and MacPhail 2002).

Holt *et al*. (2002) re-examine the four pedagogical principles of sampling, modification–representation, modification–exaggeration and tactical complexity that Thorpe *et al*. (1984) introduced and they explain how these principles may be integrated with the original model. They also call for a need to explore the learner-centred feature of the model by suggesting future research that would consider the implications of games pedagogy for the cognitive, affective and behavioural domains.

Metzler (2000) argues for a move toward model-based instruction (e.g. cooperative learning, sport education, teaching for social responsibility, TGfU) and away from activity-based instruction (e.g. teaching volleyball, tennis, basketball, soccer, etc.) in the teaching of physical education and offers guidelines for research on model-based instruction. In relation to TGfU, he suggests the following research questions to begin model-based research: how effective is TGfU as a way to teach students situated skills and tactical decision-making, and what are the essential prerequisites needed by children to get full advantage of TGfU's features?

Rationale and key assumptions of a tactical games model

Proponents of the tactical games model (TGfU, game sense, play practice and concept-based games) believe that games are an important part of the physical education curriculum because they are highly motivating for students (Griffin *et al.* 1997; Thorpe and Bunker 1986). Most physical education teachers are familiar with the common question from students in sport-related units: 'when do we get to play the game?' This suggests two positions on the part of the students. The first of these is that they have 'been there, done that' and are bored with the same skills; they see the regime of skills practice as a constant reiteration of things they (or at least some of the most vocal ones) already know. Many students, as learners, approach a games unit, such as volleyball with prior knowledge about volleyball. In other words students have their own picture of how volleyball is played. The challenge for teachers is to facilitate the learning process by linking their picture of volleyball with new knowledge about volleyball (Dodds *et al.* 2001).

Research on the development of learners' domain-specific knowledge confirms the importance of studying the specific content of the prior knowledge (Griffin and Placek 2001). Findings indicate that students vary in the type and range of experiences, as well as the source of their knowledge. Researchers have verified that students not only need to be aware of their own knowledge, but they must also have opportunities to articulate and publicly share their knowledge if changes in their mental models are to occur (Wandersee, *et al.* 1994).

In requesting the game, the second position students take up is that games, as compared to skills practice, are fun! One reason games are more fun is that they have structure and outcomes which give meaning to performance which could be directly tied to situational interest. Situational interest is a multisource construct in which students report that an activity provides a sense of novelty and challenge, demands exploratory action and high-level attention and generates a feeling of instant enjoyment (Deci 1992). Chen (2001) points out that situational influence may have a stronger impact on students' motivation to learn than goal orientations. The decision-making process of games which precedes the use of skills and movement execution, we argue, places students into situations that are developmentally appropriate. At the same time, these demand exploratory action and high levels of attention. As a result, games help students develop a sufficient level of skillfulness so that they experience the joy and pleasure of games that will perhaps afford them continued motivation and increased competence to continue to play later in life.

Having provided a rationale for games as a valued activity, there are three major assumptions about games that underpin the tactical games model. First, games can be modified to be representative of the advanced game form, and conditioned (i.e. exaggerated by rule changes) to emphasise tactical problems encountered within the game. The use of small-sided games helps to slow down the pace and momentum of the game so that there is a better chance for the development of game appreciation, tactical awareness, and decision-making. Teachers should view the small-sided games as building blocks to the advanced form, not as ends in themselves.

Second, games have common tactical problems, which form the basis of the games classification system and serve as the organising structure for the tactical games model. Advocates of the model argue that many games within each category have similar tactical problems and understanding these similar tactical problems can assist in transferring performance from one game to another.

Third, games provide an authentic context for assessment. Assessing students during a game is the most meaningful way for them to receive formative feedback and help focusing the learner's development toward skillfulness and competence as a games player (Corbin 2002). As is commonly espoused in physical education, assessment should be an ongoing part of instruction such that students are provided with continuous feedback for reflecting on and self-managing of learning. Proponents of the tactical games model argue that games teaching is dramatically enriched through the use of assessment, particularly when that assessment is aligned with instructional objectives (Griffin *et al.* 1997; Mitchell *et al.* 2003). For example, if improved tactical awareness is the goal of instruction then assessment should be conducted within the context of the game. Having students play games allows them the opportunity to reflect upon their decision-making abilities. To be aware of students' prior knowledge and its relationship to performance, teachers need to evaluate this knowledge (Placek and Griffin 2001). To this end, game performance assessment tools, such as the Game Performance Assessment Instrument (Griffin *et al.* 1997; Mitchell and Oslin 1999; Oslin *et al.* 1998) and the team sport assessment procedure (TSAP) (Grehaigne *et al.* 1997; Richard *et al.* 2002) have been developed to measure outcomes during game play.

Developing problem-solving skills using the tactical games model

The purpose of this section is two-fold. First, we will outline the role of the teacher as a facilitator. The tactical games model is a student-centred model in that the teacher facilitates the learning process. As the facilitator, the teacher sets problems or goals, by organising the game or game form, and students are given an opportunity to seek solutions to these problems. One of the basic premises of the tactical games model is that to become a good games player, students need to become good problem-solvers. Students need to be able to: (a) define the problem; (b) gather information about the problem; (c) identify the decision-making options; (d) make the decision; and (e) put the decision into action. To do this, students need to have many games-playing experiences to help them develop their problem-solving skills. The teacher helps the students explore possible solutions to the problem through questions, which then become the focus of a situated practice. The teacher also facilitates practice by either simplifying the game, or introducing more challenging game conditions, based on student abilities. In this way the teacher is working with the students' prior knowledge to develop new knowledge.

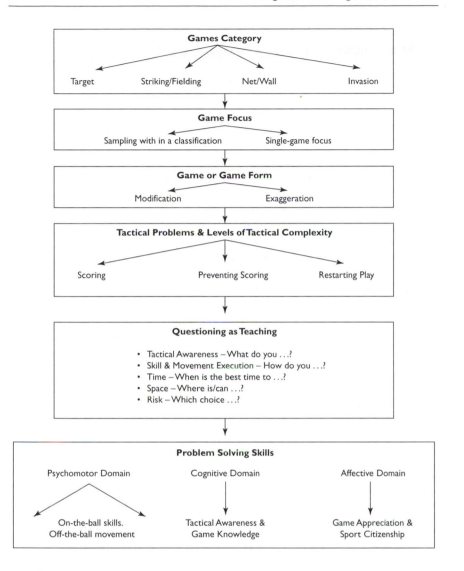

Figure 3.2 A conceptual framework for problem-solving using a tactical games model

Second, we propose a conceptual framework to help the teacher foreground problem-solving in the tactical games model (see Figure 3.2). The primary features include: (a) the games classification system; (b) game or game form focus; (c) the tactical problems and levels of tactical complexity; (d) game or game form modification; (e) questioning as teaching; and (f) problem-solving skills as outcomes.

The games classification system

At the core of the tactical games model is the games classification system, which is a category scheme based on similarities among the primary rules that define games (Bunker and Thorpe 1982; Griffin *et al.* 1997). Primary rules of a game identify how the game is to be played (tactics) and how winning can be achieved.

The classification system has four major categories that are positioned within the conceptual framework from left to right in an order of increasing complexity and labeled target, fielding/run score, net/wall and invasion games (see Figure 3.3). Target games are defined by propelling objects with great accuracy towards targets. Fielding/run score games are defined by primary rules that require one opponent to strike an object so as to elude defenders on the field. Net/wall games, such as tennis, volleyball and badminton, are defined tactically as propelling an object in ways that cannot be returned by an opponent. Games such as soccer, ultimate Frisbee, basketball and field hockey are tactically similar in that the objective is to invade your opponent's territory to score.

Classifying games provides students with a more expansive view of games and helps students identify the similarities of games that are usually considered quite different in terms of the specialised skills they employ. In using this model, teachers may explicitly teach students to transfer knowledge they may have about one game to another, simply because they are in the same classification. For example, it needs to be pointed out that volleyball is a net/wall game sharing tactical similarities with tennis and badminton.

Target	Fielding/Run-scoring	Net/Wall	Invasion
Golf	Baseball	Badminton	Basketball
Croquet	Softball	Tennis	Netball
Bowling	Rounders	Table Tennis	Team handball
Lawn bowls	Cricket	Pickle ball	Water polo
Pool	Kickball	Volleyball	Soccer
Billiards		Racquetball	Hockey
Snooker		Squash	Lacrosse
		Fives	Speedball
			Rugby
			Football
			Ultimate Frisbee

Figure 3.3 A classification system for games (Griffin *et al.* 1997)

Game or game form focus

In the context of the tactical games model, games refer to small-sided competitive challenges where there are an even number of players on each team (e.g. 3v3), while game forms refer to highlighted tactical situations, often encountered during a full version of the game, where there are an uneven number of players on a team (e.g. 3v2). Within game forms, tactical problems are foregrounded thereby allowing the students multiple opportunities to problem-solve and practise the appropriate tactical response (French and McPherson 2003). When creating games experiences (games or game forms), the teacher may organise the unit in one of two ways: (a) game sampling; or (b) single game focus.

Game sampling

The purpose of game sampling is to provide students with a variety of experiences that show similarities and differences among games (Thorpe *et al.* 1984; Griffin *et al.* 1997; Holt *et al.* 2002). The game classification system can facilitate the sampling process by providing a selection of various games with similar tactical problems, rather than the traditional selection of teaching one specific sport as a unit topic (Thorpe *et al.* 1984). For example, a teacher might want students to experience solving the tactical problems of setting up to attack and winning the point across various net/wall games, such as pickle ball, badminton and volleyball. To assist students' ability to transfer their learning from one game to another, the students can encounter and the teacher points out, when appropriate, the common tactical elements or problems in each of the three games.

Single game

The purpose of a single game focus within a unit is to provide students with an in-depth experience of the tactical problems and decision-making options associated with one particular game (e.g. volleyball). Selecting a single game focus for a unit in which the teacher holds a high level of content knowledge is strongly advocated for first-time tactical games model users. Either choice – game sampling or single game focus – provides a context for teachers to facilitate students' development of and effective use of problem-solving skills, however, to maximise the effect of the game modifications are necessary.

Tactical problems and levels of tactical complexity

Central to the tactical games model are the tactical problems presented by various games. Tactical problems are those which must be overcome in order to score, to prevent scoring, and to restart play. Having identified the relevant tactical problems a game presents, students need to solve these problems by making appropriate decisions and applying appropriate movements and skills. Again, many games within each category have similar tactical problems, an understanding of which can assist in transferring performance from one game to another.

In order to help teachers and students identify and break down relevant tactical problems, as well as associated skills and movements, Griffin *et al.* (1997) developed game frameworks. Two questions guided the development of the frameworks:

1   What problem or set of problems does this game present for scoring, preventing scoring, and restarting play?
2   What off-the-ball movements and on-the-ball skills are necessary to solve these problems?

For example, in net/wall games the tactical problems for scoring include: (a) setting up to attack; (b) winning the point; and (c) attacking as a pair or team. The tactical problems for preventing a score include: (a) defending space in your own court; (b) defending against an attack; and (c) defending against a pair or team. The frameworks develop the content for facilitating problem-solving. They ensure that students become familiar with the game and that skills and movements, when taught, relate to game context.

Levels of tactical complexity help teachers match tactical complexity with students' problem-solving skills development. Some tactical problems are too complex for novice players to understand. For example, in the net/wall game of volleyball teachers might anticipate that novice players would understand the necessity to set up for an attack, since it is by scoring points that games are won. Level one would include the basic skills of passing, setting, opening up and pursuing the ball, which are the skills and movements novice players need to play a basic small-sided game. On the other hand, level five teaches offensive strategies (e.g. 4–2 or 6–2), which require the introduction of a variety of defensive and offensive set plays. Playing large-sided games (e.g. 6v6) would also not be appropriate for level one novice players, but would provide excellent challenges for level five players (see Griffin *et al.* 1997). As students develop an understanding of tactical problems and appropriate solutions, the complexity of the game can be increased; that is, working with levels of tactical complexity affords teachers a way of teaching games in a developmentally appropriate manner.

We offer three ways that the teachers could develop appropriate progressions for increasing tactical complexity. First, students can move gradually from cooperative situations to competitive situations. For example, in a soccer unit, students would be asked to mark (guard) their opponent using a passive (less active) type of defence to foreground offensive. Second, students move from simple to complex with regard to skills, movements and game conditions. Again using soccer, to keep the game simple students are involved in a pass-only game in which they are trying to solve the tactical problem of maintaining possession of the ball. Finally, students move from individual (1v1 soccer), to small group (4v4 soccer), to large group games (6v6 soccer).

Game or game form: modification and exaggeration

Proponents of the tactical games model argue that all students can play a game if that game is modified to enable meaningful play to occur (Ellis 1986; Mitchell *et al.* 2003; Thorpe 2001). This may mean beginning with few skills, few rules and as few players as possible. Modified games or game forms, however, should be representative of the mature form and conditioned (i.e. exaggerated by rule changes) to emphasise tactical problems encountered within the game (i.e. changing the secondary rules) (Mitchell *et al.* 2003; Thorpe 1989). The following are five aspects of the game or game form that can help the teacher exaggerate a particular tactical problem.

1 *Rules*. Rules define what players can and cannot do in a game. Rules can be changed (the game conditions) to create a specific learning emphasis. For example, in 3v3 volleyball there might be a rule to alternate serve using a free ball toss. Alternating the serve using a free ball toss makes initiation of the game simple and highly successful and allows both teams an equal chance to receive serve.

2 *Number of players*. Small-sided games or game forms (3v3 or 2v1) slow down the tempo and flow of a game thus limiting the tactical complexity which, in turn, simplifies the decision-making process. They also maximise the potential for every student to be a decision-maker within a game or game form.

3 *Playing area*. Altering the size of the playing area or changing the size of the goal may help students focus on learning a particular aspect of the game. For example, in a 3v3 volleyball game, the court conditions might be narrow court (e.g. half of a regular size court) and lower net. Narrowing the court and lowering the net allows the students to focus on a small playing area.

4 *Equipment*. Modifying the playing equipment makes the students feel safer which allows for more successful execution of skills and movements. For example, students are more likely to attempt the forearm pass or dig in volleyball when trainer volleyballs are used.

5 *Scoring or modifying the goal*. Scoring allows the game to be shaped to reinforce practice. For example, in a volleyball lesson the final game goal might be to have teams earn points for containing the first pass on their side of the court.

Questioning as teaching

Questioning is a critical teaching skill used in the tactical games model and helps the teacher guide their students in identifying solutions to the tactical problem presented in the game. As facilitators, teachers will need to know when to use questions and when to provide answers. Literature on tactical games teaching has been consistent in emphasising the importance of high quality questions (Australian Sports Commission 1997; Bunker and Thorpe 1982; Griffin *et al.*

1997). The quality of questions is critical to problem-solving in a tactical games model and should be an integral part of the planning process. As indicated in Figure 3.2, these questions fall into five categories:

Tactical awareness	What do you . . . ?
Skill and movement execution	How do you . . . ?
Time	When is the best time to . . . ?
Space	Where is/can . . . ?
Risk	Which choice . . . ?

It is important to remember that each type of question is not necessarily asked during a single questioning session. The number and types of questions are determined by the teacher and are based on the readiness of the students.

Games, as content provide the teacher with endless opportunities to create opportunities for integration and interaction across all domains (psychomotor, cognitive and affective) (see Figure 3.2).

• The psychomotor domain consists of the on-the-ball skills (e.g. passing, setting and spiking) and off-the-ball movements (e.g. adjusting and covering) across games.
• The cognitive domain consists of tactical awareness (i.e. decision-making skills) and game knowledge (e.g. rules and communication).
• The affective domain consists of knowledge that addresses the various feelings and emotions students have developed about games.

We argue that it is the integration and interaction across the domains that have the potential to increase students' tactical awareness. Tactical awareness is defined as the ability to identify problems and their solutions in game situations. We argue that in identifying problems and their solutions, students learn to be better decision-makers.

A tactical games model with an emphasis on authentic performance, promotes an active in-depth learning setting for students. An underlying goal of the tactical games model is to appeal to students' interest in games playing so that they value (i.e. appreciate) the need to work toward improved game performance. Improving game performance we hope will lead to greater enjoyment, interest and perceived competence to become lifelong games players (Corbin 2002; Griffin *et al.* 1997).

Putting the problem-solving framework in action

Having explained the thinking behind our conceptual framework, in this section we will provide an example, by way of a scenario, of the decisions a teacher makes that put the tactical games problem-solving framework into action. The scenario is as follows. Using the conceptual framework (Figure 3.2), a middle school physical education teacher decides to further student understanding of net/wall games and chooses a single game focus on volleyball, since the students had completed a net/wall game sampling unit last year. The game sampling unit focused on setting up to attack and winning the point in pickle ball, table tennis and volleyball. The teacher knows that the students are novice players and selects scoring as the main tactical problem and determines the level of tactical complexity to be a level one.

The tactical problem for the first lesson is setting up to attack, with a lesson focus on base position and containing the first pass to set up. The 50-minute lesson begins with students involved in 3v3 games (a total of twelve students per court) with the goal of attempting to contain the first pass on their team's side of the court. The conditions of the game include a narrow court with a lower net, the game initiated from a playable, two-handed, overhead toss (free ball), an alternate free ball toss, rotate after each rally, and use up to three hits on a side. As the students play, the teacher observes.

After approximately 7 minutes, the games break down (meaning that students cannot direct consistent passes to the middle, the ball does not go over the net, etc.) and at that point, the teacher begins to ask students questions with the purpose of encouraging self-directed, reflective analysis of their game play. The following is a representation of a typical exchange, designed to foreground problem-solving skills within the psychomotor domain:

TEACHER: Were you able to set up for an attack? Why or why not?
STUDENTS: No. Cannot get the ball to thc hitter or spiker.
TEACHER: What do you need to do first to have the opportunity to set up for an attack? (tactical awareness)
STUDENTS: Forearm pass
TEACHER: Where must you pass the ball? (space)
STUDENTS: To setter or target, front line
TEACHER: How do you perform the forearm pass? (skill and movement execution)
STUDENTS: Medium body posture, feet to ball, flat platform, and finish to target
TEACHER: OK, let's practise the forearm pass.

(Griffin *et al.* 1997)

As illustrated through the questioning process, the students verbally identify issues related to solving the tactical problem of containing the first pass. Now that the students have identified these solutions there is a need to situate students in practice that rewards and reinforces good decision-making, not just good skill execution (French and McPherson 2003). Further, when the skill is placed within the game context, the importance of being able to execute it consistently is highlighted thereby increasing the focus level of the students during practice.

At this point, students return to their playing courts and practise in a triad formation with one tosser, one passer and one setter. From a location on the court that simulates actual game play, the tosser sends a rainbow toss to the passer who uses a forearm pass to direct the ball to the setter. The setter then catches the ball and bounce passes it back to the tosser. After five trials, the students switch roles allowing each student to practise each of the roles during the majority of the class time. During practice, the teacher circulates and asks students what they are thinking. Just asking questions can focus attention toward thinking about tactics (French and McPherson 2003). The lesson then ends with a 3v3 game using the same conditions as the initial game, however, the goal is now that a team earns a point (change in secondary rule) when they contain the ball on their side of the court on the first pass (for detailed lessons, see Griffin *et al.* 1997).

Conclusion

The tactical games model is a student-centred model in which the teacher facilitates the learning process. All parts of the process are important and teachers must take care in planning and teaching for understanding. First, games are modified appropriately to encourage student thinking relative to the tactical problem on which instruction is focused. Second, questions are designed to develop tactical awareness (understanding of what to do to solve a problem) and are well thought out. Third, skill practices teach essential skills to solve problems in as game-like a manner as possible. Finally, the final game provides students with the opportunity to apply their practice in an authentic setting in which points are earned for using the tactics that were the focus of situated practice. Each component of the lesson process is valued and must be planned to ensure that: (a) games are modified appropriately to encourage students to use their problem-solving skills to focus on the tactical problem of the lesson; (b) questions are designed to develop tactical awareness; and (c) situated practice teaches essential skills and movements to solve problems in a game-like a manner (Mitchell *et al.* 2003).

The tactical games model is grounded in a constructivist learning perspective that recognises the centrality of the learner to the construction of meaning across psychomotor, cognitive and affective domains. The tactical games model places the students in dynamic game-playing experiences that require them to make decisions and reflect upon their decisions through assessment and teacher facilitation. As Rink (2001) states, learning requires processing and knowing how learners' process should be a concern for teachers and researchers. Having the teacher emphasise authentic performance puts students in an active learning situation so that they can use and develop their problem-solving skills (Darling-Hammond 1997).

References

Allison, S. and Thorpe, R.D. (1997) 'A comparison of the effectiveness of two approaches to teaching games within physical education: a skill approach versus a games for understanding approach', *British Journal of Physical Education* 28(3): 17–21.
Australian Sports Commission. (1997) *Game Sense: Developing Thinking Players*, Canberra: ASC.

Bunker, D and Thorpe, R. (1982) 'A model for the teaching of games in the secondary schools', *Bulletin of Physical Education* 10: 9–16.

Chandler, T. (1996) 'Teaching games for understanding: reflections and further questions', *Journal of Physical Education, Recreation and Dance* 67(4): 49–51.

Chen, A. (2001) 'A theoretical conceptualization for motivation research in physical education: an integrated perspective', *Quest* 53: 35–58.

Corbin, C.B. (2002) 'Physical activity for everyone: what every physical educator should know about promoting lifelong physical activity', *Journal of Teaching in Physical Education* 21: 128–44.

Darling-Hammond, L. (1997) *The Right to Learn*, San Francisco: Jossey-Bass.

Deci, E.L. (1992) 'The relation of interest to the motivation of behavior: a self determination theory perspective', in K.A. Renninger, S. Hidi and A. Krapp (eds) *The Role of Interest in Learning and Development*, Hilldale, NJ: LEA.

Dodds, P., Griffin, L.L. and Placek, J.H. (2001) 'A selected review of the literature on development of learners' domain-specific knowledge', *Journal of Teaching in Physical Education (Monograph)* 20(4): 301–13.

Ellis, M. (1986) 'Making and shaping games', in R. Thorpe, D. Bunker and L. Almond (eds) *Rethinking Games Teaching*, Loughborough, UK: University of Technology Loughborough, Department of Physical Education and Sports Science.

French, K.E. and McPherson, S.L. (2003). 'Development of expertise', in M. Weiss and L. Bunker (eds) *Developmental Sport and Exercise Psychology: A Lifespan Perspective*, Morgantown, WV: Fitness Information.

Grehaigne, J.-F. and Godbout, P. (1995) 'Tactical knowledge in team sports from a constructivist and cognitivist perspective', *Quest* 45: 490–505.

Grehaigne, J.-F., Godbout, P. and Bouthier, D. (1997) 'Performance in team sports', *Journal of Teaching Physical Education* 16: 500–5.

Griffin, L.L. and Placek, J.H. (2001) 'The understanding and development of learners' domain specific knowledge: introduction', *Journal of Teaching in Physical Education* 20: 299–300.

Griffin, L.L., Mitchell, S.A. and Oslin, J. L. (1997) *Teaching Sport Concepts and Skills: A Tactical Games Approach*, Champaign, IL: Human Kinetics.

Holt, N.L., Strean, W.B. and Bengoechea, E.G. (2002) 'Expanding the teaching games for understanding model: New avenues for future research and practice', *Journal of Teaching in Physical Education* 21: 162–76.

Kirk, D. and MacPhail, A. (2002) 'Teaching games for understanding and situated learning: rethinking the Bunker-Thorpe model', *Journal of Teaching in Physical Education* 21: 117–92.

Launder, A.L. (2001) *Play Practice: The Games Approach to Teaching and Coaching Sports*, Champaign, IL: Human Kinetics.

Lave J. and Wenger, E. (1991) *Situated Learning: Legitimate Peripheral Participation*, New York: Cambridge University Press.

Mauldon, E. and Redfern, H.B. (1969) *Games Teaching: A New Approach for Primary School*, London: MacDonald & Evans.

McInerney, D. and McInerney, V. (2002) *Educational Psychology: Constructing Learning*, Sydney: Pearson.

Metzler, M. (2000) *Instructional Models for Physical Education*, Boston: Allyn and Bacon.

Mitchell, S.A., Oslin, J.L. and Griffin, L.L. (2003) *Sport Foundations for Elementary Physical Education: A Tactical Games Approach*, Champaign, IL: Human Kinetics.

Mitchell, S.A. and Oslin, J.L. (1999) *Assessment in Games Teaching. NASPE Assessment Series*. Reston, VA: National Association of Sport and Physical Education.

Mitchell, S.A., Griffin, L.L. and Oslin, J. L. (1995) 'The effects of two instructional approaches on game performance', *Pedagogy in Practice: Teaching and Coaching in Physical Education and Sports* 1(1): 36–48.

Placek, J.H. and Griffin, L.L. (2001) 'The understanding and development of learners' domain specific knowledge: concluding comments', *Journal of Teaching in Physical Education* 20: 402–6.

Oslin, J.L., Mitchell, S.A. and Griffin, L.L. (1998) 'The game performance assessment instrument (GPAI): development and preliminary validation', *Journal of Teaching in Physical Education* 17: 231–43.

Richard, J.-F., Godbout, P. and Griffin, L.L. (2002) 'Assessing game performance', *Physical Education and Health Education Journal* 68(1): 12–18.

Rink, J.E. (ed.) (1996) 'Tactical and skill approaches to teaching sport and games (monograph)', *Journal of Teaching in Physical Education* 15: 397–516.

Rink, J.E. (2001) 'Investigating the assumptions of pedagogy', *Journal of Teaching in Physical Education* 20: 112–28.

Rink, J.E., French, K.E. and Tjeerdsma, B.L. (1996) 'Foundations for learning and instruction of sports and games', *Journal of Teaching in Physical Education* 15: 399–417.

Thorpe, R. (1989) 'A changing focus in games teaching', in L. Almond (ed.) *The Place of Physical Education in Schools*, London: Kogan Page.

—— (2001) 'Rod Thorpe on teaching games for understanding', in L. Kidman (ed.) *Developing Decision Makers: An Empowerment Approach to Coaching*, New Zealand: Innovative Print Communication.

Thorpe, R. and Bunker, D. (1986) 'Is there a need to reflect on our games teaching?', in R. Thorpe, D. Bunker and L. Almond (eds) *Rethinking Games Teaching*, Loughborough, UK: University of Technology Loughborough, Department of Physical Education and Sports Science.

Thorpe, R.D., Bunker, D.J. and Almond, L. (1984) 'A change in the focus of teaching games', in M. Pieron and G. Graham (eds) *Sport Pedagogy: Olympic Scientific Congress Proceedings*, vol. 6, Champaign, IL: Human Kinetics.

Turner, A.P. and Martinek, T.J. (1992) 'A comparative analysis of two models for teaching games (technique approach and game-centred (tactical focus) approach)', *International Journal of Physical Education* 29(4): 15–31.

Wade, A. (1970) *Coach Yourself Association Football*, London: Educational Publications.

Wandersee, J., Mintzes, J. and Novak, J. (1994) 'Research on alternative conceptions in science', in D. Gabel (ed.), *Handbook of Research on Science Teaching*, New York: Macmillan.

Chapter 4

PlaySMART

Developing thinking and
problem-solving skills in the context
of the national curriculum for physical
education in England

Tom Bell and Dawn Penney

The national curriculum and national curriculum for physical education: designed with what learning and what learners in mind?

At the time of the most recent revision to the national curriculum in England, the government stated its desires for young people to become 'healthy, lively and enquiring individuals capable of rational thought and discussion and positive participation in our ethnically diverse and technologically complex society' (Blunkett 1999). A subject-focused framework for the national curriculum was retained, but with a renewed expectation that all subjects would make a collective contribution to the development of a number of identified 'key skills' and specifically, 'thinking skills'. (Identified key skills were: communication, application of number, information technology, working with others, improving one's own learning and performance, and problem-solving.) The opening pages to the new NCPE highlight opportunities for the development of these skills. This document states that physical education provides opportunities for thinking skills 'through helping pupils to consider information and concepts that suit different activities and critically evaluate aspects of performance and to generate and express their own ideas and opinions about tactics, strategy and composition' (DfEE/QCA 1999: 9). Attention is thus directed towards a greater sophistication in pupils' thinking about skills and, in particular, an awareness and understanding of the potential application of skills in various physical activity contexts, and of the principles that relate to performance. Thinking is thus portrayed as integral to performance.

Thinking skills and the NCPE: embedded? Marginalised? How defined?

The revision of the NCPE formally identifies four aspects of skills, knowledge and understanding as the focus for teaching and learning in physical education, to be developed in and via a range of activity contexts stipulated as the 'breadth of study' for the subject:

- Acquiring and developing skills;
- Selecting and applying skills, tactics and compositional ideas;
- Evaluating and improving performance;
- Knowledge and understanding of fitness and health.

(DfEE/QCA 1999: 6)

The development of thinking skills can be seen as integral and essential to each of these, supporting the contention that in physical education, 'pupils learn how to think in different ways to suit a wide variety of creative, competitive and challenging activities' (DfEE/QCA 1999: 15). Yet in the NCPE text and accompanying guidance, thinking skills have arguably become positioned and defined in ways that appear uncritical and that relate to a technical-rationalist view of teaching/learning. The document *Terminology in Physical Education* (QCA 1999), produced to accompany the new NCPE, explicitly foregrounds physical skills in its description of the aspect 'acquiring and developing skills'. Four categories of physical skills are presented: travelling skills, whole or part body actions, manipulative skills, and performance skills, with the latter associated with 'technical and physical accuracy and the overall quality of movement' (QCA 1999: 3). There is no attention to the possibility of the cognitive skills that are associated with learning in the context of physical activity. In the specific context of games, sending, dribbling, receiving, interpreting, marking, tackling, dodging and covering are highlighted and described in exclusively 'physical terms'. The document does allow for the development of evaluation skills that are described in terms of enabling pupils 'to be able to recognise and explain what is happening and what has just happened and to make and take decisions which lead to more efficient and effective performance' (QCA 1999: 15).

In many respects the national curriculum and the NCPE can be viewed as highly authoritative texts, stating categorically what is to be taught in all state primary and secondary schools in England. Yet there has always been an accompanying caveat, that the national curriculum is only a framework and, furthermore, does not constitute the 'whole curriculum'. Its requirements are to be met, but how they are met and what schools and teachers see fit to do beyond what is required is where the flexibility lies. Viewed in this light there is substantial scope to foreground the development of thinking skills in teaching and learning in physical education. This is the challenge taken up by staff at Manchester Metropolitan University who have developed the innovative programme to be discussed in the remainder of this chapter.

Exploring the flexibility: the 'PlaySMART' programme

The PlaySMART project was established to promote teaching and learning practices in physical education that will contribute to improvements in the performance of secondary school pupils in a range of physical education contexts, as well as to learning outcomes across the curriculum. It is directed towards the development of skills, knowledge and understanding that clearly relate to national and international interests in establishing foundations for lifelong learning. A key learning goal for PlaySMART is to encourage learners to take greater responsibility for their own learning. This is within a cyclic problem-solving process involving the planning, execution and subsequent review of self-generated solutions.

Problematising skill development and what constitutes 'skilful thinking' is central to the project. It has explicitly sought to challenge the 'traditional' view of skill development that Read (1993), for example, found to predominate in UK schools. Read describes 'orthodox' teaching in physical education as characterised by an almost exclusive preoccupation with the promotion of narrowly defined and usually decontextualised techniques that often produced pupils who were frustrated by the limitations of the approach and who failed to perform 'skilfully' during 'end of lesson' competitions. Read also draws attention to the fact that during competition, the problems team game players encounter vary constantly as they interact dynamically with other performers. She argues that if they are to deal effectively with such variations, performers' solutions need to reflect sound and sophisticated knowledge of performance in those dynamic contexts.

In response to these concerns, PlaySMART is underpinned by an integrated and holistic conceptualisation of skill that sees cognitive and motor control components as fundamentally inter-related, with a change in one reflected in a reciprocal effect upon the other (Oslin and Mitchell 1998) and a view of technique as dependent upon both task and environmental techniques (Newell 1986). PlaySMART is therefore designed to develop both cognitive and motor control components in tandem and 'in (real/authentic) contexts', but with a focus on enhanced awareness and sophistication in the cognitive element. This reflects the view that the key discriminator between the performances of expert and novice children may well be their knowledge and thinking skills, rather than their level of motor control or technical ability. French and Thomas (1987) make the very optimistic point that while the technical and physiological components of skill seem resistant to change in the short term, players' thinking and knowledge can be improved significantly in a short time scale.

With this emphasis on the development of the thinking skills and problem-solving knowledge components of sports performance, the development of PlaySMART has drawn particularly on Anderson's (1982) work on the acquisition of cognitive skill. He proposed the 'If–Then Production' theory in which a 'production' solved a problem by offering the performer an appropriate association between certain problem conditions and an action (solution): that is, if the challenge is situation (A) then an appropriate response would be to use these game principles to satisfy condition (B). PlaySMART has adapted Anderson's idea so that each production also includes an explanation to facilitate understanding of the conceptual basis of the solution. In PlaySMART a production would be phrased as: 'if this is the situation, then create this moment of advantage, because it offers these tactical advantages that can be exploited in this way'. Below we explain in more detail the problem-solving cycle inherent to PlaySMART and the acronym SMART that is used as a mnemonic for teachers using the programme's methodology.

PlaySMART methodology, structure and pedagogy

The PlaySMART methodology has been designed to promote teaching styles and pedagogical relations aligned with notions of guided discovery. That guiding sees teachers and learners going through three development phases:

- Experience of the full game;
- A focus on a 'core task' that relates to one identified part of that game;
- Participation in 'SMART challenges' that are directly linked to the core task.

SMART is an acronym for five stages in a problem-solving cycle: Situation, Methods, Adapt, Reduction and Transfer. The progression here owes much to the work of Adey and Shayer (1994) who were responsible for the cognitive acceleration work in science and mathematics (CASE and CAME), designed to accelerate learners from what Jean Piaget termed a 'concrete' to a more 'formal operational' level of cognition, and thereby enable them to generate and employ abstract concepts to solve their own problems. Like CASE, PlaySMART has specifically sought to help pupils deal with problems and understand their solutions at a conceptual level. There is recognition that in order to solve their own problems pupils need to be capable of applying their knowledge beyond the narrow context in which it was learned (Fisher 1993). Expert problem-solvers in sport, but also in other life situations/contexts, are able to deal systematically yet flexibly with novel problems and situations. They are able to do this because they understand solutions in terms of their underlying principles (rather than as rigid instructions, as novices do). They have the conceptual knowledge that enables them to adapt their solutions in response to problem constraints.

The five stages of SMART are an adaptation of Adey and Shayer's (1994) five pillars or phases in CASE: concrete preparation, cognitive conflict, construction, metacognition and bridging or transfer. Concrete preparation introduces the leaner to the task and facilitates goal setting. It is also an opportunity to limit the learner's focus to a pivotal issue and to identify those things that can and cannot be varied when searching for a solution. Finally it provides both teacher and learner with an opportunity to explore how they define and understand relevant linguistic concepts. This ensures that there are shared reference points for analysing the task. Cognitive conflict owes much to Piagetian thinking, which proposes that by deliberately presenting learners with ideas that appear to challenge their existing and possibly partial knowledge, they would be prompted to re-examine that knowledge and thereby deepen their understanding of a given phenomena. Piaget also recommended that learners in this state of conflict could be 'scaffolded' or assisted to reconstruct their knowledge in such a way that understanding was facilitated. The construction phase refers to the point in a lesson where pupils explore possible solutions. Metacognition describes the ability to reflect not only upon what has been done, but also the thinking processes that contributed to a performance. In a games-playing context, metacognition refers to the conscious methods players employ to monitor the effects of their own and opposing teams tactics and strategies and subsequent decisions relating to adaptations to these. Finally transfer refers to the notion that an idea developed in one context can act as an analogy for the use of a similar idea to solve a problem situated in another context. Feuerstein (1980) suggests that transfer crucially requires some form of bridging, perhaps by the teacher, where the value of and the means by which the idea to be transferred is made apparent.

Figure 4.1 depicts the relationship between PlaySMART and the CASE 'pillars' and outlines each of the five phases of SMART. It shows that in PlaySMART the situation, method and adaptation phases have borrowed ideas from CASE's cognitive preparation, construction and cognitive conflict phases, respectively. In PlaySMART there is no specific metacognitive phase but pupils are encouraged to reflect collaboratively throughout the programme and particularly in the transfer phase, which borrows ideas from the CASE bridging section. PlaySMART also differs from the CASE programme by having a reduction section in which learners are encouraged to synthesise information into solution principles and to 'chunk' all the components of a solution into one exemplar movement pattern. This movement pattern is then named to create shared terms of reference between team members and teachers and to stand as an analogy for all variations of that pattern.

Before discussing specific examples of SMART challenges, it is important to note other central facets of PlaySMART's methodology and pedagogy.

Understanding purposes

Bailey and Chambers (1996) suggest that effective problem-solving is purposeful and reasoned. PlaySMART is designed to make learners aware of the purpose of the challenges put before them and instil in them belief in their own abilities. This reflects the view that pupils learn best when they are interested in and motivated to achieve the tasks set and when they believe that they have the ability to succeed. PlaySMART methods teach pupils explicitly how to analyse problems

S	**SITUATION:** *Cognitive Concrete Preparation Phase*

Performers determine the following knowledge:
- Task: (Ball/player movement goals)
- Psychomotor tools (With what)
  'Technical ability' available to achieve movement goal.
  (Throwing/catching, hitting/running)
- Constraints on ball/player movements (What cannot)
  (Things that prevent movements i.e. games rules)
- Key moments (When)
  What moment(s) during the task is a ball/player movement <u>advantage</u> most required?
  (Before, during, immediately after an event etc.)

M	**METHOD:** *Construction Phase*

Performers attempt to understand the nature of the advantage required at this particular moment and the means by which they could create that kind of advantage:
- <u>Endgame</u> (Why)
  Explain what kind of (ball/player pathway) advantages you want to create <u>at this moment</u>.
  (Easiest/shortest/quickest B/P pathways etc.)
- <u>Moment of Advantage MOA</u> (What)
  Alternative relationship configuration that provides required advantages at a key moment in time.
- <u>Setup</u> (How)
  Alternative ball and player movement patterns that set up required MOA relationships.

A	**ADAPTATION:** *Cognitive Conflict Phase*

Teams are challenged to adapt their solutions by forcing (by constraints?) changes in their relationships and movement patterns:
  Teams create and evaluate adapted and/or alternative plans.

R	**REDUCTION:** *Synthesise Learning into Principles*

Performers are asked to compare, contrast and categorise potential solutions so as to synthesise them into:
  - ○ Relationship rules *(between, next to, opposite etc.)*
  - ○ Movement rules *(using <u>these</u> movement methods along <u>these</u> pathways)*
  Rules take the form of:
  'If –Then do this/Because' contingencies.
- Chunk Set Up/MOA/Endgame ideas into a SMARTPlan.
- Develop an **analogy** to stand for variations of this SMARTPlan.
- Practise executing SMARTPlan decisions.

T	**TRANSFER:** *Consolidation of Learning, Testing and Review*

Pupils test, evaluate and review their own and others' practical and cognitive performance:
- Use team game rules developed as performance criteria.
- Record a team score over a series of trials.
- Rate team members' responsibility for the development and execution of their solutions.

Figure 4.1 The SMART framework

and plan solutions that suit their current level of development and for which they can also offer a rationale.

Responsibility and creativity

In order to enable pupils to take more responsibility for their own learning, PlaySMART challenges staff to adopt a dialectic teaching approach. PlaySMART is also designed to equip pupils to go beyond the information given, to adopt a critical attitude to information and argument, as well as to communicate effectively, and to have the confidence to be creative in their thinking (particularly about possible solutions). Reflecting McGuiness' (1990) contention that the creation of dispositions for 'good thinking' is crucial to the development of better thinking and reasoning skills, the PlaySMART programme is committed to finding ways to create an educational atmosphere where talking about thinking – questioning, predicting, contradicting, doubting – is not only tolerated, but actively pursued. Pupils are expected to review their own and their peers' 'thinking achievements' and are helped to learn to take responsibility for correcting their own errors.

PlaySMART in practice

As indicated above, experience of the full game is a crucial first phase that will enable contextualisation of the activities that follow and ensure their authenticity. Recognising that full games are from a learning perspective, overly complex in their multiple and dynamic demands, the second phase in PlaySMART provides a clear and restricted focus on one part of the game. The phase could be corners in soccer, or the transition phase of play in basketball, when control of the ball changes from one team to the other. Moments of transition are particularly significant in basketball, not only because they occur frequently, but also because they require team-game roles to be switched rapidly (attackers become defenders and vice versa) in a highly dynamic game environment. Switching roles efficiently in these circumstances can be challenging, and players are often at their most ineffective during these moments. Consequently 'smart teams' need to attempt to reduce the time taken for them to make these changes, and exploit opponents who are slow to react in these situations. The focus on the particular phase of play is achieved via an appropriate 'core task' that is then followed by a series of 'SMART challenges'.

A 'core task' – end game

This is an adaptation of play in basketball, emphasising the transitional phase of play. It uses normal basketball rules with the following limitations. All attacks start from the three point line so that the game is played predominantly at one end of the court. The team on attack maintains possession of the ball as long as they keep scoring. Teams on defence can only become the attack if they can gain control of the ball and progress it at least as far as the opposite three point area within a three to five second time limit. If this is done (irrespective of whether they also score or not), the game is stopped, the teams swap roles and reposition themselves at one end of the court ready to play again. The constraints placed on the teams by these rules (particularly the time limit) encourages teams on defence to fast break as soon as they gain possession. Being given possession of the ball and therefore allowed to attack rewards teams that react efficiently at the transitional points in the game.

SMART challenges

SMART challenges are typically highly simplified adapted versions of the focus sport, usually involving small numbers of players and restricted rules, thereby reducing the number of variables that players have to deal with and technical challenges faced, to manageable levels. The activities are designed to offer authentic cognitive demands and technical challenges. The game principles that emerge and their inherent technical and tactical dimensions are expected to link with the core task and the full game. Burton and Miller (1998) argue that highly adapted tasks are only useful in developing the appropriate kinds of knowledge and understanding if learners can be reassured that they are authentic, that is, that the movement solutions developed through them can be transferred by the players to solve the kind of 'real' problems they will encounter later in the full game version. In PlaySMART, teachers are prompted to adapt the basic structure and rules both to differentiate on the basis of the learners' capabilities and make the task developmentally more challenging as learners progress, while also making challenges enjoyable in their own right. SMART challenges have an inherent hierarchy, starting with developmentally less challenging activities and building in difficulty until ultimately they resemble the core task once again. Below we provide an example of this development, with challenges derived from the Asian game, Kabbadi. The challenges and activities have been specifically designed to help learners to develop an understanding of effective performance at a point of transition in an invasion game. They exemplify the inter-connected and developmental nature of PlaySMART pedagogy.

PlaySMART: Kabbadi

At its most basic level, this version of Kabbadi requires an attacker to enter a square defensive area (marked out by small cones) through one side (designated as the entrance/exit). Within a time limit, the attacker must tag one of two 'defenders' located in this box and run back to a target mat located several metres outside this box before one of the defenders can tag them back. The defenders are constrained in their response by a series of rules: First defenders are not allowed to leave the box or attempt to tag the attacker until one of them is tagged first! However when one defender has been tagged their team-mate can then leave the defensive area to chase the attacker. Second, the defender who is tagged may not tag the attacker back or leave the box. This defender is therefore reliant upon his or her team-mate to chase the attacker. Typically this game is played in teams of four, with defenders rotating in and out and the attacking team taking it in turns to attack. When all four attackers have had a turn the teams swap roles. The remainder of the discussion takes us through the progressions of S-M-A-R-T that can be developed in this context.

Situation

In the situation phase, teachers demonstrate the whole task and invite teams to familiarise themselves with the task by playing against their own team-mates. The learning objectives for students for this phase are to identify the nature of the task from the perspectives of the attack and the defence, the movement skills required for its solution and the constraints the rules place upon them in this respect. The movement 'tools' available for use in this particular task are chasing, dodging and sprinting. The expected knowledge outcome is for the defence to realise that the real challenge is not to avoid being tagged which in such a confined area is probably impossible, but to interact effectively with colleagues in order to prevent the attacker from escaping back to the target zone after one of them is (inevitably) tagged. Many novices will misunderstand the task as finding ways to avoid being the one who is tagged. Consequently they will employ non-cooperative evasive manoeuvres, such as sudden changes in direction and speed. Within this phase the teacher will also ask the pupils to identify problem variables and constraints, that is, things that they can and cannot alter. They will also be alerted to the concepts of movement pathways and temporal issues such as sequencing. This ensures that pupils know which relationship and movement factors to focus on when they come to develop their own solutions in the next section.

Method

In this part of the session, performers explore ways of establishing a tactical advantage. Pupils are required to generate four kinds of knowledge relating to this goal namely: when, why, what and how?

Key moment (*when*): The first task here is to ask players to analyse the game problem from either a defensive or attacker's perspective, in order to establish if there is a key moment in time when they would most like to have an advantage. It is highly likely that the players will recognise that the moment when the attacker tags a defender is literally pivotal in this game and is the moment when they would most like to have a tactical advantage.

Why: This component requires performers to identify and understand the nature of the tactical advantage that they want to exist at the moment when a defender is tagged. Pupils should also be asked to explain why they want these kinds of movement opportunities at this moment in time. They are likely to couch their answer in terms of descriptions of movement pathways, that is, easiest/shortest/ quickest pathways, etc. The expectation is that they will identify the movement opportunity they would like to exist at this point in time as one where their runner will have a significantly shorter pathway to the target mat than their opponent's.

Moment of advantage (*MOA*) (*what*): The information sought here is a description and a rationale for the way in which game variables should be configured when a defender is tagged, if the advantage they require is to exist. The idea of an MOA is a difficult concept to address, but asking players to imagine a short, video sequence, involving a 'still picture' (or 'freeze frame') can help. Players are prompted to imagine key game variables configured (realistically) in a way that is helpful to them and then to imagine that the pause button is released and the video runs forward, showing the viewer how the team exploit the opportunity provided by this particular set of circumstances. This 'mind movie' idea owes much to a similar idea developed by David Leat (1999) for his thinking skills programmes. When pupils believe that they have devised a static configuration that they like, they predict the likely outcome and then trial it for real, starting the game at the moment when a defender is tagged. As with most PlaySMART challenges, it is emphasised that there is no absolutely correct answer to this problem. Teams are encouraged to devise different ideas and explore these practically. Many defending teams will construct an MOA that involves one defender being tagged in a corner most distant from the target mat, with the other defender occupying a corner diagonally opposite. This configuration is viable because it offers the tactical advantage of a shorter pathway to the target for the second defender player. During this part of the lesson, teams also start to consider the movements that they would use to exploit opportunities arising at and from the MOA, that is, to chase down the retreating attacker. Defenders will recognise that they must react as soon as possible when their colleague is tagged. In order to help with timing, teams may develop auditory and/or a visual signals (the tagged player usually decides to yell 'Go'!). Chasing defenders will also experiment with the pathways that they take to intercept the attacker and might develop a 'sprint start' technique that they believe will get them into motion faster.

How: Finally players have to consider what movement ideas they could use to construct the MOA they have selected. With respect to the possible solution outlined above, teams have to work out how to draw the attacker down to a bottom corner. They can achieve this situation if they initially fill both bottom corners. They then have to find a way of moving a player into the corner diagonally opposite the attacker. These positional switches are relatively straightforward from a motor control perspective. However their timing is not and usually requires practice and a series of adjustments before some degree of competence is achieved.

Adapt

During this part of the session, ideas are presented to pupils that challenge their existing and partial knowledge. The purpose is to encourage them to develop knowledge in the form of movement or relationship principles. This is done by placing constraints that require them to adapt their knowledge. For example, we can introduce a demand for players to swap sides, encouraging the under-standing that these changes do not affect the nature of the tactical advantage and that the same solution principles are applicable. The teacher may also pose challenges such as: 'What if the attacker fakes to tag one defender and then reverses direction to attack the other defender in the safety role?' By both observing and playing against various teams, adaptive knowledge is developed.

Reduction

In this phase the challenge is now to reduce information processing demands by pupils finding memory efficient ways of restructuring their knowledge and specifically using the 'If then (because) production rules'. For example, defenders in Kabbadi might reduce what they know to the following form:

If the attacker is not trying to tag anyone, defenders should fill both bottom corner;

If the attacker tries to tag you, then only be tagged in a bottom corner. (Yell 'Go' if this happens);

If the attacker decides to tag your colleague then move to a position in the opposite top corner;

Because this MOA presents the attacker with the longest possible distance to travel after they have tagged an opponent and provides the covering defender the time and space to move into a position where they can either prevent the attackers escape or return to a bottom corner if the attacker changes direction to attack them instead.

Transfer

The final goal is to promote the use of the game principles and the more general thinking processes developed through the earlier phases in other contexts. Transfer requires careful bridging to be effective, with the bridging process endeavouring to demonstrate to pupils that their team game rules and perhaps the analogies they have developed are also applicable in a new, yet related, context. One way this is done is to adapt the SMART game. In Kabbadi, this could be by locating an extra defender at the far end of the court beside the target mat. The object for the defence is now different. Rather than chasing the attacker when one of them is tagged, the defence has to pick up one of two balls balanced on cones in the back corners of their box and pass the ball down the court to their new colleague, so that it arrives ahead of the retreating attacker. In this version the original defenders may not leave their bases and must make one pass within the defensive box before they are allowed to throw the ball to their new colleague down the court. Although initially quite daunting differences are presented, exactly the same

solution principles will work in this game, although now the movement requirements include passing and catching the ball.

This is only one of a series of adaptations that are organised hierarchically to
provide learners with developmentally appropriate challenges in both cognitive
and motor terms. The final stage in the evolution of the games is to return to the
original core task and ultimately, the full game of basketball. If the learning that
has taken place en route is as profound as expected, pupils' performances should,
in cognitive terms at least, show real signs of improvement.

Conclusion: emerging practice and extending possibilities

Development of the PlaySMART programme is ongoing and data are currently
being gathered that will provide a sound basis upon which to judge its success in
relation to its identified aims. Here we briefly reconsider some of the issues raised
in our earlier discussion and reflect on the type of thinking skills being engaged
with by teachers and learners who participate in the PlaySMART programme.

The practices described in our example mark a distinct shift in focus, from
teaching a game as an end in itself, to teaching in a game context as the basis
for the creation of various learning opportunities. In this respect PlaySMART is a
significant development and one that openly challenges conservative boundaries
of interpretation and implementation of the NCPE. Its focus and recommended
pedagogy undoubtedly raise professional development issues for teachers and
teacher educators. It also raises issues for pupils, for whom PlaySMART activities
may seem new and strange in comparison to their prior experiences and expectations of physical education lessons.

PlaySMART has the potential for other outcomes related to social justice and
equity which have not been developed in this chapter and have yet to be assessed.
The challenges set by PlaySMART are designed to both encourage and empower
all pupils, including those who may be/feel marginalised in other physical
education teaching contexts, to take responsibility for their own decisions and the
consequences of these. PlaySMART tries to set challenges that pupils can with
some effort and thought solve. Furthermore, it encourages pupils to believe that
the situations in which they must solve both academic and social problems are
not beyond their control. By thinking things through, situations can be improved
and realistic goals can be achieved. The further development of the PlaySMART
programme thus presents possibilities to explore social justice and equity issues
within contexts of implementation of the NCPE and in particular, games teaching.
It is a programme that, in arguably difficult policy and professional contexts, is
extending possibilities for future practice.

References

Anderson, J.R. (1982) 'Acquisition of cognitive skill', *Psychological Review* 89: 369–406.

Adey, P.S. and Shayer, M. (1994) *Really Raising Standards*, London: Routledge.

Bailey, C. and Chambers, J. (1996) 'Interactive learning and technology in the US Science and Mathematics Reform Movement', *British Journal of Educational Technology* 27: 123–33.

Blunkett, D. (1999) 'Letter of introduction', *The Review of the National Curriculum in England. The Secretary of State's Proposals*, London: QCA.

Burton, A.W. and Miller, D.E. (1998) *Movement Skill Assessment*, Champaign, IL: Human Kinetics.

Department for Education and Employment (DfEE)/Qualifications and Curriculum Authority (QCA) (1999) *Physical Education. The National Curriculum for England*, London: QCA.

Feuerstein, R. (1980) *Instrumental Enrichment: An Intervention Program for Cognitive Modifiability*. Glenview, IL: Scott, Foresman & Co.

Fisher, R. (1993) *Teaching Children to Think*, New York: Simon and Schuster Education.

French, K.E. and Thomas, J.R. (1987) 'The relation of knowledge development to children's basketball performance', *Journal of Sports Psychology* 9: 15–32.

Leat, D. (1999) 'Rolling the stone uphill: teacher development and the implementation of thinking skills programmes', *Oxford Review of Education* 25(3): 387–401.

McGuiness, C. (1990) 'Talking about thinking: the role of metacognition in teaching thinking', in K.J. Gilhody *et al.* (eds) *Lines of Thinking*, Chichester: Wiley.

Newell, K.M. (1986) 'Constraints on the development of coordination', in M.G. Wade and H.T.A. Whiting (eds), *Motor Development in Children: Aspects of Coordination and Control*, Dordrecht: Nijhoff.

Oslin, J.L. and Mitchell, S.A. (1998) 'Form follows function', *Journal of Physical Education, Recreation and Dance* 6: 46–9.

Qualifications and Curriculum Authority (1999) *Terminology in Physical Education*, London: QCA.

Read, B. (1993) 'Practical knowledge and a games education at Key Stage 3', *British Journal of Physical Education* (Spring): 10–14.

Chapter 5

Problem-solving in teaching sports

Peter Hastie

The field of sport offers numerous opportunities for student problem-solving. The games themselves present tactical problems (do I pass, dribble or shoot?), but too often, sports units are conducted in situations that rarely reflect the authentic sport experience. Units are often too short to develop any significant skills, let alone involve students in substantive problem-solving or decision-making.

This chapter will first describe the essential features of a sport education curriculum model that promotes authentic sport experiences. In addition, the chapter will describe the various ways in which participatory democracy and problem-solving can be incorporated into a sport education season.

> It is a Saturday afternoon at the football. Be it in Melbourne, Australia, Manchester, England, or on the campus of the University of Michigan, there is a common theme. Fans are gathering to watch their teams play against a vaunted rival. Most are dressed in their team's colours, some even have their faces painted. There is passionate support for the game and an air of festivity is easily felt by even casual passers-by. As the game begins, the excitement level builds as the teams struggle for supremacy.

As noted in the scenario I have created above, in almost all countries of the world, sport is a significant cultural practice. That is, sport as an activity is embraced by many of the populous, and is taken seriously. As Siedentop (2000) notes, sport is organised and dramatised in a manner that is almost religious. Nonetheless, varying social forces including politics and economics, and more recently, science, technology and globalisation, all influence sport as a cultural practice. To that extent, as Tinning and Fitzclarence (1992) note, physical education has often ignored these changes so that sport within physical education is now seen by many children and young people as not only boring, but irrelevant. Consider the follow-up scenario from two students' weekend involvement with sport.

> The following Monday, brother and sister James and Sarah attend their local high school. James never misses a Saturday game, while Sarah herself is an avid soccer play and competes in the local leagues each weekend. For James

and Sarah, their current softball unit in physical education hardly provokes any excitement. There are 18 students on each side, sides that are formed in an ad hoc manner each lesson, and the games count for nothing of great consequence. Few students get turns to pitch, and many are satisfied playing in the deepest of outfield positions in order to have minimal involvement in the game at all.

While in most countries, the practice of sport is a fundamental component of school physical education, Siedentop (1994) suggests that most sport within physical education rarely reproduces those features of sport that lead to its attractiveness, resulting in student claims of irrelevancy and boredom. Typical physical education sports units involve very little (if any) of a sport's culture, in particular, those six key features of what Siedentop calls authentic sport, the sport played by Sarah in her soccer league and that watched by James and his mother and father. Sport, according to Siedentop, is characterised by the following features: (a) sport is done by seasons; (b) players are members of teams and remain in that team for the entire season; (c) seasons are defined by formal competition; (d) there is a culminating event to each season; (e) there is extensive record-keeping; and (f) there is a festive atmosphere in which the season (and particularly the culminating event) take place.

The sport education model

As a result of the misconnection between sport in physical education and the sport experienced by students outside of school, Siedentop (1994) developed 'sport education', a curriculum and instruction model to provide students with authentic sport experiences. During a season of sport education seasons, students become members of the same team for the entire length of the unit (usually at least twenty lessons). The students also take greater responsibility for the organisation and management of the sporting experience. A typical sport education season also involves students not only in skill learning and game play, but adopting leadership positions and taking responsibility for the conduct of the unit. Student roles may include coaches, captains, referees, scorers, statisticians and members of the sports-organising board. Sport education, thus, is designed to offer a more complete sport experience than that of simply player. The following vignette provides an example of how a sport education softball season might work.

A class of thirty students is divided into six teams. Each of these teams selects its own captain, coach and manager. They also chose a name, have team pictures taken, and select a uniform color. The first part of the season involves a training camp, where the teacher provides a number of skills drills in which the group participates as a whole. A small segment of time at the end of each lesson is allocated for team coaches to conduct independent practices with their teams. Each team is assigned a 'home space'.

After a series of lessons in which the basic skills are learned and practiced, a pre-season competition is held. During this phase of the season, students practise becoming umpires, learn how to keep score and take statistics, and are involved in many of the managerial tasks, such as setting up the field and having all the equipment ready for play.

As the season progresses, refining and practising skills takes less of the class time, and formal competition becomes the focus. It is a team competition, so the major goal is to win the competition by compiling points for winning matches, but also for good sportsmanship, being organised, and completing any set managerial duties. At the completion of the finals series, a variety of awards are presented: final ranking, referee awards, fair play awards and participation awards.

Sport education then, aims to replicate sport within the legitimate social context that it is enacted in the community. As a cultural practice, sport has many aspects that seem attractive. These are those features of sport that are claimed to promote teamwork, cooperation, honesty and fair play. Alternately, there are many socially and culturally significant components of sport that those looking for a positive experience for all participants would also like to change, and we do not have to search far to find evidence of negative student outcomes from their participation in sport in physical education when it is replicated directly from the community setting (see Ennis 1996). It is not by accident that Boswell (1994) has described professional sport as a playground for thugs and goons! In designing the sport education model, Siedentop (1994) purposefully highlighted three significant important ways in which sport education differs from sport in communities and schools. These are (a) participation requirements – by which all students play all the time; (b) developmentally appropriate involvement – by which team sizes are reduced and games rules are modified to match the experiences and abilities of the students; and (c) diverse roles – by which students do not participate simply as players, but learn to referee, keep score, compile statistics, publicise team performance, or help as coach, manager or trainer.

As we shall see later in this chapter, these deliberate changes in the way sport within physical education is structured through the model provide us with ways in which we can accommodate Kirk's (1997) call for physical education to assist students in becoming critical of the practices associated with popular physical culture.

Research on sport education has shown that many students prefer this format of sport to others within physical education (Hastie 1996; Hastie and Carlson 1998). Further, both female and male students report that they work harder during sport education than during traditional sports units in regular physical education (Taggart and Alexander 1993). Students particularly enjoy being on the same team for a season, and lower skilled students, in particular, describe how they feel useful and can make a serious contribution to their teams (Carlson 1995; Hastie 1998a).

Problem-solving potential of the sport education model

The nature of the sport education model presents numerous opportunities for students to solve problems. Further, these problems are legitimate ones, and are situated within legitimate participation. That is, in line with community-based sport, by adopting the format of seasons (rather than units), and by recasting physical education lessons as matches and training sessions, the school reproduces aspect of the contemporary community of practice as it exists outside the school (see Kirk and Macdonald 1998).

The legitimate problems presented to students through participation in sport education can be placed into three categories: (a) problems relating to team administration; (b) problems relating to game preparation; and (c) problems relating to participation in game play situations.

Team administrative problems

The first task of any new team in a sport education season is to create an identity. This involves selecting a name, choosing colours, and sometimes a chant or slogan. Some teachers chose to set a caveat or limitations on the types of names that are acceptable (for example, some teachers prefer that students do not pick names that suggest violence, aggression or sexism), but in the main, teams are free to determine their own personality. In some cases, teachers will incorporate some form of cross-disciplinary learning when it comes to team names and identity. For example, where students are studying a particular country or region in social studies, the teacher may ask students to select a city located in that area. However, students will not only select a particular city, but will then be required to research that city's football team, adopt its colours and nickname.

Another team administrative problem-solving task is the division of labour of the students into various team roles. In all sport education seasons, students will have some role in officiating matches, be this as referee, lines person, statistician or scorekeeper. In some seasons, teachers will also require students to take managerial roles within their teams, such as equipment manager, publicist, coach or sport board member, to name a few. In all of these cases, teachers can provide minimal to no leadership, and simply let students work things out on their own, or they may provide structured guidelines to help the students to determine who will follow a certain role.

Preparing to play

All sport education seasons incorporate time within lessons for students to practise and plan independently of the teacher. During these independent practice sessions, teachers may provide teams with the opportunity to work on skill-related practices, or ask them to develop some team tactics and strategies. Again, the sophistication of the problem can range from a selection from a limited number of options ('here are some drills you can chose from'), to a more open-ended problem, such as 'devise a series of plays for use in your first three offensive possessions'.

Many sport education seasons operate on the concept of graded competition. That is, students will compete for their team against students of similar ability. For example, a hockey team of eight members may divide into two teams of four. The 'A' team will then compete against another team's 'A' players, while the two 'B' teams compete against each other. The winning team for the day is determined by combining the scores of the two matches. In this way, students are consistently engaged in small-sided games that maximise the opportunity for participation in developmentally appropriate competition. In a similar vein, a tennis team of five students may be required to provide three singles players and a doubles team.

While not all season plans call for graded competition, teams will still be faced with the problem of maximising their playing potential. While this problem can be totally open-ended and left to the students' devices, some teachers provide guidelines through which teams can work to determine playing responsibilities. Figure 5.1 provides one example from a four-a-side hockey season.

```
Team Analysis Sheet
To help make you a better team!!

1.   Do you have a player who really wants to play goalie?      Y      N

     If 'NO', how are you going to deal with this?
     a.  rotate players each game
     b.  rotate players during a game
     c.  another solution

2.   Find out your players' major stick side (right or left).
     Is this balanced with an equal number of right and left players?      Y      N

     How does this affect how your team lines up.
     (Left-handed players normally play left wing)

3.   Who is your most powerful shooter? ..............................
     Should this player perhaps be your major defender? ..................

4.   Who is your best dribbler? ........................................
     Might this player be your primary forward – the center?

5.   So what is your best line up?      1 – 1 – 2
     or maybe                           1 – 2 – 1
```

Figure 5.1 A team analysis sheet for a four-a-side hockey season

Match-play problems

It is within games that students will be faced with questions of whether to pass or shoot, or to maintain possession if that is within the rules. They will be faced with decisions about whether to attack or defend, depending upon their position on the field, the state of the game and the quality of their opponents. One of the significant findings of sport education research is that students do improve some of their tactical understanding through the playing of games (see Hastie 1998a). In one study of Frisbee, a team improved its percentage of passes that put the opposing defence under pressure (called 'jeopardising passes'), from a little more than one in two, to more than three in four as the season progressed. In addition, the correlation data between the number of short passes and successful catches and overall efficiency, suggest that the players learned that shorter passes lead to more successful receptions and hence fewer turnovers (Hastie 1998a).

The key to the skill and tactical development engendered through sport education however, occurs when students feel valued as legitimate team members. Most studies of this model reinforce the idea that students do indeed embrace the persisting team concept. They enjoy playing with the same players over a long period of time (Hastie 1998b), and for the lower skilled, find this a particularly attractive component of sport education (Carlson 1995). For those who are frequently picked last and are alienated in large teams, being on a small team of four or five where they have some responsibility and their team-mates are helping them improve, this format is particularly empowering (see Hastie 1998a).

Going beyond the structural problems

The issues or problems examined in the previous section relate particularly to the many structural problems associated with sport seasons. That is, how many games should be played, what rules might be incorporated to make games more fair, and how scoring should be conducted (if at all), are all related to the context of the competition. However, there is no need to be limited to purely technical issues when giving students opportunities to give voice to their physical education experiences. While sport education can be more engaging to students when they make contributions to game structures, there can also be places for students to examine more critical questions about sport and its management. That is, students can be focused upon many of the issues that exist within community sport, and work towards addressing these within their seasons. For example, issues of gender and race-related discriminatory practices are two commonly identified issues in contemporary sport. Likewise, students can be asked to explore the mass media's coverage of selected athletes and their sports. Both these areas of concern can be addressed easily within the curricular structures available within sport education – most notably through the sport board, but also through the potential for having student committees within seasons.

The sports board

One of the basic organising features of sport education is the formation of a 'sports board'. The sport board is comprised of a group of students who advise the teacher on issues related to the overall policies that govern the season. Depending upon the degree of problem-solving that the teacher wishes to present to students, board members can be involved in both the planning and implementation stages of a season. Some examples of these include: (a) the selection of teams; (b) potential rule modifications; (c) competition schedules; (d) violations of fair play rules; and (e) planning the culminating event. The inclusion of a sport board provides a mechanism whereby decisions can be made and disputes arbitrated by students themselves, thus contributing to the personal-growth goals of the curriculum.

Committees

In an effort to involve all students, it is also possible to set up a number of separate committees, each being responsible for a specific component of the season. Examples of these committees include, but are not limited to, a rules committee, a competition committee, an ethics and fair play committee, a dispute resolution committee, and an awards and ceremonies committee. The following list provides a sample of the areas that would be the responsibility of each of the committees mentioned above.

Rules committee
*   All issues and decisions relating to the playing rules of the game
*   Determination of playing boundaries

Competition committee
*   All issues and decisions relating to the conduct of play
*   Number of games per lesson
*   Time length of games
*   Finals competition format

Ethics, equity and fair play committee
*   Ethical issues, including appropriateness of team names (e.g. racially insensitive team names, or those promoting aggression or violence)
*   All issues and decisions relating to sportsmanship, player behaviour and appropriate class conduct
*   All issues relating to the reproduction of gender order

Dispute resolutions committee
*   Respond to complaints from officials

Awards and ceremonies
*   Season awards – type and criteria
*   Format of the culminating event

It is important for the teachers to provide a clear explanation to students about these roles and responsibilities. In particular, the teacher should remind students that membership to some committees would involve a willingness to spend time in meetings and discussions outside regular class time.

Allocating students to committees

In the initial lessons of a season, the teacher has one of two options. The first is to require students from each team to provide one member to each of the committees incorporated for that season. The second is to allow students to join the committee whose functions and responsibilities they find the most attractive. The advantage of the first option is that various committees will have balanced numbers, while in the second, students may be more motivated to contribute to the committee given they have made a purposeful choice.

Designing decision tasks

The first task for a teacher following the formation of committees is to design a series of 'decision tasks'. These decision tasks will be in the form of problems that students are required to discuss and resolve. The sophistication of these tasks will depend upon two factors: (a) how much time the teacher wishes to allocate to committee meetings; and (b) how much freedom the teacher is prepared to give students relating to the problem. Let us take one scenario to explain this situation:

> Mr. Brown is using committees for the first time in his fifth grade floor hockey season. He presents the following decision tasks to his 'rules committee'.
>
> - The goalie can wear a softball glove to help in defence. This is so that he can sprawl on the floor to cover up the ball without getting injured. A face-off follows.
> - Discuss this rule. Do you agree or disagree with the goalie being allowed to wear a glove?
> - If not, what other option do you wish to include?

> Ms. Jones, on the other hand, has a tenth grade class who is also playing floor hockey. Prepared to spend a little more time in class and with the expectation that students will continue to discuss issues outside of class, her decision tasks are presented as follows.
>
> - What equipment restrictions (if any) are you going to place on the goalie? That is, can they wear anything different from other players?
> - With regard to your solution to the above question, what other rules might you want to incorporate as a result of goalie clothing/equipment?

It's a balancing act

In designing decisions tasks, the teacher must first decide what part of the programme is, and is not, negotiable. For example, if the teacher specifically wishes to teach the concept of off-side rules in hockey, then it would be problematic to introduce a decision-task that allows students to dispense with off-side rules altogether. Some of the teacher's agenda for a unit may be compromised when students present some alternative that follows a different path. Take another example (see Hastie and Carlson 2002):

TEACHER: OK, competition committee – what was your brief for today?

STUDENT: (reading the sheet) How should the league be scored. That is, how should the scoring system work for winning and losing?

STUDENT: We reckon that you just get the number of points as goals you score. That's a simple way to do it. Like, not three for a win and zero for a loss, but if you score five goals you get five points, and if you score two, you get two points.

TEACHER: OK, but that means a team that wins five–one, scores more points than a team that wins three–two, is that reasonable? What do you other guys think?

STUDENT FROM CLASS: Well, if they score more, they deserve more (chorus of 'yeah, that's fair').

TEACHER: Well, have you considered this? What about a team who wins two–one – they would score less for the day than a team that loses seven–three. Did you consider that?

STUDENT: No, but you should get more points if you score more goals.

TEACHER: OK, what does everyone else think – anyone with a specific suggestion?

STUDENTS FROM CLASS: I say it's OK, the aim is to score goals.

TEACHER: So, read your resolution again (student reads). Anyone unhappy with the idea that the score is simply the number of goals a team gets becomes their league score?' (chorus of 'no') OK, then you get what you score. It's decided.

This outcome certainly biases the game towards attack, negating defensive skills, and the question is whether the teacher should have more strongly worked toward a more balanced solution. To follow the teacher's agenda without incorporating the students' ideas is to somewhat diminish the notion of voice, while also reinforcing the notion of higher status knowledge (or at least process). As Holdsworth comments:

> for students, really 'having a voice' is much more than being consulted . . . It is much more concerned with having a valued and recognised role within that community – where what we think and say is measured against what we do, how we are appreciated and what difference we make. To have a

'voice' and make no difference is possibly more profoundly alienating than having no voice at all!

(Holdsworth 1999)

Implementing committee meetings

At the beginning of a lesson, the teacher will give each committee its decision task. Students in the committee are asked to discuss and resolve a decision during the specified time. At the end of the designated time, a member from each committee presents its proposal, and the class then votes on this resolution. Failure to reach a consensus can lead to one of two options. First, the plan defaults to the original wording of the relevant rule or suggestion as prepared by the teacher. Second, the committee is asked to revisit their resolution and present an alternative at the next class meeting.

Words of caution

One of the most recent studies (Brock 2002) on sport education examined the nature of student interactions within one team as it progressed through a season. The results of this study are particularly relevant as they apply to the idea the problem-solving tasks are very often group tasks. An essential message of Brock's (2002) dissertation is that students' status has a particularly powerful influence on the decision-making process. In essence, students considered to be of 'high status' (that is, those who were rich, attractive, athletic and with personality) appeared to be the dominant voices for not only making team decisions, but in serving in power roles. Take the following scenario as one example.

> Amy and Angela, two high status students dominated all decisions for the Cougars team. Beginning with the first team meeting Amy and Angela decided team captains, team colours, and the team name. The instructions for and the intent of the meeting was for the team to make decisions together, however these two students continually overpowered and silenced the other students in this meeting and throughout the unit. When deciding team captains, Amy announced, 'Our captain is Angela Adams' and the other students complied. Amy and Angela also picked Paul, a low status student as the second captain, after two high status boys declined the role. In addition, while all the students were making suggestions, Amy and Angela decided the team colors should be lime green and black and the team should be called the Cougars. Again, the students complied and never challenged the two girls. Even Paul, the other captain, did not appear to have much input into team decisions.
>
> (Brock 2002: 179)

Of more significance, however, was that the other students in this team viewed Amy and Angela's dominance as inevitable and therefore futile to resist or question.

At this point we should recall Cohen's (1998) findings that since high status members talk much more than other people, their suggestions often become the group's decision. Similarly, because low status members talk less than others, no one takes their ideas seriously and other members may not even listen to what they have to say; even when they do speak up. Teachers, then, need to put in place strategies that help to ensure that group decisions are not simply those of a few high status students that may not represent the opinions of the group members.

Conclusion

By incorporating student voice within the design of sport education seasons, through a series of committees with the agendas of solving problems, we have provided students with the capacity to critically engage with the conduct of sports practices. As noted in the earlier chapters of this book, there is an increasing expectation that physical education should provide students with opportunities to engage in activities which require critical thinking, critical inquiry, problem-solving and collaboration with others in the process of learning.

Sport education fits comfortably within a constructivist theory of learning that emphasises the active role of the student in building or constructing their own understanding and performance. What better way for students to better understand sane and equitable sport practices than through the construction of seasons that provide opportunities for those very outcomes? The active learning so implicit to the sport education curriculum should increase students' interest and arousal through a sense of personal ownership of the new knowledge and increased responsibility. To paraphrase one student's comment from a season where the class negotiated most of the learning goals 'since we made up the rules and how the game was to be played, everyone understood them – they were clear, and everything went way more smoothly – we certainly learned a whole lot more'.

Sport education also fits comfortably within the context of critical inquiry. Students are put in situations where not only do they have to solve problems, but examine the consequences of their decision answers. Moreover, while sport education presents a student-centred curriculum and instruction model, it also asks students to critically reflect upon their solutions to problems in an effort to present a more sane and equitable sporting context.

References

Boswell, T. (1994) 'Ugly defense is NBA's big offense', *The Washington Post* (June 1): F1.

Brock, S.J. (2002) 'Sixth grade students' perceptions and experiences during a sport education unit', PhD dissertation, The University of Alabama, published by UMI Dissertations Services, UMI number 3067263.

Carlson T.B. (1995) '"Now I think I can": the reaction of eight low-skilled students to sport education', *ACHPER Healthy Lifestyles Journal* 42(4): 6–8.

Cohen, E.G. (1998) 'Making cooperative learning equitable', *Educational Leadership* 56(1): 18–21.

Ennis, C.D. (1996) 'Students' experiences in sport-based physical education: (more than) apologies are necessary', *Quest* 48: 453–6.

Hastie, P.A. (1996) 'Student role involvement during a unit of sport education', *Journal of Teaching in Physical Education* 16: 88–103.

—— (1998a) 'Skill and tactical development during a sport education season', *Research Quarterly for Exercise and Sport* 69(4): 368–79.

—— (1998b) 'The participation and perceptions of girls within a unit of sport education', *Journal of Teaching in Physical Education* 17(2): 157–71.

Hastie, P.A. and Carlson, T.B. (1998) 'Sport education: a cross cultural comparison', *Journal of Comparative Physical Education and Sport* 20(2): 36–43.

—— (2002) 'The inclusion of participatory democracy in a season of sport education', presented at the American Education Research Association National Convention, New Orleans, LA.

Holdsworth, R. (1999) 'Authentic student participation in action: some observations on contagious institutional deafness, selective hearing and acquired laryngitis syndrome', presented at the Annual Meeting of the Australian Association of Research in Education, Melbourne, Australia.

Kirk, D. (1997) 'Schooling bodies for new times: the reform of school physical education in high modernity', in J.-M. Fernadez-Balboa (ed.) *Critical Aspects in Human Movement: Rethinking the Profession in the Postmodern Era*, Albany: SUNY Press.

Kirk, D. and Macdonald, D. (1998) 'Situated learning in physical education', *Journal of Teaching in Physical Education* 17(3): 376–87.

Siedentop, D. (1994) *Sport Education: Quality PE Through Positive Sport Experiences*, Champaign, IL: Human Kinetics.

—— (2000) *Introduction to Physical Education, Fitness and Sport*, Mountain View, CA: Mayfield.

Tinning, R. and Fitzclarence, L. (1992) 'Postmodern youth culture and the crisis in Australian secondary school physical education', *Quest* 44: 287–303.

Taggart, A. and Alexander, K. (1993) 'Sport education in physical education', *Aussie Sport Action* 5(1): 5–6, 8.

Chapter 6

Student-centred research
Working with disabled students

Hayley Fitzgerald and Anne Jobling

In this chapter we discuss the use of student-centred research as a classroom-based pedagogical technique for exploring young people's physical education and sporting experiences. According to Arnold (1985), physical education can be understood as a subject that is not merely the doing of physical activity. Indeed, Arnold (1985) believes students can learn 'in', 'about' and 'through' physical education. This chapter draws on this understanding of physical education to illustrate how students can learn 'about' physical education by participating in classroom-based, student-centred research. Initially, we discuss the use of student-centred research with young disabled people. Given the many organisations that now claim to support and develop opportunities for these young people (Department of Culture, Media and Sport 2001; English Federation of Disability Sport 1999) and the increasing recognition of the importance of personal autonomy and empowerment (Children and Young Peoples Unit 2001), it is appropriate that when we explore physical education and sporting experiences we include young people within the process. We review a number of examples of student-centred approaches that have been used. We then consider the usefulness of student-centred research for researchers, school staff and students. Finally, we explore the relevance and possibilities of the pedagogic principles underpinning student-centred research for other groups of young people in the context of physical education.

Disabled people and new times

Like many groups in society, disabled people[1] continue to be affected by the new times discussed in Chapter 1. These new times are complex and contradictory and have seen the mobilisation of disabled people through support for independent living, self-advocacy, civil rights and equal opportunities (Barnes *et al.* 1999; Campbell 2002). These developments have sought to challenge professionals and change thinking about the way disabled people are perceived, treated and understood. This politicisation has been coupled with the increasing recognition of the social model of disability that provides accounts of disability from materialist (Finklestein 1980; Oliver 1990) and cultural perspectives (Morris 1991; Thomas 1999). The social model rejects the individualist medical approach to disability that emphasises personal tragedy, the need to be treated by experts and for disability to be seen as an individual problem. Instead, the social model positions society as the cause of disablement through economic, environmental and cultural barriers (Barnes and Mercer 2003). To this end, the social model enables the social exclusion and oppression of disabled people to be seen as a construct of society, rather than as practices centred on the individual with the impairment. Undoubtedly, the momentum created by campaigners and the recognition of the social model has prompted much change within society. Internationally, there has been new legislation, changes in policy direction and to some degree new practices have been encouraged to overcome the exclusion of disabled people in social life (Priestley 2001).

Although there is much optimism in these new times that society will be more just, there is also caution and scepticism (Hughes 2002). Our consumer culture has little to offer those who do not have the economic capital to retain their membership in this kind of society. Many disabled people are unable and/or cannot respond through these economic terms and will remain at the margins (Russell 2002). Other developments associated with advances in technology (television and electronic media) continue to reinforce the oppression of disabled people by placing greater value on a non-disabled norm. Consequently, popular culture tells us it is best to be young, white, male, straight, fit, educated and competitive (Gard and Meyenn 2000; Oliver 2001). For example, the messages created through the popular media portray idealised notions of normality in which 'others', including disabled people, are seen as deficient in some way. Barton (1993) for example, highlights the prominence given to body image in the following quotes:

> What is important as far as the question of body image and disabled people is concerned is their powerful personal awareness that they do not, in various ways, match up to the physical ideas able-bodied society sets.
>
> (Barton 1993: 47)

Barton goes on to argue:

> Dominant images surrounding sexuality, attractiveness and the body-beautiful as well as the expectations, identities and practices associated with them are a means of oppression in the lives of disabled people.
>
> (Barton 1993: 48)

In these new times, it is clear that many aspects of social life have the potential to both emancipate and oppress disabled people. And until society is more socially just, marginalised groups including disabled people will continue to pursue and advocate for the human rights that many of us take for granted. One aspect of social life that may be given some consideration in these new times is physical education and school sport. What does physical education and sport mean to young disabled people?

Disabled people and physical education

Recently, and as a response to some of the more oppressive aspects of new times, educators and other providers of public services have become increasingly concerned with issues relating to inclusion and equity (DePauw and Doll-Tepper 2000). Physical educators and sports providers have also recognised the need to address these issues and have responded within syllabuses (Ministry of Education 1999; Qualifications and Curriculum Authority 2001), guidelines (Block 2000; Downs 1995; NASPE 1995), with resource innovations[2] and in some countries through the development of professionals associated with adapted physical education (Sherrill 1998). However, the extent to which young disabled people are touched by and gain longer-term benefits from these kinds of developments is unclear. In some instances, physical education and sport can be a positive and fulfilling experience for young disabled people. Indeed, Blinde and McClung (1997) found that sport enables disabled people to experience their bodies in new ways, improves perceptions of physical characteristics and increases confidence to participate in new activities. Tanni Grey-Thompson in her autobiography reports that after watching TV coverage of the 1984 London marathon when Chris Hallam 'the bad boy of wheelchair racing' won, she was inspired: 'I could do that . . . at the time I thought it would be basketball but the specific sport was always changing . . . I really really want to do archery' (Grey-Thompson 2001: 26).

In other instances physical education exposes disabled youngsters to an environment that reinforces the disadvantage experienced in other areas of life. Tannie, for example, remembers hating her school experiences of physical education:

> When I moved to up to St Cyres, I wasn't allowed to stay in mainstream school for PE. I was meant to go back to the special school but I didn't like it because I didn't know most of the kids. They were doing daft things like musical movement and pretending to be trees. I hated it.
>
> (Grey-Thompson 2001: 22)

A recent large-scale survey in England concluded that young disabled people participate less and undertake a narrower range of physical education and sporting activities than their non-disabled peers (Sport England 2001). Rather than providing a positive experience, physical education can sometimes contribute to a young disabled person's sense of marginalisation:

> The reality of underachievement and exclusion from most sporting and other physical activities, within a school which placed great emphasis on competitive achievement, meant that I was unable to make my mark through officially sanctioned paths. There was, too a sense of humiliation as my peers had their identities defined in terms of everything they could do, while I felt mine was being defined in terms of what I could not do.
>
> (Swain and Cameron 1999: 72)

In cases such as this, participation in physical education has broader implications for a person's sense of self and serves to reinforce dominant discourses of disability that emphasise lack and inability. Some would not be surprised by this situation and have argued that the very foundations of physical education are based on ableist notions and at odds with those that do not neatly fit into this restricted understanding of physicality (Barton 1993). In this context, normalising values associated with physical education are imposed upon all and little consideration is given to the consequences this may have on those that fail to match up to these ideals. Indeed, even within a climate where inclusion is vigorously promoted it is difficult to see how experiences of physical education can be enhanced if the composition and nature of this subject remains largely unchanged (Penney 2002). As teachers navigate the requirements of new curricula, we are left wondering if young disabled people are now better positioned in these new times to become physically educated. Do these young people place any kind of value on physical education and/or does physical education have any relevance for them beyond the school context?

As young disabled people are at the centre of these questions we believe they should also be at the centre of any discussion that attempts to explore these issues. However, as Graham (1995) points out, teachers often take for granted these insights and draw their own conclusions about the experiences of young people. Often they see only barriers and problems and the array of adaptations deemed to be required in physical education. This has been coupled with a general apathy by educational researchers to engage with young people (Cook-Sather 2002). Indeed, when consideration is given to young disabled people, it is evident that much research mirrors the way in which these youngsters are perceived by our disabling society. Typically, researchers listen to the views of parents, carers and professionals and dismiss young disabled people as illegitimate sources of research information (Davis and Watson 2002; Priestley 1999; Shakespeare and Watson 1998; Ward 1997). This dismissal adds to their already diminished sense of self and lack of control over their own lives. Without insights from young people it is difficult to see how teachers or researchers can effectively and legitimately advance change within physical education. Quite simply, how can we advocate for young disabled people within physical education when we actually know very little about their experiences? We believe that student-centred research is one approach that can be adopted to ensure importance is placed on the views and experiences of young people and that these youngsters learn through this process of active engagement.

Student-centred research

Initially, the student-centred research reviewed in this chapter developed in response to an awareness that there is a lack of consideration given to young disabled people within the physical education research context. In particular, the physical education field seems to be preoccupied with observing, experimenting or talking about these young people. Student-centred research is an alternative to what is considered the conventional wisdom and promotes many of the values associated with the social model of disability. In particular, student-centred research enables young disabled people to be seen as active social agents who are well positioned to articulate their experiences and express their own views. They are as Barnes and Mercer (1997: 7) put it 'expert knowers'. The process of student-centred research reflects this understanding and responsibility is placed on the students themselves to shape and then be actively involved in and influence the research process. The Vygotskian concept of 'the zone of proximal development' (ZPD) informs the pedagogy of student-centred research. In particular, we share the view of Renshaw (1998) that ZPD is an interactive and negotiated space in which the students we work with and ourselves co-construct the process of inquiry.

A learning environment supporting critical inquiry also promotes student-centred research, an environment that provides the catalyst to facilitate active and positive learning experiences. Following Brooker and Macdonald (1999), we believe that working in this way has the potential to contribute to broadening participants' capacity to explore and critique their physical education and sporting experiences. This student-centred approach fosters many characteristics of the learning environment advocated by Darling-Hammond (1997) and discussed in Chapter 2. Of particular relevance to the case studies reviewed in this chapter is the 'appreciation of diversity' and a desire to value the contributions of all participating students. Placing emphasis upon learning as part of the research process extends our work beyond what some would call research to that of curriculum. To this end, the goal of the research process becomes far more than merely the generation of data to be analysed and reported. Instead, student-centred research promotes engagement with students, as participants and learners. We believe like others including Oliver (2001) this fusion is desirable as it leads to a research experience that can be educationally relevant and meaningful to the young people involved.

Initially the case studies reviewed in this chapter were facilitated by Hayley and Anne and driven by the desire to generate some research data. However, it soon became apparent that student-centred research yielded considerable potential as a curricular approach for practising teachers. That is, it was an approach that contributed to many of the learning outcomes stipulated in physical education syllabuses. Two special school[3] environments provided the 'interactive and negotiated space' in which the work was framed. At the first school, a student-led research case study was undertaken that illustrates how students can effectively take on the role of co-researcher and work collaboratively to generate research data about themselves and their peers. The second case study at Ashdale School reviews a task-based approach undertaken by eight participating students in order to generate research data about themselves. Although the approaches adopted in each of these case studies differ, the pedagogic principles underpinning the process remain the same and emphasise learning in which the experiences, contributions and views of all participating students are valued and seen as essential to the development of the research process.

Case study one: Woodland School

The first case study took place at Woodland School, a special school for young people experiencing physical disabilities and learning difficulties. Five students aged between 14 and 15 years participated in the project as research students. The purpose of the project was to engage in student-led research activities to find out more about their experiences and those of their peers relating to physical education and sport. Students worked on this project during a class usually scheduled for a vocational qualification. The teacher anticipated that the student-centred project work would contribute to the achievement of a several components of this award. Research strategies were identified, planned and carried out by the students. These included peer interviews, undertaking a physical education survey and photographing physical education lessons, sporting and free-time experiences.

Peer interviews

In order to undertake the interviews the students initially worked through specific aspects of the interview process. They considered 'who to ask', discussing the possibilities of involving students from different schools, other classes at their school, their siblings, teachers and parents. The students then considered the practicalities and possibilities of interviewing these groups and came to the conclusion that it would be most viable to ask children from other classes at their school. As one student suggested 'I'd like to find out from the other classes here [at this school]. That'd be good, what do them in class four do?' (Mark Discussion Notes 13 March 2001). The students also discussed 'what questions to ask' and considered if the questions they had identified were clear and understandable. In order to facilitate this process the students practised the questions with the teacher and support staff as respondents and after this made a number of modifications to the questions. At this practising stage the students also decided who would ask the questions and how they would remember the questions they were going to ask. For example, one student was happy to read written text, another student used symbols, another was going to remember the questions he would ask and the question of the final student was recorded on 'Big Mac'.[4] The students decided that they would like to video the interview sessions. They wanted to see themselves on video afterwards. In addition, they recognised that this approach would provide a visual record of their peers' responses that would be particularly useful for those communicating nonverbally.

As a group and individually the process of conducting the interviews demonstrated the ability of the students to make decisions and with support to reach a stage of actually doing the interviews. During this process the role of the researcher became one of facilitator. This included drawing students' ideas on the white board so they could all remember what was said, promoting discussions between the group, giving ideas when asked to, encouraging students to make choices and decisions and supporting students so that they kept on task.

The students became very excited at the prospect of going into other classes to conduct the interviews. By the time they were ready to do their first interview, word had already got around to other students of the group's project. The teacher explained that a number of the research students were 'leavers' (at the end of the academic year they would be leaving the school to take up a place at a college or adult training centre) and this generally gave them increased status with their peers. The teacher felt the research project had increased this status even further as the research students were perceived as having the kind of responsibility usually only afforded to school staff. After completing each interview, it was evident from the discussions between research students that they felt a real sense of achievement. In an enthusiastic tone James explained, 'I was really nervous, can you see, can you see my sweat, I'm really sweating, did you see, I did it on my own' (Discussion Notes, 27 March 2001).

From each interview session, Hayley generated a results sheet. Sometimes the research students had little to say about what was found out and at other times the results provided a catalyst for conversations between students. In response to the result sheet in Figure 6.1, the students talked about the circumstances that affected their involvement in free time activities away from home. For example, this sheet prompted one conversation about getting to and from evening clubs

Figure 6.1 Results sheet – video, toy box, computer, music, TV

and illustrated an acute awareness of the reliance students had upon their family. One student suggested 'It's a pain mum, dad or me sister take me out and around. It has to be sorted out with them' (Mark, Discussion Notes, 3 April 2001). Another student remarked, 'I stay at home, I like it there, I like going bowling, I go bowling sometimes. Mum takes me. She has to take me so I can get there' (James, Discussion Notes, 3 April 2001). On occasion students expressed frustration with their life-style. One student frequently compared himself with a younger sibling, 'I'd like to be my sister, she gets to do lots, going out when she wants to, with her friends. But not me I can't do that' (David, Discussion Notes, 3 April 2001). This student believed that using a wheelchair had contributed to his restricted lifestyle.

Survey

The idea for a survey came from one research student who had noticed that during the interviews not all students identified the activities they undertook or said what they thought about them. In a very practical way this student had seen a limitation of group interviewing and identified an alternative strategy for data collection. The research students decided to focus on school physical education lessons and consider how other students rated physical education activities. The research students discussed and then debated which physical education activities to include. The final selection caused much disagreement as different ideas and preferences emerged. Eventually, after a series of 'votes' initiated by the students, twelve activities were included in the survey. The students decided that the survey should be in a 'pictured' format with smiley faces used as the rating scale. Figure 6.2 illustrates a line of the physical education survey.

Hayley drafted the survey and the research students administered it to other classes. She then generated and presented the results to the research students. The subsequent discussions between the students and teacher stimulated an interesting exchange. The physical education teacher expressed his surprise that the survey indicated unfavourable responses to 'parachute games' and 'big ball' and explained that he had regularly included these activities in physical education lessons as he thought the students liked these activities. The research students responded to the teacher by suggesting reasons why they and fellow students did not like these activities. In relation to big ball one student suggested, 'I hate

Figure 6.2 One line of PE survey

it when it hits my face, you know its going to, but can't stop it, push it away. It's this big thing coming at you' (David, Discussion Notes, 15 May 2001). Based on similar discussions the teacher decided to offer alternatives to these activities and consider giving students the choice to decide what activity they would like to undertake.

Photographs

All students were given a disposable camera in response to one of their data collection ideas to take photographs in physical education lessons and during their free time away from school. A number of students were particularly looking forward to the prospect of taking and then showing their photographs to other class members. Eventually, three of the students returned their cameras. On reflection, perhaps the two students who had not returned their cameras were not as fully included in this activity. In particular, they were not given adequate support to facilitate the process of taking their photographs. However, all the students contributed to the discussions that were stimulated from the photographs. These discussions were sometimes initiated by the researcher: 'What were they doing?', 'Did other students do this activity?', 'Where did they do this?', 'Did they like it?', 'Who did they do it with?' As the discussions unfolded, the students began to recognise that a number of them undertook the same activities and they discussed specific aspects of this between themselves. These discussions highlighted how activities including sport can be an important site of resistance for these young people. In an objecting tone, James said, 'When people think I can't do things, it's them with the problem'. In an equally defiant manner, David remarked '. . . to prove you can, so people think and can see you can' (Discussion Notes, 27 March 2001). This resistance was targeted at nondisabled people's discriminatory opinions and illustrates the contempt and frustration felt by these youngsters.

In response to student suggestions a corridor display and 'pictured' report of the research work that had been undertaken was developed. Although this process marked the end of our work with the students we anticipated that both of these resources would provide an additional means of promoting the work of the research students within and beyond the school. In particular, we felt the display would provide a continuous reminder to students of the work they had undertaken and the things they had found out. When we were constructing the display we were encouraged that many students had conversations with us about the findings and we hoped this exchange would continue between students when we were no longer visiting the school. We also anticipated that other members of staff would be interested in replicating the project in other curriculum areas and that the display and report would prompt them to find out more from the students, teacher and support staff who attended the sessions.

The nature of the work undertaken in this school met the curricular requirements of the vocational qualification the class was working towards, it fitted into the school's timeframe and accounted pedagogically for the abilities of the participating students. As can be seen from Fitzgerald *et al.* (2003), work in other schools may evolve somewhat differently. In particular, the presence of multiple student groups is likely to result in greater differentiation of project tasks and a need to initiate inter-group reporting mechanisms. Higher literacy levels may increase the use of written text. For example, rather than drawing pictures on the white board as a reminder to students of their ideas alternative strategies can be implemented. For example, a 'research road map' was effectively used in one school project to generate ideas and remind students of their options.

At this school, greater student involvement was also achieved in other aspects of the project work including the development stage of the surveys, the production of posters and the analysis of data. Dissemination of the project work was also extended to include meetings and discussions with officers responsible for the community provision of sporting and recreational opportunities.

Case study two: Ashdale School

The second case study took place at Ashdale School, a special school for young people experiencing severe learning difficulties. Eight students aged between 14 and 18 years participated in the project. Like case study one, we wanted this project to focus on finding out more about student experiences of physical education and sport. However, after preliminary meetings with students and staff at this school it became clear that the student-led approach adopted in case study one would not be the most effective means of engaging students. Instead, a task-based approach was developed. Our exploratory meetings informed the initial task developed. In particular, we were keen to ensure this task was relevant and meaningful to the students' experiences of physical education, challenging and interesting. After this, tasks evolved as the sessions unfolded. We evaluated a completed session and then considered ways to approach the next one. By reflecting in this way the tasks were developed in response to students' interests in and reactions to tasks. In total, thirteen tasks were developed incorporating the use of 'pictured symbols'. These tasks related to four key themes: physical education lessons at school, free time activities, interactive news reporter interview and activities and well-being (Fitzgerald *et al.* 2003). The tasks reviewed below specifically relate to the PE theme.

Task 1: Physical education and sport thinking box

Each student worked with a 'thinking box' task sheet illustrated in Figure 6.3. Students considered a range of activities positioned outside the thinking box. Students selected a physical education activity they had undertaken. The student then moved this activity from outside to inside the thinking box. This was repeated until the student was happy with the selections made. As a consequence, the activities chosen represented their current and/or past engagement with the selected activitiy. During this task, students were encouraged to discuss their selections

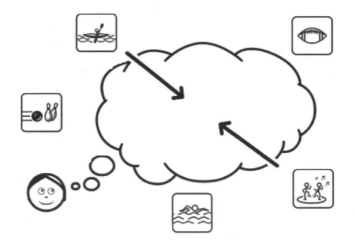

Figure 6.3 Thinking box

with fellow classmates, the support worker, Hayley and Anne.[5] Conversations varied and included students recalling the last time they had undertaken a particular activity, who they were with, some rules, if they liked or disliked the activity and if their team won. Some students also demonstrated a skill or technique relating to the activities they were considering.

Students then removed the symbols they had not selected from the task sheet. This left each student with a number of activities within the thinking box that they had identified as having participated in during physical education and/or school sport. As a group, students then shared with each other some of the activities they had included. This stimulated further exchange between the students and teacher.

Task 2: Thumbs

Each student used the activities they had placed inside the thinking box as a frame of reference for the next task. Students selected individual physical education and sporting activities and decided if the activity was 'good' (thumb up), 'okay' (thumb parallel) or 'not good' (thumb down) by moving the activity symbol into the appropriate area of the task sheet. This task was designed so that students could express their views about each activity. Again, students were encouraged to share their opinions about activities.

Task 3: Favourite

From the 'good' box, students ranked their 'top three' physical education activities. We anticipated this activity would encourage students to consider the activity preferences they might have. Once all students had ranked their top three activities students were keen to find out if any other students had made the same selection for their favourite activity. As a group, students listened to other student preferences and were able to establish if any one in the group had identified the same activities. By discussing preferences we hoped students would begin to see that some of their peers enjoyed similar activities to themselves and that this might prompt further engagement between students.

Task 4: News reporter interview

Students used their completed 'top three' physical education activities task sheet (from task 3) to help them answer news reporter questions. In addition, a 'free-time booklet' created during the tasks associated with the free-time theme was also used to stimulate the students' thinking. We undertook the role of news reporters and questioned students about their physical education and free-time activities. In order to make the session animated a range of props was used including a rugby ball, CDs, food packaging, swimming goggles and news reporter microphones. These props were particularly useful tools in facilitating additional responses from students who were less vocal. The following short segment illustrates this:

[holding the swimming goggles and towel up]
RESEARCHER: Is there anyone here today that likes swimming?
STUDENT 1: Yeh, I like swimming, swimming at the deep end!
RESEARCHER: What strokes do you do?
STUDENT 1: Crawl.
[researcher puts goggles on and gets ready for action]
RESEARCHER: Show me how to do crawl.
STUDENT 1: [demonstrates stroke]
RESEARCHER: Why do you like doing crawl?
STUDENT 1: I can see where I go, I can put my head in the water, I go the fastest doing crawl.
RESEARCHER: Do you always do front crawl when you swim?
STUDENT 1: No.
RESEARCHER: What other ways do you swim.
STUDENT 1: On my back, with my head up, like in bed.
[another student interrupts and the discussion continues]

The interview session enabled some questions from previous tasks to be repeated and then developed further. This strategy was particularly effective for gaining more detailed responses from students. Apart from adding an element of fun and informality to the session, we anticipated that the props would enable a closer association between the questions asked and the activities they related to. For example, the questions relating to swimming were framed within the context of a pair of goggles and a towel. This prompted a student to demonstrate a swimming stroke, in response to this we were able to ask further questions and encourage other students to contribute.

After considering physical education and free-time experiences we then developed a number of tasks focusing upon lifestyles and in particular the relationship between physical education, free-time and well-being. As a starting point for these tasks we used the physical education and free-time preferences already stated by the students and began to explore issues relating to health, physical vigour and enjoyment (Fitzgerald *et al*. 2003). However, the work at this school finished after the completion of thirteen tasks, as the class was moving on to other curricular areas. With additional curricular time it might have been possible to assist the students to explore even further the relationship between physical education, free time and healthy lifestyles.

Usefulness of student-centred research

The programmes of student-centred work which we developed can be viewed from the perspectives of the researchers, the school staff and the students. Each of these perspectives is briefly explored in the following section.

Researchers

There are a number of questions that researchers will inevitably ask about the student-centred research presented in this chapter that will frame judgements made about the usefulness of this kind of project work. Some may question the appropriateness of engaging with young disabled people within the research process, particularly young people experiencing severe learning difficulties. We suggest that this argument is grounded within perspectives associated with the medical model of disability as it fails to see these young people beyond their disability and places no responsibility on researchers to rethink or refine their practices. We have already seen in case study one that practitioners can become inclusive in their work with young people when they actively engage with young people. We suggest that this challenge remains largely unmet by researchers within this field. Indeed, we believe that until our research community accepts responsibility for promoting inclusive research practices we will continue to privilege those groups that respond best to the restrictive and limiting research approaches that are extensively used. For example, designing and using research methods that assume literary competence will continue to restrict contributions from those who cannot respond in this way.

Others may express concerns about the reliability and quality of the data generated. We would see the central issue here as being one of authenticity. We believe that adopting a student-centred approach captures authentic constructions of the participant's physical education experiences. We believe authenticity was achieved in our case studies through a combination of actions. In particular, we worked *in situ* with the students and were thereby engaging them in the setting in which they experience physical education. In this context, the research became physically and experientially associated with the participants and was not abstract from their school environment. In addition, we placed value on what the students were telling us by thinking beyond the boundaries of words and written text. We achieved this by embracing the language and communication systems familiar to the students. We saw this as an essential dimension of our work and were committed to ensuring every stage of the research process, including dissemination, was accessible to the students. Furthermore, we worked with the students to co-construct the focus and direction of the research process. For example, in case study one we worked in a manner that encouraged the research students to make their own decisions about the way they would like to work and the activities they would like to complete in order to find out about their peers' physical education and sport experiences. The students' insiders perspective, enabled them to develop data collection strategies that their peers would likely respond to.

The student-centred nature of this project work also raises another important issue relating to the data generated. In particular, we were relatively unable to control the kind of information collected. For example, in both case studies students broadened the parameters of the research from a physical education and school sport focus to one that also included what we would describe as free-time activities. Although we may not have wanted to initially explore this additional aspect of the students' lives we supported the research process that enabled the students to do this. We also later recognised that the students conceptual understandings of physical education, sport and free time were somewhat different than ours and if we had not embraced the students' understandings we may have limited the nature of the insights we captured.

School staff

Following Rose (2002) we were keen for this work to have relevance and meaning to the school staff, as well as the students. Consequently, we encouraged staff to attend and participate in some aspects of the sessions. This participation was on the understanding that they adopted a facilitating role similar to our own. We recognise that by involving the staff in this way we may have compromised, to some degree, the autonomy of the students. Indeed, at one of our schools during the early stages of the project we became particularly frustrated with one member of staff who whispered ideas and suggestions to students in an attempt to 'help' them. This staff member was also at times unsupportive and negative about the students' experiences and frequently made comments that emphasised 'can't,' 'won't' and 'not able to'. In this instance, we encouraged this member of staff to continue to attend the sessions, as we believed the research project would serve as an important learning experience. As the project progressed we promoted informal discussions with staff members and anticipated that these conversations would reinforce our ethos underpinning the project and the role we expected participating staff to adopt. It is difficult to determine if attending the sessions changed the attitude of this unsupportive staff member. However, it was noted that her negative comments became less frequent and in a number of instances this worker enthused, rather than criticised the abilities of students.

As the projects progressed, it was evident from the teachers and support workers that they were gaining wider and new appreciations of their students' physical education, sporting and free-time experiences. In particular, this student-centred research enabled school staff to develop a more detailed understanding of individual students or a class's experience(s). For example, in case study two although the teacher believed he knew the students reasonably well he was pleased to find out new things about the students. The tasks relating to physical education confirmed his view that horse riding, swimming and basketball are the overall favourite activities in physical education lessons. In a number of instances, the teacher was surprised by individual responses and this prompted him to rethink the type of activity options and choices to give to students in physical education. The teacher felt that he knew very little about students out of school experiences and was therefore particularly interested in the responses given relating to the free-time tasks. Again, the teacher believed valuable new insights were gained about all the participating students. In particular, the teacher had wrongly assumed that one of the students did not like swimming. The teacher was surprised to discover that swimming was in fact this student's favourite free-time activity. In response to this new insight the teacher suggested he would send more information home to the student's parents about aquatic-based opportunities that the family could access.

Beyond the schools, local sports development officers received the students' reports and visited one of the schools. Clearly, extending the project work by engaging other providers of sporting opportunities may serve to enhance the understandings of these practitioners and contribute to the decisions these stakeholders make on behalf of young disabled people. We believe that it is crucial that other stakeholders responsible for planning, promoting and providing wider sporting opportunities utilise the insights from this project work and in partnership with the student researchers seek to enhance the nature of opportunities available. We believe that engagement between the students and stakeholders is vital as it has the potential to strengthen the links and continuity between school and community provision. However, we are also aware that these practitioners may be reluctant to listen to and act upon the students' insights.

Students

We began our work in these schools with a desire to create an environment in which the students would personally benefit from their involvement in the project. It was evident from the students' responses that they enjoyed the activities they completed. This was particularly the case during the 'news reporter interview' in case study two, where many students became animated, excited and full of anticipation. It is also clear that this project elicited responses from students that would indicate an increased sense of value and importance. As we saw in case study one, the research students felt a great sense of importance when undertaking the peer interviews and were considered by their peers to have been afforded a privileged status usually only associated with school staff. The teachers and support workers also believe that the project provided a useful setting in which the students were able to develop important skills associated with respectful listening. In case study one this was evident during the planning stages of the project where students shared and listened to ideas before making a group decision about how to progress. Similarly, in case study two the teacher felt that the project promoting an environment in which students were encouraged to listen to one another and that through this students had also learned more about each other.

We also wanted the research students to become more aware of their own experiences of physical education. In a sense, we were attempting to use the student-centred work in both schools as a catalyst to stimulate their awareness. There were many instances in the schools where the students discussed their experiences and began to reflect upon them. In case study one this often happened when the results from the surveys or interviews were reviewed. While in case study two the students would often engage in discussions during the tasks and this would lead to conversations about their personal experiences. Our concern to provide opportunities for such conversations sometimes created an unforeseen tension. We wanted students to keep on task (designing a survey, practising interviewing or completing tasks) in order that the school research project could progress. However, at the same time we wanted to encourage discussions. We recognise that sometimes it was difficult to gain the right balance particularly as we were aware of the time constraints imposed by our participating schools.

Although we believe our student-centred work facilitated many positive responses from the students we are also conscious that these responses may not be evident beyond the parameters of the project. We had hoped that by involving teachers some aspects of our work would be replicated in future practice. However, we provided no support mechanism after the project to facilitate this process. A challenge for future student-centred work in this area is to collaborate with schools in a sustained manner in order to assist them to find ways of extending the boundaries of our project work into broader dimensions of the school experience.

Working with other groups of young people

The student-centered research reviewed in this chapter was undertaken with a group of young people that have typically not been given a voice on issues affecting their lives. We believe other groups that are repressed in similar ways could also benefit from engaging in a learning experience in which they become active social agents. This may include young people from ethnic minority backgrounds, those that are socially disadvantaged and young people under judicial care. We also believe that the principles underpinning student-centred research are relevant to all young and that this approach is particularly effective for addressing pertinent issues relating to physical education. Indeed, Oliver and Lalik (2001) have shown the innovative ways in which body image can be explored with girls. We will also see later in Chapter 8 how a student-centred approach can be used to explore diverse cultural perspectives in physical education. There are also many other issues that would be worth exploring, such as those relating to physically active lifestyles. In this context, the outcomes from this kind of student-centred work could contribute to informing changes in curriculum design within schools. We believe that student-centred research presented in this chapter was effective within the school settings we worked in. However, we would also support the wider use of student-centred research within youth work environments and with organisations that promote self-advocacy for young people. Indeed, partnerships between schools and these organisations could extend this kind of project work beyond a school or curriculum context and provide a channel through which issues relevant to broader aspects of young peoples' lives can be explored.

Notes

1 It should be noted that the notion of 'disability' or to be 'disabled' can be understood and defined in a variety of ways. It is not our intention to review these complex and contested understandings. For an insight into this debate see, for example, Barnes *et al.* 1999.
2 See for example the programmes offered by the Youth Sport Trust (www. youthsporttrust. com) including 'TOP Sportsability' and 'Elements'.
3 Special schools refer to institutions that provide segregated educational opportunities for disabled young people.
4 Big Mac is an audio recorder that enables the teacher, support worker or student to record a sentence that is spoken and then enables another student to activate the recording.
5 The terms 'discuss' and 'conversation' are used in their broadest sense and include any exchange between students for example, using Makaton and other forms of communication technology.

References

Arnold, P. (1985) 'Rational planning by objectives of the movement curriculum', *Physical Education Review* 8(1): 5–61.
Barnes, C. and Mercer, G. (1997) 'Breaking the mould? An introduction to doing disability research', in C. Barnes and G. Mercer (eds) *Doing Disability Research*, Leeds: The Disability Press.
—— (2003) *Disability (Key Concepts)*, Cambridge: Polity Press.
Barnes, C., Mercer, G. and Shakespeare, T. (1999) *Exploring Disability A Sociological Introduction*, Cambridge: Polity Press.
Barton, L. (1993) 'Disability, empowerment and physical education', in J. Evans (ed.) *Equality, Education and Physical Education*, London: Falmer Press.
Blinde, E.M. and McClung, L.R. (1997) 'Enhancing the physical and social self through

recreational activity: accounts of individuals with physical disabilities', *Adapted Physical Activity Quarterly* 14: 327–44.

Block, M.E. (2000) *A Teacher's Guide to Including Students with Disabilities in Regular Physical Education*, Baltimore: Paul H. Books.

Brooker, R. and Macdonald, D. (1999) 'Did we hear you? Issues of student voice in curriculum innovation', *Journal of Curriculum Studies* 31(1): 83–98.

Campbell, J. (2002) 'Valuing diversity: the disability agenda – we've only just begun', *Disability and Society* 17(4): 471–8.

Children and Young Peoples Unit (2001) *Learning to Listen: Core Principles for the Involvement of Children and Young People*, London: HMSO.

Cook-Sather, A. (2002) 'Authorizing students perspectives: towards trust, dialogue, and change in education', *Educational Researcher* 31(4): 3–14.

Darling-Hammond, L. (1997) *The Right to Learn*, San Francisco: Jossey-Bass.

Davis, J. and Watson, N. (2002) 'Counting stereotypes of disability: disabled children and resistance', in M. Corker and T. Shakespeare (eds) *Disability/Postmodernity Embodying Disability Theory*, London: Continuum.

Department of Culture, Media and Sport (2001) *A Sporting Future for All: The Governments Plan for Sport*, London: Department of Culture, Media and Sport.

DePauw, K.P. and Doll-Tepper, T.G. (2000) 'Towards progressive inclusion and acceptance: myth or reality? The inclusion debate and bandwagon discourse', *Adapted Physical Activity Quarterly* 17: 135–43.

Downs, P. (1995) *An Introduction to Inclusive Practices*, Belconnen: Australian Sports Commission.

English Federation of Disability Sport (1999) *Building a Fairer Sporting Society. A four year sports development plan for disabled people in England 2000–2004*, Alsager: English Federation of Disability Sport.

Finklestein, V. (1980) *Attitudes to Disabled People*, New York: World Rehabilitation Fund.

Fitzgerald, H., Jobling, A. and Kirk, D. (2003) 'Listening to the "voices" of students with severe learning difficulties through a task-based approach to research and learning in physical education', *Support for Learning, British Journal of Learning Support* 18(3): 122–8.

—— (forthcoming) 'Valuing the voices of young disabled people: exploring experiences of physical education and sport', *European Journal of Physical Education*.

Gard, M. and Meyenn, R. (2000) 'Boys, bodies, pleasure and pain: interrogating contact sports in schools', *Sports, Education and Society* 5(1): 19–34.

Graham, G. (1995) 'PE through students' eyes and in students' voices: introduction', *Journal of Teaching in Physical Education* 14: 364–71.

Grey-Thompson, T. (2001) *Seize the Day: My Autobiography*, London: Hodder and Stoughton.

Hughes, B. (2002) 'Bauman's strangers: impairment and the invalidation of disabled people in modern and post-modern cultures', *Disability and Society* 17(5): 571–84.

Ministry of Education (1999) *Health and Physical Education in the New Zealand Curriculum*, Wellington: Learning Media.

Morris, J. (1991) *Pride Against Prejudice*, London: Women's Press.

NASPE. (1995) *Moving Into the Future: National PE Standards: A Guide to Content and Assessment*, Boston, MA: McGraw-Hill Education.

Oliver, K. (2001) 'Images of the body from popular culture: engaging adolescent girls in critical inquiry', *Sport, Education and Society* 6(2): 143–64.

Oliver, K. and Lalik, R. (2001) 'The body as curriculum: learning with adolescent girls', *Journal of Curriculum Studies* 33(3): 303–33.

Oliver, M. (1990) *The Politics of Disablement*, Basingstoke: Macmillan.

Penney, D. (2002) 'Equality, equity and inclusion in physical education and school sport', in A. Laker (ed.) *The Sociology of Sport and Physical Education: An Introductory Reader*, London: RoutledgeFalmer.

Priestley, M. (1999) 'Discourse and identity: disabled children in mainstream high schools', in M. Corker and S. French (eds) *Disability Discourse*, Buckingham: Open University Press.

—— (2001) 'Introduction: the global context of disability', in M. Priestley (ed.) *Disability and the Life Course Global Perspectives*, Cambridge: Cambridge University Press.

Qualifications and Curriculum Authority (2001) *Planning, Teaching and Assessing the Curriculum for Pupils with Learning Difficulties Physical Education*, London: Qualifications and Curriculum Authority.

Renshaw, P. (1998) 'Sociocultural pedagogy for new times: reframing key concepts', *The Australian Educational Researcher* 25(3): 83–100.

Rose, R. (2002) 'Teaching as a "research-based profession": encouraging practitioner research in special education', *British Journal of Special Education* 29(1): 44–8.

Russell, M. (2002) 'What disability civic rights cannot do: employment and political economy', *Disability and Society* 17(2): 117–35.

Shakespeare, T. and Watson, N. (1998) 'Theoretical perspectives on research with disabled children', in C. Robinson and K. Stalker (eds) *Growing Up with Disability*, London: Jessica Kingsley.

Sherrill, C. (1998) *Adapted Physical Activity, Recreation and Sport: Cross-disciplinary and Lifespan*, Dubuque: WCB/McGraw-Hill.

Sport England. (2001) *Disability Survey 2000 Young People with a Disability and Sport, Headline Findings*, London: Sport England.

Swain, J. and Cameron, C. (1999) 'Unless otherwise stated: discourses of labelling and identity in coming out', in M. Corker and S. French (eds) *Disability Discourse*, Buckingham: Open University Press.

Thomas, C. (1999) *Female Forms: Experiencing and Understanding Disability*, Buckingham: Open University Press.

Ward, L. (1997) 'Funding for change: translating emancipatory disability research from theory to practice', in C. Barnes and G. Mercer (eds) *Doing Disability Research*, Leeds: The Disability Press.

Chapter 7

Movement, art and culture

Problem-solving and critical inquiry in dance

Michael Gard

My purpose in this chapter is to suggest some ideas for teaching dance in physical education classes. This means that I will not spend time discussing the uncomfortable and marginal place dance has tended to occupy within physical education. As important as it is, a number of thoughtful analyses and discussions of this issue exist elsewhere (for example, Brennan 1996; Evans 1988; Flintoff 1991, 1994; Talbot 1997; Wright 1996). However, it is an issue that we can never really put behind us, particularly if one is interested in what is distinctive about dance. In other words, I think we need to admit that dance is qualitatively different from activities such as competitive and recreational sports, and that the things which make it distinctive can also be the things which make it unattractive to physical educators. To take a straightforward example, unlike sport, dance is often explicitly concerned with emotional expression. For many school and university physical educators, expressing emotion for and/or with students is seen as either outside what they perceive as physical education's 'core business' or outside of their own personal 'comfort zones', or both.

By no means should this imply that physical educators should wear all the blame for devaluing dance within education. Bolwell (1998) argues that dance educators themselves have tended to be narrow and unimaginative in terms of their educational vision for dance, often preferring (much like physical educators) to focus only on the acquisition of movement skill. One obvious consequence of this has been that dance educators have not always been able to put forward convincing reasons why physical education should be interested in dance. And as Bannon and Sanderson (2000) point out, the question of how dance might fit within and contribute to physical education remains largely unexplored.

With these points in mind, my emphasis in this chapter will be on the distinctive contribution dance might make to promoting critical inquiry in physical education. There are at least two reasons for doing this. First, there is little to be gained by duplicating points made elsewhere in this volume. But more importantly, physical education is the poorer for its neglect of dance regardless of who is to blame, a point I have made more fully elsewhere (Gard 2001, 2002). Implicit in this second point is both a belief that dance can enrich the school experience of children in distinctive ways, and also a realisation that some of the teaching ideas that

I present here will push at the boundaries of what is normally considered physical education's subject matter.

As the various chapters in this volume indicate, there are many ways in which teachers might help children to develop critical inquiry and problem-solving skills while learning about sport. The study of dance presents us with a similar (if not greater) range of possibilities and a single chapter about teaching dance inevitably entails omitting many potential approaches. Therefore, I have chosen to concentrate on three approaches to dance education, two relatively well known and a third which I am currently developing in my own teaching. These traditions are in many ways discreet and represent different, and sometimes opposing, visions of what children should learn. For each tradition I will outline the kinds of thinking skills which proponents claim can be developed and describe examples of activities. While I would welcome more physical educators with technical expertise in dance, none of the suggestions I make in this chapter assume any level of formal dance training on the part of teachers.

Movement

Perhaps the approach to dance education with which physical educators will be most familiar is the one called 'creative dance' or 'creative movement'. Historically, creative dance grew in popularity and credibility in tandem with more general educational trends towards more liberal, holistic, child-centred and process-oriented approaches to teaching. Consequently, proponents of creative dance have emphasised concepts such as 'body awareness', 'creativity' and 'expressivity'.

Creative dance has its critics. In particular, there are those who see it as a frivolous waste of precious classroom time and seriously doubt the educational benefits which are claimed by its proponents. This is not the place to buy into this debate, suffice to say that my inclusion of it in this chapter indicates my belief that carefully planned and sequenced creative dance programmes can be extraordinarily rewarding and valuable experiences for teachers and students.

Whether or not one believes creative dance can be used to develop problem-solving and critical inquiry skills depends largely on how one defines these skills. For example, what if we decided that the body and its infinite movement possibilities represented 'movement problems' to be explored? In this case, one approach in creative dance might be to ask students to solve age-appropriate 'movement problems'. With early secondary students this could mean focusing on one body part (arm, hand, finger, head, elbow, foot and so on) and exploring its movement possibilities. It could also mean experimenting with different methods of locomotion and different ways of doing each method. Varying the 'way' in which students locomote could mean varying the direction, speed, tempo, pathway and quality (smooth, languid, robotic, jerky, etc.). Students might work alone (for example, free movement to music), in pairs (for example, where one child 'mirrors' the movement of another) or in small groups (for example, where several students line up behind a leader and follow her around the room).

As always, how these experiences are taught is central to. their potential to achieve desired educational outcomes and, in keeping with other chapters in this volume, the development of problem-solving skills, rather than simply making choices, is pivotal. So we are not talking about teachers suggesting that children 'move like this' or 'move like that'; we are talking about children working out, by using their bodies, how to move in new ways. To facilitate this process, most creative dance teaching resources advocate structuring lessons around what are usually called 'the elements of dance'. Although the exact list of elements tends to vary, the rationale is that the elements of dance provide children with 'thinking tools'. For example, students might be challenged to vary the level, direction, energy, speed and pathway with which their body and/or body parts move. Early lessons in dance units could ask students to devise short movement phrases that conform to a set of criteria (for example, fast, low and circular).[1] In later lessons they could be asked to devise longer movement sequences, perhaps involving small groups of students, utilising a more complex set of dance elements. As well as the elements of dance, a wide range of other stimulus material, such as stories, images, music, historical events and current affairs, can be used to generate movement. While a now considerable creative dance literature provides teachers with further ideas for stimulus material, in general, the more successful approaches tend to be those which strike a balance between being open-ended enough to allow children space to create their own unique movement sequences, but not so open-ended that students are 'paralysed' by freedom. Teachers should bear in mind that for many of us, there are few things more terrifying than being asked to 'move any way you want' in front of other people.

At this point, some readers may be wondering about the relevance of creative movement to critical inquiry, as opposed to problem-solving which I have emphasised so far. Although I will say more about critical inquiry in the next two sections, the more thoughtful dance educators would ask teachers and students to think about the body as a site of infinite movement possibilities (see Shapiro 1998, for a more detailed discussion of this point). So if/when students are discomforted, amused or excited about being challenged to move their bodies in new ways, these reactions represent important teaching opportunities. A variety of questions for discussion and critical reflection present themselves: What is the difference between 'normal' and 'weird' movement? Why does it feel good/bad to move in new ways? To what extent are these feelings influenced by the expectations of other people? Do we go through our lives without exploring our bodily possibilities? Is this a good or bad thing? To what extent is bodily conformity forced on people? Can we think of examples of where bodily conformity is enforced? Does bodily conformity take different forms for male/female, able/disabled, young/old, gay/straight, English speaking/nonEnglish speaking or white/black people?

These questions could then feed back in as stimuli for further movement exploration exercises. One obvious example that I have used in my own teaching is where students set up familiar social situations using props and performers (perhaps a crowded train, a restaurant, a classroom, a bank queue) and then 'comment' about the movements which are 'normally' associated with that situation. This 'commentary' may take the form of parody (where students exaggerate the level of conformity of bodily movement in that situation), disruption (where they depict people moving in ways that are 'inappropriate' in that situation) and/or juxtaposition (where they create contrast by depicting 'appropriate' and 'inappropriate' movement side-by-side). These exercises have yielded some of the most creative and critically thoughtful (not to mention funny!) student work I have seen. In short, these student-centred activities create spaces for the students to ask their own questions about the world in which they live.

Before concluding this section, it is also important to say something about assessment, evaluation and critical enquiry. As Zakkai (1997) points out, asking students to evaluate the movement phrases, sequences and dances that they create is a crucial and yet often overlooked part of creative dance programmes. Asking students to talk or write about movement gives teachers a chance to check students' understanding of the concepts being taught. So we are not simply talking about students saying whether or not they liked a particular movement; we are talking about them using the concepts that underpinned the lesson to justify their opinions. But perhaps just as importantly, by asking students to give and justify their opinions we can help them to see that their opinions matter. While there are many reasons why students at all levels of education might resist or fail at tasks which require them to think critically, one important reason is surely that some students simply do not value their own voice. Dance movement, more so than sport movement, is something about which we can form subjective and evaluative opinions. This evaluative dimension is something which some teachers have sought to de-emphasise, particularly when it is the students' own movement creations which are being evaluated. This is a mistake. In fact, without this dimension, the criticism that creative dance is a frivolous use of classroom time becomes considerably more difficult to refute.

Art

I now want to extend this point about critical inquiry and dance evaluation by drawing on the work of the philosopher of dance, Graham McFee (1992, 1994, 1997). As I will show later, McFee's views are by no means universally accepted. In addition, his work does not specifically address classroom practice. However, in this section I want to draw on his particular rationale for using dance to educate children, suggest some ways in which his ideas might work in practice and prepare the scene for the final section of this chapter in which I address more recent thinking about dance education.

McFee (1994) argues that when deciding matters of curriculum content (what to teach), there are usually many more things that we could or would like to include than is practically possible. Therefore, although we might consider dance important, there may simply be more important things for schools to concern themselves with. Of course, whether or not dance is seen as important enough for inclusion is, in the end, a value judgement, and while dance may be a compulsory area of study in many physical education curricula, this has clearly not been enough to guarantee that it will be taught – far from it.

For McFee, these realities mean that a distinctive rationale for teaching dance must be put forward, and particularly one that is different from those given for teaching sport. Without this distinctive rationale McFee argues that we should neither be surprised nor particularly worried if dance is not taught. But this rationale must not only be distinctive, it must also argue credibly that dance is sufficiently important to warrant inclusion. McFee's answer to this challenge is to focus on dance as a performing art.

It will be immediately clear that the study of dance as art is a very different vision of dance education from the creative movement approach. A study of 'art' suggests that we can talk about 'good' and 'bad' dance, while the tendency of creative movement is to make fewer judgements of this kind. At this point readers may be concerned by the elitist overtones in McFee's focus on artistic dance. I have similar concerns which I will return to in the next section, but for the moment I want to explore the pedagogical possibilities that this approach suggests.

The first thing to be said is that an 'art' focus in dance teaching suggests that students should be exposed to the work of professional dancers and choreographers. There is now a well-established tradition of classical music appreciation programmes for children of all ages and there have been and continue to be similar, if not always so well-known, dance programmes (in both ballet and modern dance) in which children are able to watch live performances, listen to artists talk about their work and ask questions. And while attending live performances can be economically and geographically prohibitive, the last decade or so has seen a proliferation of text, video and computer-based resources which present the work of dance artists and which invite viewers to consider the art of dance-making. However, the issue here is not simply about watching dance, but also thinking about it. McFee wants teachers and students to think about what makes a piece of dance art 'good' or 'bad' in much the same way as a dance critic might.

There are at least two ways we can approach the issue of evaluating artistic dance. The first and most straightforward is the one I touched on briefly at the end of the previous section. That is, students are asked to view works of artistic dance as movement sequences. What kinds of movement were used? Can particular movement themes be identified? How were the dancers arranged in space and relative to each other? What were the effects of these aspects of the performance? For these kinds of questions it may be useful for students to refer back to the 'elements of dance' (discussed in the previous section) in order to articulate their answers. If music was used, how did the music relate to the movement? What qualities did the movement and the music share or not share, what about the clothes the dancers wore, the arrangement of the stage or props if there were any, the lighting? We should also not forget that students may want to express their opinions in less prosaic terms. For example, their reactions may be more emotional, personal or intellectual. So by posing these questions I am not suggesting that whether or not students liked or disliked the dance work is unimportant. What I am highlighting is the importance of focusing on the process of evaluation.

This approach to critical inquiry raises the question of whether subjecting dance (or any art form) to this kind of structured analysis necessarily diminishes the pleasure students might derive from watching dance. This is a difficult and complex issue for which there are no straightforward solutions. My own teaching suggests the choice of dance work is absolutely crucial if one hopes to engage students. Another important consideration is whether the students are able to 'personalise' the dance work and it is to this aspect that I now turn.

A second approach to dance evaluation, focusing on the 'meaning' of dance, is conceptually more complex but potentially more rewarding. It is also probably more useful to think of it as an extension of the more structured movement analysis I described above. After all, part of our personal and emotional response to a dance work is likely to be connected to the actual movements that were used. However, this is surely not the whole story. A dance work may excite, move or make us think because of its mood, its narrative or because it connects with something in our own life. Once again, this would seem to present us with a rich vein of learning experiences which are more easily tapped via dance movement, because of its explicitly expressive qualities, than through other movement disciplines. In order to develop these ideas, consider the following examples.

During 2002, the Australian contemporary dance company Chunky Move presented their work *Australia's Most Wanted: Ballet for a Contemporary Democracy*. The preparation of this work involved the distribution of questionnaires to the public in which people were asked to nominate the elements they most liked to see in dance performances. For example, people had to select their preferred distance from the stage, kind and volume of music, balance between entertainment and intellectual stimulation, whether or not they wanted dance which told a story and so on. Taking the results of the questionnaires, the company created dance pieces which conformed to the preferences of men, women and the public in general. They also created an item out of all the 'least wanted' elements. The different dance items were extremely thought-provoking in themselves and could easily provide stimulus material to help students discuss their own preferences. However, behind the performances lay deeper questions about the society in which we live. Specifically, the artists wanted to draw attention to the tendency of governments and other organisations to base their decisions on the results of opinion polls and to consider what is meant by the word 'popular'.

On a slightly different level, the English dance company DV8 Physical Theatre has also created a number of superbly original dance pieces, many of which are available on video, dealing with different aspects of personal and sexual relationships. In much of this work, the viewer is asked to consider what is 'normal' sexual behaviour and how our ideas about what is 'normal' are socially produced and maintained.

It is not hard to see how these examples of contemporary dance could serve to stimulate thinking and discussion about sensitive political and cultural issues and what are sometimes called values. McFee writes:

> when speaking of the education of 'values' here, as the centre of education, the intention is not the teaching of a specific value system – that would be preposterous in a multi-cultural, multi-ethnic society (if not anywhere). No, what is intended is the provision of the sorts of intellectual 'tools' needed for questioning preceptively and thinking independently.
>
> (McFee 1994: 31)

But apart from thinking generally about values, what exactly does McFee want students to do? McFee says that thinking, writing and talking about dance should engage students in 'personal inquiry', where the emphasis is on the word 'personal'. Personal inquiry is where students consider other people's feelings, ideas and actions, and listen respectfully to their reasons for feeling and acting as they do. Its purpose then is to challenge students to understand and empathise with other people, even those with whom they disagree. He writes:

> Now this possibility – the possibility of respecting another – is a distinctly human one. If we succeed in mastering it, we will have taken an important step towards becoming a moral agent: we will have begun learning to be a *human being*.
>
> (McFee 1994: 32, emphasis in original)

It will come as no surprise to learn that McFee is interested in notions of social change. But his argument is that worthwhile social change does not happen when people simply learn new standards of behaviour for social interaction. Instead, he sees meaningful social change as tied to the concepts each of us has at our disposal to think about the world. Put another way, his argument is that our experiences of the world, including our feelings, beliefs and attitudes, are strongly influenced by the concepts that shape our thinking. Thus, dance can act as a medium for what he calls 'emotional education' because of the way dance (such as the dance pieces I described above) deals with 'life issues'. For McFee, artistic dance offers students new concepts with which to think about the world:

> A conceptual change – a change in the concepts available to a person – might change the range of desires open to her or him – and hence the range of experiences open to that person. The experience of the arts allows us to experience finer shades of feeling, and may do so because it may allow the refining of those concepts under which those feelings are experienced, and under which those experiences are characterised.
>
> (McFee 1994: 40)

Readers will probably notice that this approach to dance education mirrors somewhat the use of literature in English teaching. As something of a traditionalist, McFee is interested in 'high-culture' art and clearly believes that high-culture dance can have a kind of 'civilising' effect on students. While this belief is vulnerable to the same kind of criticisms that have been levelled at 'traditionalist' English teaching, we can take from McFee the point that a great deal of artistic dance does deal with important 'life issues', and that dances can be treated as 'texts' to be analysed. In the case of the dance work of DV8 Physical Theatre, the stability of constructs such as sex, sexual orientation and gender identity is problematised and, at times, fractured. As with a great deal of other modern and contemporary dance, this work has been, in part, explicitly created in order to communicate with audiences and to engage them in dialogue. This is rarely if ever the case with organised sport[2] and it is this communicative intent which makes artistic dance a potentially rich starting point for critical thought about how the world is and might be.

Culture

McFee's work raises a number of issues. For example, his focus on dance as an art form means that he is exclusively interested in western high-culture artistic dance, particularly ballet and modern dance, and this apparently leaves little space for dance forms with different cultural and ethnic roots. McFee (1994) argues that teaching children how to do ethnic folk dances is nothing more than tokenism and is hardly likely to give students a realistic appreciation of the countries from which these dances originate. He also reminds us that students from non-western backgrounds may be no more likely to identify with folk and traditional dances from their country of origin than western students are with their own ethnic traditions. There is some truth in these arguments. Certainly, as physical educators, we have tended to see our contribution to multiculturalism as extending no further than learning the names and steps of a handful of folk dances.

Yet, McFee's vision for dance education seems impoverished on a number of levels. While it is true that simply doing the dances of another country is unlikely to make authorities of its history and culture out of any of us, what students derive from these experiences will depend largely on how they are framed by teachers and by the thinking that students are asked to do. It is also a mistake to think that our purpose for studying nonwestern dance is to develop an anthropological appreciation of other cultures. For one thing, some would point out that this kind of knowledge belongs to other areas of the curriculum. More importantly though, in making this argument it is clear that McFee has lost sight of the point he started with: that we should focus on what is distinctive about dance. And if anything is distinctive about dance it is the act of dancing itself. In the remainder of this section I want to suggest an alternative reason for doing nonwestern dance by exploring the idea that different forms of dance embody different ways of thinking. And although 'critical inquiry' can be defined in a number of different ways, the ability to transcend the ideas, concepts and beliefs we take for granted is undoubtedly a crucial, if not fundamental element.

The anthropological and ethnographic study of dance around the world suggests that the act of dancing is always related to who the dancer is, his/her identity and his/her place in a particular society. Therefore, I am proposing that we need to find space within the notion of critical inquiry for a kind of embodied inquiry, where the challenge is to become someone else, to imagine what it is like to be them and to understand the significance of dance in their life, a task which is not exhausted by simply learning a new set of movements. This is similar to McFee's idea of 'emotional education' through dance appreciation, although I am focusing on movement itself as the primary pedagogical medium, as opposed to discussion and reflective thought.

Let us take some practical examples. Working with primary school children, Bond (1994) wanted to transcend the gender stereotypes which tended to lock the boys and girls in her class into particular ways of moving. Her strategy was to develop dances using 'tribal' or 'African' themes, as well as having children design and make their own masks which they wore during performances. According to Bond, the masks created a kind of performative 'license' for students to move in new ways and to immerse themselves in their characters.

In my own teaching I have made use of the expertise of indigenous Australian and Indian dancers with secondary students. In both cases, the dancers/teachers combined story-telling, music and detailed movement instruction to take students through the religious and cultural meanings of different dances and the ways in which these meanings were embodied in movement. In the case of Indian dancing, the meanings of different gestures, the cultural importance of precision and control, and the significance of the different male and female movement qualities served to enrich what might otherwise have been a purely mimetical exercise. What was striking was the dancer/teacher's emphasis on the need to 'feel' the movement and to 'imagine' who one was meant to become. Likewise, indigenous Australian dancing is also tightly bound up with culturally specific narratives, such as those concerned with life, death, time, the relationships between people and between people and their land. Both are examples of an embodied critical inquiry in that students were asked to think their way into the movement, on the one hand, and move as a way of imagining, on the other.

Needless to say, these were not completely comfortable experiences for all students and it has become increasingly clear to me that experiences of this kind are much less likely to be successful if they are appear as 'one-offs' during the school year. In fact, they may even be counter-productive unless these experiences, and the discussions and activities which support and build on them, are seen as a 'normal' part of doing physical education. For example, dance instruction which is meant to facilitate 'embodied critical inquiry' needs also to be embedded within a physical education programme which is explicitly concerned with critical inquiry generally, and in developing cross-cultural understanding in particular.

It would also be more effective where dance *per se* is seen as a legitimate, regular and valued activity by students and teachers.

Can we be sure about what students will learn through this kind of embodied critical inquiry? In developing this approach to teaching dance, I have sought to embed it within a wider curriculum framework in which the study of cultures is seen as a way of generating new insights. Therefore, they are preceded and followed by discussions and reflective writing which attempt to make explicit the modes of thinking which underpin western cultural and social practices. For example, in what ways does the treatment of older people in the west differ from other cultural traditions, and what kinds of beliefs make these different social practices possible? Put more simply, what are some of the different ways in which we can think about older people and what effects might these ways of thinking have? These kinds of activities and questions do not, however, make 'learning' inevitable, mainly because I am dealing here with a form of learning about which little is known; nobody has yet found a foolproof way of engendering both critical, tolerant and ethical modes of thinking amongst students. Nor is anyone ever likely to, not least because the meaning of the terms critical, tolerant and ethical are themselves disputed. However, what I have tried to suggest here is a mode of teaching in which the distinctiveness of dance (as a form of movement) and dancing (as a mode of learning) is central, and where the culturally and socially inscribed nature of bodily movement is the starting point for critical inquiry.

Thinking critically about physical education

As well as surveying some current thinking about dance education, I have attempted to think critically about dance in particular and physical education in general. And while readers will form their own opinion about the success or otherwise of this exercise, one point is fundamental: as physical educators, we need to continue thinking critically about why and how we use dance in physical education. The current situation in which dance is often seen, at best, as a syllabus obligation will not change unless we can think of good reasons to offer dance and interesting things for students to do.

However, for the development of problem-solving and critical inquiry skills to be a realistic objective of dance education, both dance and pedagogies which promote these skills need to be a normal part of the practice of physical education. As many teachers know, students are often resistant to dance instruction. But who could blame them if their understanding is that physical education is primarily concerned with the development of sporting skills or simply participation in sport?

Therefore, the suggestions I have made in this chapter return us to the question of the status of dance within school physical education and teacher education programmes. But they also raise questions about the position and status of the social sciences and humanities. If my discussions of art and culture in this chapter seem far removed from 'normal' physical education, then it is because of the extent to which physical education as a discipline has generally come to see itself as a pseudo-science, concerned mostly with the body as a machine and only incidentally with the body as a culturally and socially located entity. Dance, as a primarily social (as opposed to competitive) and aesthetic (as opposed to instrumental) form of physical activity, has the potential to greatly extend the pedagogical possibilities of physical education. As yet, this potential remains largely untapped.

Notes

1   David Spurgeon's *Dance Moves: From Improvisation to Dance* (1991) offers teachers a large variety of stimulus ideas and movement games designed to help students create movement phrases and to move students past any initial anxieties they might have about moving in new or 'weird' ways.
2   This comment is not intended to suggest that sporting movement cannot also be treated as a 'text' which communicates meaning to an audience. My point is that this is rarely the primary or explicit purpose.

References

Bannon, F. and Sanderson, P. (2000) 'Experience every moment: aesthetically significant dance education', *Research in Dance Education* 1(1): 9–26.

Bolwell, J. (1998) 'Into the light: an expanding vision of dance education', in S.B. Shapiro (ed.) *Dance, Power and Difference: Critical and Feminist Perspectives on Dance Education*, Champaign, IL: Human Kinetics.

Bond, K. (1994) 'How "wild things" tamed gender distinctions', *Journal of Physical Education, Recreation and Dance* 65(2): 28–33.

Brennan, D. (1996) 'Dance in the Northern Ireland physical education curriculum: a farsighted policy or an unrealistic innovation', *Women's Studies International Forum* 19(5): 493–503.

Evans J. (1988) 'Introduction: teachers, teaching and control', in J. Evans (ed.) *Teachers, Teaching and Control in Physical Education*, Brighton: Falmer Press.

Flintoff, A. (1991) 'Dance, masculinity and teacher education', *The British Journal of Physical Education* (Winter): 31–5.

—— (1994) 'Sexism and homophobia in physical education: the challenge for teacher educators', *Physical Education Review* 17(2): 97–105.

Gard, M. (2001) 'Dancing around the "problem" of boys and dance', *Discourse: Studies in the Cultural Politics of Education* 22(2): 213–25.

—— (2002) 'What do we do in physical education?', in R. Kissen (ed.) *Getting Ready for Benjamin: Preparing Teachers for Sexual Diversity*, Lanham, MD: Rowman & Littlefield.

McFee, G. (1992) *Understanding Dance*, London: Routledge.

—— (1994) *The Concept of Dance Education*, London: Routledge.

—— (1997) 'Education, art and the physical: the case of the academic study of dance – present and future', in G. McFee and A. Tomlinson (eds) *Education, Sport and Leisure: Connections and Controversies*, Aachen: Meyer & Meyer Verlag.

Shapiro, S.B. (1998) 'Toward transformative teachers: critical and feminist perspectives in dance education', in S.B. Shapiro (ed.) *Dance, Power and Difference: Critical and Feminist Perspectives on Dance Education*, Champaign, IL: Human Kinetics.

Spurgeon, D. (1991) *Dance Moves: From Improvisation to Dance*, Sydney: Harcourt Brace Jovanovich.

Talbot, M. (1997) 'Physical education and the national curriculum: some political issues', in G. McFee and A. Tomlinson (eds) *Sport and Leisure: Connections and Controversies*, Aachen: Meyer & Meyer Verlag.

Wright, J. (1996) 'The construction of complementarity in physical education', *Gender and Education* 8(1): 61–79.

Zakkai, J.D. (1997) *Dance as a Way of Knowing*, York: Stenhouse Publishers.

Chapter 8

Understanding and investigating cultural perspectives in physical education

Lisette Burrows

Introduction

Curriculum frameworks, at least in Australia, New Zealand and the UK, are increasingly acknowledging that physical education must contribute to students' understanding of the diverse meanings and practices attached to physical culture. As pointed out in Chapter 1, concepts like critical thinking, critical inquiry and problem-solving feature prominently in syllabus documentation, reflecting the now widespread educational interest in fostering students' capacity to learn how to learn and to engage with the proliferation of uncertain knowledge characterising 'new times'. An investment in sociocultural aspects of physical education is also evidenced in new syllabuses. In New Zealand, for example, the health and physical education curriculum requires students to explore topics such as 'societal attitudes and beliefs', 'people and the environment' and 'identity, sensitivity and respect'. 'Social and cultural' factors are explicitly foregrounded as key constituents of learning in the 'movement concepts and motor skills' domain (Ministry of Education 1999). Respect for the diverse ethnic and cultural heritage of New Zealand people, and the acknowledgment of the unique place of Maori is also specified as a requirement of curriculum in the National Education Guidelines (Ministry of Education 1993) of New Zealand.

As suggested in Chapter 1, neither of these orientations is new, but rather what has changed is the incorporation of this twin attention to cognitive theories of learning and sociocultural knowledge in mainstream physical education. This shift from the margins to mainstream potentially opens up opportunities for students' own cultural heritages and preferences in health and physical education to be valued and included in curriculum and learning processes. It also establishes opportunities for physical educators to position themselves as facilitators of young peoples' understanding of culturally diverse values and social practices linked to physical activity and (in the case of New Zealand and Australia) health.

English-speaking countries such as the UK, Canada, the US, Australia and New Zealand are now generally understood as ethnically diverse by both definition and make-up. Extensive migration in the US for example, has meant that bicultural, rather than monocultural, populations have almost become the norm in urban centres like Los Angeles, San Francisco, Chicago and New York (Darder 1991).

In New Zealand and Australia, there has been a rapid influx of students from South Asia, South Africa and the UK. These migratory trends coupled with an increased recognition of indigenous cultures in places like Canada and New Zealand have produced an expectation that schools not only recognise differences, but provide opportunities for individuals to be educated in their own diverse languages and learning styles. An expectation that schools will endeavour to create educational climates, materials and approaches that are sensitive to and celebratory of the diverse histories, cultural orientations and experiences students bring with them to schools is now fairly commonplace. Furthermore, there appears to be a recognition that culture is not a homogeneous concept.

Within and across cultural groups commonly lumped together (for example, Asian, African-Caribbean, Native-American, Maori) ethnocultural diversities invariably exist. Every day, students identify and associate with a diversity of cultural practices. As many scholars have pointed out, if the notion of 'one culture' is actually rather meaningless, then the concept of 'multicultural' is equally problematic (Irwin 1989). Nevertheless, until recently, school syllabuses and teaching practices have, even in their most 'progressive' guises, assumed the existence of a 'common culture' around which a range of 'other' multicultural expressions circulate. As Darder points out, 'multicultural initiatives' in the US tend to emphasise activities like bringing cultural artefacts into the classroom and participating in activities of 'different' cultures.

> Many situations exist in which students are presented with games, food, stories, language, music, and other cultural forms in such a way as to strip these expressions of intent by reducing them to mere objects disembodied from their cultural meaning.
>
> (Darder 1991: 113)

In New Zealand too, multicultural educational initiatives of the 1970s and 1980s emphasised activities like making poi, playing Maori stick games, and presenting cultural artefacts and traditions to students in ways that function to dissolve cultural differences and promote Eurocentric interpretations of the way 'other cultures' operate (Hirsch 1990). These processes, while often enacted with good intent, contributed little to an understanding of cultural differences and indeed often served to distort depictions of students' cultural histories (Irwin 1989).

What is both exciting and challenging about current ways of thinking about culture and ethnicity is the opportunities they afford for addressing issues related to power and equity in schooling. Expectations that physical education has a responsibility to understand and work with the diversity of cultures with which students identify and associate on a daily basis open up spaces for physical education to do things differently. When culture is not regarded as predictable, deterministic and shared by all the members of a specific ethnic group, the notion that the dominant culture should make all decisions about what counts as curriculum, how curriculum gets taught and for what ends has little purchase.

Physical educators often assume that religion, culture and parental constraint are responsible for the relative nonengagement of students from nondominant cultures in sport and physical activity. The stereotyping and categorising of all people of Asian descent, for example, as less able and willing to participate in sport is commonplace in British physical education and elsewhere (Chappell 2002). It is only recently, that we have begun to recognise that current forms of physical education are premised on interests and values that inevitably result in the alienation of large numbers of children. That is, physical education, not students from nondominant backgrounds is 'the problem' (Evans and Davies 1993). Addressing these issues is neither easy nor straightforward, yet there are some examples, within physical education, of educators who are taking up the challenges implicit in affirming cultural diversity in their practice.

In the first section of this chapter, I describe New Zealand-based initiatives that point to the utility of physical education and health education as contexts within which cultural perspectives can be valued and explored. In the second section, I describe two generic strategies that may encourage students in the junior and middle years to critically analyse the interrelationships between cultural identity and physical activity. I suggest that the critical inquiry, critical thinking and problem-solving approaches that are currently being foregrounded in constructivist theories of learning and sociocultural perspectives of physical education, are processes that potentially enable both students and teachers to understand the ways in which ethnicity informs their own and others' orientation toward and experiences of physical activity. Critical inquiry processes can facilitate an understanding that engagement in physical activity does not happen in a social and/or cultural vacuum; that people who engage in similar activities may derive a plurality of meanings from this engagement; and, that sport and physical education can function as a medium for both the production and reproduction of ethnic difference. These processes may also create opportunities to honour and maintain the distinctiveness of different cultural values and beliefs about physical activity and simultaneously contribute to a developed sense of community within wider physical culture.

Multiplying meaning in physical education

'Culture' is a highly contested and relational concept. If I were writing for a New Zealand context only, culture would explicitly refer to practices and world views embraced by indigenous Maori. In the context of this paper, which speaks to an audience both within and outside New Zealand, I am using the phrase 'cultural perspectives' to refer to the perspectives of (any) individuals, groups and/or communities 'which see themselves as different by virtue of history, religion and/or language' (Epstein 1997: 4). In doing so, I do not wish to imply any essentialist biological basis for culture or any kind of homogenous category. Rather, I draw on Epstein's suggestion that differences between groups are constructed 'over time and in relation to socio-economic and political change, and will also carry varying salience for different (groups) of people at different times' (Epstein 1997: 3).

Regarding culture as 'relational' invites us to interrogate the plurality of meanings physical education and health practices may potentially have for students and consider the variety of cultural resources that students bring with them to the study of physical education. Employing a relational notion of culture also demands consideration of the historical, social, economic and political circumstances within which students construct their identities as 'healthy' citizens and make choices in relation to physical activity. Finally, thinking about culture relationally requires analysis of the consequences of privileging dominant cultural values and traditions in physical activity over those embraced by children of diverse cultural heritages. Questions like, 'Whose interests are privileged when large ball skills are the major constituent of a physical education programme?' and 'What happens to children when they rarely recognise themselves as capable or interested participants in school-based physical education programmes?', are integral to such an approach.

One defining feature of physical education and health curricula is the certainty attached to both the uptake and delivery of knowledge about physical activity. As discussed in Chapter 1, rapid changes in specialist and technical knowledge mean that students need skills to negotiate the vast amounts of often confusing and contradictory information they engage with. Uncertainty, rather than certainty characterises knowledge production in the realms of physical activity and physical culture, yet in physical education there has been a tendency to represent established knowledge about motor skills, exercise, health, fitness and sport as if it were the 'truth'. For example, a programme largely comprised of sports and fitness activities continues to dominate school curricula, despite contemporary trends that indicate youths are preferring a range of individual recreational activities to team sports (Fitzclarence and Tinning 1992; Penney 2002). Many teachers continue to prescribe daily fitness activities and dietary practices premised on biophysical principles that have been seriously challenged in recent times (Gard and Wright 2001). Knowledge about healthy lifestyles is distributed to students in ways that suggest particular practices (e.g. not smoking, eating the correct foods) will produce a healthy person (Burrows *et al.* 2002). As Atrens (2001) and others suggest, definitions of 'health' and information about how to achieve has always been contestable, contradictory and subject to variations across time and place.

The assumption that principles derived from one particular frame of reference are universally applicable, that has been widely critiqued both in physical education (Evans and Clarke 1988; Tinning *et al.* 2001) and in education more generally (Dahlberg *et al.* 1999; Morss 1996). The notion that all children learn in similar ways, that people progress through a series of chronological stages of growth and development and that particular types of activities are universally 'good' for children at particular ages and stages continues to underpin much of what goes on physical education despite this critique (Burrows and Wright 2001). This assumption of a 'normal' child for whom a particular physical education curriculum is appropriate yields little opportunity for recognising or celebrating cultural diversity in the classroom.

In New Zealand, for example, the Heart Foundation's food pyramid is the most widely used teaching resource for nutrition education (Burrows *et al.* 2002). The food pyramid represents a hierarchical ordering of 'healthy' food groups, with many Maori and Pacific Island-preferred food types being those represented as those one should eat least. As Hokowhitu (2001: 267) suggests, 'for a variety of economic, cultural and historical reasons, Maori have been physiologically and culturally geared towards the reverence of fat', yet foods rich in fat are now invested with notions of 'risk' and 'unhealthiness'. Research on the health beliefs of young New Zealanders (Burrows *et al.* 2002), shows that year four and year eight students in New Zealand regardless of ethnicity, consistently refer to fatty foods as 'dangerous' and 'unhealthy'. As Atrens (2001) has convincingly shown, what is regarded as 'healthy' in both popular and biomedical discourse is far from universal, yet a particular notion of what a healthy diet comprises is represented in most school-based resources.

In another example, Wright (1997) has written about the privileging of particular sports skills in fundamental motor skills programmes. She suggests that skills like kicking, striking and throwing linked to male-preferred sports like football, rugby, cricket are consistently foregrounded as 'fundamental' whereas balance and flexibility – capacities linked more often to girls – are marginalised. These findings have implications for all students for whom the particular sports granted elite status in schools have little interest. For example, activities, such as badminton, table tennis, volleyball, martial arts, tai chi and yoga are often marginalised or missing altogether in the subject matter of school-based physical education classes.

It is not only the content of physical education that requires scrutiny. As Bishop and Glynn (1999a, 2000), Durie (1994), Hokowhitu (2001) and Salter (1999) point out, theories of learning premised on western ways of knowing (e.g. developmental psychology) inform most school-based teaching. Self-responsibility narratives, commitments to rationalist forms of inquiry and the grounding of teaching practices in normative notions of how children 'develop' and what capacities they 'need' en route to becoming autonomous adult citizens (Burrows and Wright 2001) fuel teaching practices, yet these are notions that do not necessarily sit well with the cultural proclivities and experiences of all children (Smith 1990). For example, an emphasis on individual responsibility for learning runs contra to Maori-preferred models of learning that privilege connectedness and learning in groups (Bishop and Glynn 1999a; Salter 1999). Similarly, the notion that self-responsibility is the end-point of successful schooling conflicts with Kaupapa Maori valuing of an individual's capacity to contribute to whanau (family) and iwi (tribe) development as a measure of achievement (Bishop and Glyn 1999b). As Salter puts it:

> For Maori, knowledge, lived experiences and the processes of teaching and learning physical education might be understood and represented in quite different ways from those suggested by 'official' pedagogic discourses.
>
> (Salter 2000: 5)

Drawing on Bourdieu's (1973) work on cultural capital several physical education scholars (Hargreaves 1986; Penney and Evans 1999) have shown how the resources required for success in schooling in general and physical education in particular, are generally those displayed by middle-class, western pupils. In a climate where holistic, critical and constructivist models of teaching/learning are being taken up, there is an increasing recognition of the different cultural resources that children bring with them to schooling and the web of social relationships that surround young people both within and outside school. A shift from the individualistic cognitive developmentalist theory of Piaget to an emphasis on sociocultural contexts of learning, evident in work of Vygotsky and others (Rogoff 1990; Smith 1993), yields possibilities for fostering interdependence and collaboration, as well as independence and autonomy. It also yields opportunities for students themselves to consider how specific historical, social, economic and political circumstances have contributed to particular physical education and health practices/outcomes becoming valued over others.

Maori initiatives

In New Zealand, several challenges to the monocultural pedagogies and curricula of 'mainstream' schooling have been mounted in the past three decades (Bishop and Glynn 1999a, 1999b, 2000; Hemara 2000; Hokowhitu 2001; Salter 2000; Smith 1990; Walker 1995). Fuelled by a recognition that the needs and aspirations of Maori students were not being met in regular education institutions, initiatives such as Taha Maori (the Maori dimension), Kura kaupapa Maori (middle years schooling) and Kohanga Reo (language nests for pre-school children) have been encouraged by successive governments in an effort to counter the monocultural frame of reference that New Zealand education has been geared around (Irwin 1988). Each of these initiatives foregrounds Maori values, Maori language and Maori-preferred styles of learning and teaching. Efforts to develop physical education within Maori contexts have also been made since the late 1980s (Salter 2000; Walker 1995) with Te Reo Kori (the language of movement) and latterly Te Ao Kori (world of movement) being incorporated into junior physical education programmes throughout the country (Craig 2001; Salter 2000).

Te Reo Kori, literally translated as 'language of movement', is a school-based physical education programme that uses the medium of movement to promote an understanding of Maori cultural values and language. Students learn the physical skills required to demonstrate traditional Maori movements, Maori language is often used for instructions, and Maori customs linked to particular physical activities are explained along the way. The programme was originally conceived as one that would be accessible to Maori students in mainstream education and non-Maori students with little knowledge of Maori culture (Salter 2000). Critics have suggested that Te Reo Kori has actually functioned to benefit non-Maori more than Maori and that, in some instances, it is a simplistic and ultimately debasing version of aspects of Maori culture that has been transmitted via Te Reo Kori (Hokowhitu 2001). Nevertheless, it is widely accepted that Te Reo Kori has gone some way to acknowledging and centring a Maori dimension in physical education (Salter 2000; Stothart 2000; Walker 1995).

Te Ao Kori, described by Salter (2002) as 'the world of movement from a Maori perspective', was suggested as a replacement term for Te Reo Kori by respected Maori educationalist, Rose Pere in the year 2000. Te Ao Kori differs from Te Reo Kori in its distinctly Maori ancestry and its focus on explicitly meeting Maori students' needs and aspirations in a mainstream schooling context (Salter 2002). It includes a wider range of traditional games and pastimes than Te Reo Kori and adopts a more holistic orientation towards the teaching of these activities. While the physical dimension is still foregrounded, spirituality, the arts, science and technology and health are all integrally involved (Irwin, cited in Craig 2001). For example, students may be engaged in performing traditional dance, building waka (canoes), collecting materials to make kites or making maps. Essential to each of these activities is the promotion of respect for Maori protocols and an understanding of spiritual, intellectual, social, aesthetic and technological aspects of the activities. Perhaps what most clearly distinguishes Te Ao Kori from Te Reo Kori is the explicit valuing of Maori cultural aspirations as equal to those of Pakeha culture.

Together with opportunities to develop skills and knowledge in Maori movement, models like Te Ao Kori provides opportunity to explore the sociopolitical, economic and cultural context within which Maori movement takes place, to understand, experience and appreciate Maori cultural values through movement and to learn something of the Maori language in the process (Salter 2000). As Salter (2000) and others (Irwin, cited in Craig 2001; Pere 1994) suggest, the holistic philosophy driving Te Ao Kori, that is, the desire to connect skill learning with understandings of the cultural values and context within which those skills have meaning, sits well with the student-centred learning approaches currently being promoted in the Health and Physical Education in the New Zealand Curriculum (Ministry of Education 1999).

The notion that learning processes should build on children's life experiences and 'funds of knowledge' (as discussed in Chapter 1) is also well supported in Te Ao Kori in that such a model requires students to engage with the values and social practices associated with physical activity and culture in their world – that is, a country committed to bicultural nation building. While Te Ao Kori is clearly not a package readily transportable to contexts other than Aotearoa and its premises are not even whole-heartedly embraced by Maori or non-Maori educationists in New Zealand (see Hokowhitu 2001), the principle of growing a curriculum from movement, music, language and values unique to indigenous culture is one that can inform the work of physical educators in other contexts. Indeed, the notion of an education premised on students' own experiences and understandings is fundamental to the critical inquiry and problem-solving approaches with which this book is concerned.

Another concept that is having a profound influence on the shaping of physical and health education curricula and pedagogy in New Zealand currently is 'hauora'. Translated somewhat simplistically in the curriculum as 'well-being', hauora is defined in the dictionary of *te reo Maori* (Williams 1975: 41) as 'spirit of life, health, vigour'. As Moeau (1997) and Salter (2000) point out, hau refers to breath while ora designates being alive, well, in health. The HPE curriculum writers drew on Mason Durie's (1994) Whare Tapa Wha model to flesh out what Hauora might mean in the context of a health and physical education curriculum. The Whare Tapa Wha encompasses four dimensions that are each regarded as crucial in the establishment of a person's well-being – taha hinengaro (mind), taha tinana (body), taha wairua (spirituality) and taha whanau (social). As Moeau (1997) and Hokowhitu (2001) have suggested, a fifth dimension, whenua (connectedness with the land), is also integral to this model. The positioning of the four corner-stones of health is indicative of not only the envisaged structure and symbolism of the concept (for example, health represented as the framework of a house providing shelter and security), but also of the interrelatedness of each of the dimensions. Each side of the house and the platform upon which it stands is necessary for the whare (house) to exist and good health cannot be achieved if even one of those sides (dimensions) is not functioning.

There are inherent difficulties in aligning a concept integral to a Maori world view with understandings expressed in another world view (and language). Some commentators have observed that the way hauora is represented in the health and physical education curriculum does not do justice to the richness and complexity of the concept as construed in Maori culture (Salter 2000). Others have charged the curriculum writers with distorting and diluting hauroa to serve dominant interests, viewing its inclusion in mainstream curriculum as a further example of colonisation of indigenous concepts. Still others argue that a Maori concept, such as hauora, has little relevance for students of other nondominant groups (e.g. Asian and Pacific Island students). These are debates that will likely continue for some time. Nevertheless, hauora has been included as a key constituent of the conceptual philosophy of New Zealand's HPE curriculum (Ministry of Education 1999) with many teachers finding it a useful vehicle through which to encourage students to critique and understand their own and others' health and well-being (Heke 2002; Legge forthcoming).

The potential of hauora lies in its recognition that children's dispositions toward health and physical activity and their sense of themselves as 'players' in health and physical culture cannot be considered in a vacuum. Rather the spiritual, mental and physical components of people together with people's connectedness to family/community and place equally contribute to a sense of 'aliveness' or 'wellness' at any point in time. Conceiving of well-being in such a holistic fashion disrupts conventional mind/body dichotomies, disturbs everyday understandings that health and fitness can be achieved through individual discipline and effort alone, and creates possibilities for students to recognise and interrogate multiple meanings for their own and others' health and well-being. As a platform for critical inquiry and problem-solving, hauora seems to offer considerable potential for teachers of junior and middle years students. If nothing else, the presence of hauora in mainstream curricula points to the fact that there are as many different ways of constructing health and the place of physical activity in contributing to this as there are social and cultural groups. It would seem worthwhile to both identify and explore these to better assist students to develop a social cultural perspective on health and physical activity.

Cultivating critical inquiry and celebrating diverse cultural perspectives

Cognisant of the perils of promoting catch-all pedagogical models as solutions to diverse curriculum challenges, in this section, I describe two generic strategies that may be usefully adapted to facilitate understanding of cultural perspectives in a middle school or junior school context. The examples I use to illustrate these are drawn from my own work and that of scholars and school-based teachers in the fields of education, health and physical education. They are by no means exhaustive as examples for addressing cultural difference in physical education. Rather, my intent is to open windows of opportunity for facilitating children's capacity to both critique and understand their own and others' experiences of physical activity in ways that honour the unique cultural resources and identities they bring to the institution of schooling.

Rethinking curriculum

How does what we teach value the diverse cultural heritage and identities of children in the class? This question orients us toward considering what counts as valid physical education. If, as Penny (2002) and others (Tinning *et al.* 2001) suggest, major sports, fundamental motor skills, fitness activities and games are the main constituents of physical education programmes, then questions about whose interests these activities serve, whose cultural values and preferences are foregrounded, and with what consequences are paramount. There are several ways one could address this issue.

First, engaging students themselves in conversations about what they would like to learn in physical education is a process that potentially yields opportunities for a deprivileging of competitive mainstream sports as the core of a physical education programme. Research on young people's attitudes to, and engagement in, physical education points to the productiveness of this strategy (Carlson 1995; Graham 1995; Lineham forthcoming). Studies show, for instance, that children and young people are more than capable of discussing the relevance of current offerings to their lives and of articulating their likes and dislikes (Graham 1995), and their vision for a physical education that is responsive to their everyday engagement with physical culture in the world outside schools (Kirk 1999).

Second, in schools where syllabus requirements leave little space for pupils' input, teacher re-evaluation of the activities used to facilitate mandatory objectives may expand possibilities for students to express and perform cultural under-standings in movement. As Gard has discussed in Chapter 7 in this volume, dance provides many opportunities for not only valuing children's unique movement sequences, but also provoking critical reflection about issues of cultural diversity. When students are encouraged to move their bodies in new and different ways, for example, questions about 'how we move', 'why we move' and what social and/or cultural norms frame our capacity to move in particular ways can be posed. As Longley (2002) suggests, each student responds differently to dance activities. Dance provides opportunities to share these unique ways of knowing and students therefore learn to appreciate a range of ways to work with ideas. In contexts where sports skills are foregrounded, particular ways of doing these are valued with departures from 'the correct skill' being regarded as incorrect or faulty repre-sentations of the 'ideal'. For example, there are 'accepted' techniques for kicking a ball, swinging a tennis racket, and hurling a javelin. As Gard (Chapter 7 in this volume) has pointed out, however, dance, at least in its creative forms, involves emotional expression and a valuing of the divergent ways students respond to a piece of music, a theme or a choreographic idea. New Zealand educator Ihi Heke, for example, encourages his students to work in groups to compose dances drawing on Maori cosmology and custom. Their final performances reveal a diverse range of interpretations and understandings of Maori cultural values. Some of the compositions are emotionally charged renderings of traditional elements of Maori culture, while others point to emergent understandings of the ways tikanga Maori and Pakeha practices have informed each other to shape new ways of under-standing what it means to be bicultural.

Outdoor education also affords a space where children's histories and experiences of growing up in different cultural contexts can be brought to life. In New Zealand, for example, the meanings attached to 'the outdoors' for young Maori often differ substantially from those associated with it for many non-Maori students (Hokowhitu 2001). Notions of national parks as play spaces for the engagement in pursuits like climbing, skiing, bush walking and canoeing contradict Maori views of the land as the source of spiritual renewal, food, medicine and survival (Heke 2002). Investigating and sharing these different orientations to physical activity in outdoor environments both before and during school or excursions presents an opportunity for collaborative learning and a chance for Maori children to participate in an environment where their unique connec-tions to land are both valued and emphasised. Ihirangi Heke, a Maori tertiary educator, has incorporated the notion of using physical activity to further cultural understandings in his Akaronga Whakakori programme. His students participate in traditional Maori physical activities, such as waka-ama (canoe racing) and sea diving tutored by Maori experts who teach students not only the skills involved in these pursuits, but the cultural values and histories attached to them. Heke's students 'feel' what it is like to move in Maori-preferred ways and through the medium of waka-ama, they have opportunities to develop respect and understanding for the role and place of physical activity in a Maori world view (Heke 2002).

Interrogating knowledge

One of the key requisites in thinking critically is the capacity to re-examine previous judgements and revise them if new information becomes available (Drewe and Daniel 1998). In health and physical education a plethora of opportunities for engagement with established knowledge and reassessment of this in light of fresh inquiry exist. Many of these can be oriented toward exploring the implications of existing 'truths' for people from nondominant cultures. Whether those truths relate to what's worth doing in physical education, the health and physical activity status of different ethnic groups or the most effective way to perform a given skill, opportunities to think critically about these may produce responses that challenge the ethnocentrism of assumptions implicit in much physical education in Anglo-American countries.

Fitzgerald and Jobling suggest in Chapter 6 in this volume that student-led research is an approach that has considerable potential to both value and provide opportunities for students to explore cultural perspectives in physical education. Asking students to research the different ways that people have historically and currently thought about and engaged in leisure would seem like a worthwhile activity. The class could be divided into groups, each surveying a particular sample of the population in their local community (for example, boys, girls, parents, older children, grandparents) on what leisure means to them and how they engage in leisure activities in their daily lives. Children could then report back their findings and discuss differences or similarities and reflect upon the cultural, economic and/or social reasons why people choose to use their leisure time in particular ways. Alternatively, children could investigate different categories of leisure pursuits, researching where each originated, how they they have evolved and how their uses have changed in contemporary times. These activities are simple yet potentially facilitate an understanding that people's lifestyle choices in terms of physical activity have shifted over time and context, that particular habits regarded as 'givens' in today's climate have not always been regarded as so, and that preferences have developed for different reasons, not always the ones commonly linked to those preferences, in contemporary culture.

Hokowhitu (2001), for example, provides an illuminating viewpoint on the misrepresentations of Maori values and beliefs around health and physical activity. He analyses the stories that respected experts in Maori physical activity tell about the shifting agendas of concern and significances attached to particular practices, unsettling and disrupting many 'popular' myths attached to Maori engagement in health and physical activity. Encouraging students to investigate their own and others' stories about physical activity, to track the influences on their beliefs and their location within time and place would seem like a useful activity. When students construct knowledge in the context of their families, peer groups, communities and schools, the notion that there is more than one way of seeing the world and of doing and/or thinking about physical activity is readily understood.

As Wright discusses in Chapter 14 in this volume, popular media provides another rich source of knowledge for students to interrogate. Tracking the ways black African-Americans are represented in media coverage of sports events, teasing apart the racial stereotyping evident in movies and films that feature athletes from nondominant cultures, and critically evaluating research and media reports that suggest particular groups (for example, people of Asian descent) have lower participation rates in sport and physical activity, are activities that potentially yield an understanding of the ways sport can be used to reproduce stereotypical beliefs about race and culture. Reviewing the quantity and type of coverage devoted to different sports in news and televised reporting over a period of a week, will provide students with a data set they can examine with a view to promoting an understanding of which sports 'count' in contemporary culture and the consequent effects of this for those whose sporting identities are not represented in the coverage. These kinds of activities orient students towards an understanding that media often portrays a particular version of reality that has little purchase with many groups and individuals in their community.

Conclusion

In this chapter, I have described models and philosophies of health and physical activity indigenous to New Zealand Maori that point to the potential diverse cultural perspectives may present for engaging students in critical learning and teaching. I have also suggested rethinking current curricula and encouraging students to critically interrogate established knowledge are strategies that orient us towards centring cultural diversity in physical education practice. There are no recipes for facilitating celebration of cultural diversity in the context of physical education and single strategies will never meet the diverse needs of students in our classes. In so saying, it would seem that programmes built upon principles of social constructivism and a sociocultural view of learning are well positioned to promote and support an understanding of diverse cultural perspectives in physical education. The idea that the process of learning is as important as the outcome, that tasks should be meaningful and interesting, that learning must engage with the cultural influences that shape students' understandings of themselves as physical beings and that student inquiry should occur in a community of practice counter enduring notions of a one-size-fits-all curriculum. Rather, the principles demand that teachers critically engage with the social and cultural meanings embedded in children's experiences and knowledge of physical education, creating learning opportunities to challenge hitherto accepted assumptions and disrupt universal truths about health and physical activity.

The tensions that exist when teachers are exhorted to foster class environments that attend to cultural difference while at the same time, create learning communities that foster a sense of collective identity and unity are well rehearsed in education writing (Allard and Cooper 2001). Indeed, at times the two imperatives seem impossible to reconcile, particularly in a climate where heightened racial tensions amongst youth make a mockery of any claims to a school community identity based on a sense of belonging or collective concern for each other. Fine *et al.* (1997) argue that 'the process of sustaining a community must include a critical interrogation of difference as the rich substance of community life' (quoted in Allard and Cooper 2001: 1). Harnessing this notion to physical education would seem like a step in the right direction. Recognition of the multiplicity of ways children engage in physical culture and the cultural perspectives that inform that engagement will likely afford opportunities for a wider range of students to achieve in physical education. It may also engender an openness to otherness in our curriculum-making and teaching practices.

References

Allard, A. and Cooper, M. (2001) 'Critically interrogating classroom constructions of "community" and "difference": a case study', unpublished paper presented at the Australian Association of Research in Education, December, Freemantle.

Atrens, D. (2001) *The Power of Pleasure*, Sydney: Duffy and Snellgrove.

Bishop, R. and Glynn, T. (1999a) *Culture Counts*, Palmerston North: Dunmore.

—— (1999b) 'Researching in Maori contexts: an interpretation of participatory consciousness', *Journal of Inter-cultural Studies* 20(2): 167–82.

—— (2000) 'Kaupapa Maori messages for the mainstream', *SET: Research Information for Teachers* 2: 4–7.

Bourdieu, P. (1973) 'Cultural reproduction and social reproduction', in R. Brown (ed.) *Knowledge, Education and Social Change*, vol. 17 (pp. 819–40), London: Tavistock.

Burrows, L. and Wright, J. (2001) 'Developing children in New Zealand school physical education', *Sport, Education and Society* 6(2): 165–83.

Burrows, L., Wright, J. and Jungersen-Smith, J. (2002) '"Measure your belly." New Zealand children's constructions of health and fitness', *Journal of Teaching in Physical Education* 22(1): 20–38.

Carlson, T. (1995) 'We hate gym: student alienation from physical education', *Journal of Teaching in Physical Education* 14: 467–77.

Chappell, B. (2002) 'Race, ethnicity and sport', in A. Laker (ed.) *The Sociology of Sport and Physical Education: An Introductory Reader*, London: Routledge.

Craig, B. (2001) 'Te Ao Kori – a world of movement for everyone', *The New Zealand Physical Educator* 3(3): 7–9.

Dahlberg, G., Moss, P. and Pence, A. (1999) *Beyond Quality in Early Childhood Education and Care: Postmodern Perspectives*, London: Routledge Falmer.

Darder, A. (1991) *Culture and Power in the Classroom*, Westport: Greenwood.

Drewe, B. S. and Daniel, M. (1998) 'The fundamental role of critical thinking in physical education', *Avante* 4(2): 20–38.

Durie, M. (1994) *Whaiora: Maori Health Development*, Auckland: Oxford University Press.

Epstein, D. (1997) 'Taking it like a man: narratives of dominant white masculinities in

South Africa', paper presented at the Australian Association for Research in Education, Brisbane.

Evans, J. and Clarke, G. (1988) 'Changing the face of physical education', in J. Evans (ed.) *Teachers, Teaching and Control in Physical Education*, London: Falmer Press.

Evans, J. and Davies, J. (1993) 'Equality, equity and physical education', in J. Evans (ed.) *Equality, Education and Physical Education*, London: Falmer Press.

Fine, M., Weis, L. and Powell, L. C. (1997) 'Communities of difference: a critical look at desegregated spaces created for and by youth', *Havard Educational Review* 67(2): 247–84.

Fitzclarence, L. and Tinning, R. (1992) 'Postmodern youth culture and the crisis in Australian secondary school physical education', *Quest* 44(3): 287–303.

Fitzgerald, H. and Jobling, A. (2003) 'Student-centred research: working with students with disabilities', in J. Wright, D. Macdonald and L. Burrows (eds) *Critical Inquiry and Problem-solving in Physical Education: Working with Students in Schools*, London: Routledge.

Gard, M. (2003) 'Movement, art and culture: problem-solving and critical enquiry in dance', in J. Wright, D. Macdonald and L. Burrows (eds) *Critical Inquiry and Problem-solving in Physical Education: Working with Students in Schools*, London: Routledge.

Gard, M. and Wright, J. (2001) 'Managing uncertainty: obesity discourses and physical education in a risk society', *Studies in the Philosophy of Education* 20: 535–49.

Graham, G. (1995) 'Physical education through students' eyes and in students' voices', *Journal of Teaching in Physical Education* 14: 363–485.

Hargreaves, J. (1986) *Sport, Power and Culture*, Oxford: Basil Blackwell.

Heke, I. (2002) Personal communication about Akaronga Whakakori. Dunedin (1 October 2002).

Hemara, W. (2000) *Maori Pedagogies*, Wellington: New Zealand Council for Educational Research.

Hirsch, W. (1990) *A Report on Issues and Factors Relating to Maori Achievement in the Education System*, Auckland: Ministry of Education.

Hokowhitu, B. (2001) 'Te mana Maori – Te tatari i nga korero parau', unpublished PhD thesis, University of Otago.

Irwin, L. (1988) 'Racism and education', in W. Hirsh and R. Scott (eds) *Getting it Right*, Auckland: Office of the Race Relations Conciliator.

—— (1989) 'Multicultural education: the New Zealand response', *New Zealand Journal of Education Studies* 24(1): 3–17.

Kirk, D. (1999) 'Physical culture, physical education and relational analysis', *Sport, Education and Society* 4(1): 63–73.

Legge, M. (forthcoming) 'Sowing the seed', in B. Ross and L. Burrows (eds) *It Takes Two Feet: Teaching Health and Physical Education in New Zealand*, Palmerston North: Dunmore.

Lineham, C. (forthcoming) 'The voices of our non-participants', in B. Ross and L. Burrows (eds) *It Takes Two Feet: Physical Education and Health Teaching in New Zealand*, Palmerston North: Dunmore.

Longley, A. (2002) 'Inclusivity in dance', unpublished MPhEd thesis proposal, University of Otago.

Ministry of Education (1993) *National Education Guidelines*, Wellington: Learning Media.

—— (1999) *Health and Physical Education in the New Zealand Curriculum*, Wellington: Learning Media.

Moeau, P. (1997) 'Hauora', paper presented at the Physical Education New Zealand Conference, Christchurch.

Morss, J. R. (1996) *Growing Critical: Alternatives to Developmental Psychology*, London: Routledge.

Penney, D. (2002) 'Equality, equity and inclusion in physical education and school sport', in A. Laker (ed.) *The Sociology of Sport and Physical Education: An Introductory Reader*, London: Routledge.

Penney, D. and Evans, J. (1999) *Politics, Policy and Practice in Physical Education*, London: E and FN Spon.

Pere, R. R. (1994) *Ako: Concepts of Learning in the Maori Tradition*, Wellington: National Library.

Rogoff, B. (1990) *Apprenticeship in Thinking*, New York: Oxford University Press.

Salter, G. (1999) 'Assessing a "critical learning dimension" of physical education: stories from the field', *Journal of Physical Education New Zealand* 32(2): 4–7.

—— (2000) 'Marginalising indigenous knowledge in teaching physical education: the sanitising of Hauora (well-being) in the new HPE curriculum', *Journal of Physical Education New Zealand* 33(1): 5–15.

—— (2002) 'Te Ao Kori: a Pakeha teacher educator's perspective', unpublished essay, Hamilton.

Smith, A. (1993) 'Early childhood educare: seeking a theoretical framework in Vygotsky's work', *International Journal of Early Years Education* 1(1): 47–61.

Smith, G. H. (1990) 'Taha Maori: Pakeha capture', in J. Codd, R. Harker and R. Nash (eds) *Political Issues in New Zealand Education*, Palmerston North: Dunmore.

Stothart, B. (2000) 'Pegs in the ground: landmarks in the history of New Zealand physical education', *Journal of Physical Education New Zealand* 33(2): 5–15.

Tinning, R., Wright, J., Macdonald, D. and Hickey, C. (2001) *Becoming a Physical Education Teacher: Contemporary and Enduring Issues*, Frenchs Forest, NSW: Pearson Education.

Walker, R. (1995) 'A new direction', *Journal of Physical Education* 28(4): 19–22.

Williams, H. W. (1975) *A Dictionary of the Maori Language*, Wellington: Government Printer.

Wright, J. (1997) 'Fundamental motor skills testing as problematic practice: a feminist analysis', *ACHPER Healthy Lifestyles Journal* 44(4): 18–29.

—— (2003) 'Critical inquiry and problem-solving: locating the terms', in J. Wright, D. Macdonald and L. Burrows (eds) *Critical Inquiry and Problem-solving in Physical Education: Working with Students in Schools*, London: Routledge.

Chapter 9

Rich tasks, rich learning?

Working with integration from a
physical education perspective

Doune Macdonald

Most of the official learning within schooling occurs in compartmentalised
'subjects' derived from academic disciplines such as mathematics, art or history.
Although this model of schooling has its advantages, from the 1960s it has been
criticised for its fragmented schedules and lack of relevance to the 'real life' of
young people and the ever-changing work force (see, for example, Beare 2001;
Young 1998). Educators have since argued for a more holistic view of knowledge
made possible through an integrated curriculum. Beane, for instance, suggests
that:

> genuine learning occurs as people 'integrate' experiences and insights into
> their scheme of meanings. Moreover, the most significant experiences are
> those tied to exploring questions and concerns people have about themselves
> and their world. . . . Through the integrative process of action, interaction, and
> reflection, people have the possibility of constructing meanings in response to
> their questions and concerns.
>
> (Beane 1993: 70)

Notions of integrated curricula, interdisciplinary learning, problem-solving
and problem-based learning are not new, nor are their philosophical underpinnings.
The first section of this chapter will overview what is understood by integrated and
problem-based learning. It will overview some shared principles for integrated
and problem-based learning (i.e. relevance, timeliness, resource accumulation,
relatedness, planning and cooperative investigations (Post *et al.* 1997)), as well
as typical approaches (i.e. setting the motivational context, learners becoming
active quickly, building up of a knowledge base, knowledge application, and
learner self-management and monitoring (Biggs 1999)). Most important are the
goals for integrated and problem-based learning that aim to educate collaborative,
independent, imaginative and motivated lifelong learners who are ready to engage
with real and important problems.

The second and more substantive section will introduce multidisciplinary,
problem-based 'rich tasks' that are being trialed in some Australian schools. Rather
than learning through traditional subject structures, in years one to ten students

undertake a number of extensive tasks that include designing a personal fitness plan or organising a major community event, such as a sporting carnival. An example of a rich task that drew heavily upon physical education will be described and then analysed in terms of implications for planning, staffing, resources, teaching strategies and learning. This trial concluded that an inquiry-based pedagogy in the form of integrated, transdisciplinary tasks with the appropriate support of school personnel and changes to school structures, could provide a positive learning experience for students.

Integrated curricula

An integrated curriculum carries several labels (e.g. integrative, multidisciplinary, interdisciplinary, transdisciplinary, fused, unified studies), yet all suggest an intermingling of knowledge that goes beyond the specialised teaching of a subject or discipline (Relan and Kimpston 1993), as also occurs in problem-based learning. Integration frequently includes a focus upon general cognitive skills, such as thinking, reasoning and critical analysis, through solving 'real' problems (e.g. Beane 1993). As such it can challenge what those who have more power (e.g. employers, universities, teachers) believe are essential and rigorous knowledge and skills and bring in from the margins the voices of students and what they want to learn and develop. Indeed Beare (2001), in his advocacy for future schooling, argues that the curriculum should not be bounded by subject divisions, but rather encourage interconnectedness, give credit for group learning, and value the expressive and imaginative.

Integrated curricula frequently have a focus such as a problem (e.g. designing a community facility) or a theme (e.g. 'space'). To have problems as the focus for integrated learning is increasingly popular in tertiary settings particularly in the health sciences (Macdonald and Isaacs 2001). Students working to solve 'problems' (problem-based learning or PBL) typically collaborate to 'engage with the complex situation presented to them and decide what information they need to learn and what skills they need to gain in order to manage the situation effectively' (Savin-Baden 2000: 3). Proponents argue that PBL moves beyond problem-solving because it encourages students to explore widely, to link learning to their own needs, and become independent learners (see, for example, Biggs 1999; Hiebert *et al.* 1999).

Integrated study is squarely placed within the tradition of constructivism, given its recognition of the significance of both the individual and the group in the learning process and the influence of the social milieu. It provides students with the opportunity, alone and in groups, to analyse a relevant problem or issue and, within and beyond school, access, manipulate and understand large quantities of information, akin to adult intellectual life (Post *et al.* 1997). While integrated study should not necessarily be seen as a replacement to the study of specific disciplines, it does provide the context for substantial, interactive learning as championed by Dewey, Piaget and Vygotsky. Further, it attends to Gardner's

(1993) theory of multiple intelligences in that within cooperative and substantive interdisciplinary projects, a range of intelligences are required to address the task. For example, a student with particular abilities in spatial and bodily kinesthetic tasks can assist and learn from peers who have strong interpersonal or logical-mathematical intelligences, as the group plan and use software to model a new sports stadium for their neighbourhood.

Given the somewhat sedimented nature of schooling, integration across the curriculum can challenge conventional structures (e.g. timetabling, delegated staff rooms) and practices (e.g. teaching styles). The teacher is encouraged to become a facilitator and this can be a new and difficult role. An initial task for the teacher is to communicate with school administration, colleagues, parents and students the aims, processes and possible outcomes of the integrated approach (Post *et al.* 1997). While students will share in the planning and implementation decisions, the teacher must still thoroughly prepare background materials and motivational strategies, and plan for group processes, to name a few. In keeping with the intent of curriculum integration, teachers should employ open-ended questioning techniques, monitor group progress, encourage group cohesion, and steer reporting and evaluation (Beane 1993). According to proponents of this approach, when a teacher adopts this facilitatory role, students not only gain basic knowledge and skills, but also learn to take risks with inquiry, make judgements and choices, develop lifelong learning skills, such as patience and rigour, and refine cooperative strategies (Jackson and David 2000).

Post *et al.* (1997) outline six key instructional aspects that teachers should consider when planning for an integrated curriculum:

1   *Relevance*: where students have the opportunity to shape a project that is relevant, timely and important to them;
2   *Timeliness*: in-depth consideration of topics alongside with flexibility with how time is spent;
3   *Resource accumulation*: interdisciplinary study invariably involves the use of a wide variety of resources;
4   *Relatedness*: rather than isolated information to be memorised, interdiscplinary study draws upon a breadth of information that is 'real-world' and inter-connected;
5   *Planning*: all participants need to negotiate which topics will be included, resources required, tasks to be undertaken, groupings, etc.;
6   *Cooperative investigations*: effective planning, coordination and cooperation are essential for interdisciplinary study in contrast to individualistic and competitive contexts.

It is clear from the above that in integrating the curriculum there are important educational and procedural issues to consider. Physical education is well placed to take up these challenges given its breadth of subject matter, its history of cooperative student tasks, and its potential for student relevance. Physical educators, as with other teachers, need to ask themselves some key questions prior to integration. Given the structure of the traditional curriculum, when is it feasible to integrate? Are some clusters of knowledge and skills better to integrate than others? Are my colleagues and I equipped to implement an integrated approach? Are the school's organisation and resources able to support integration? Are the students and their parents ready for integration? Such issues will be addressed in the case study below.

The new basics and rich tasks

In the context of rapid societal changes outlined in Chapter 1, the Queensland state education system is undertaking a number of inter-related school and curriculum reform projects aimed at better preparing students for 2010 and beyond. 'New Basics', and 'Rich Tasks' are some of the change strategies being trialed in selected Queensland schools under the banner of the New Basics Project. As a university-based curriculum scholar, my goal was to spend time in a trial school as teacher/researcher attempting to implement and evaluate some of the curriculum, pedagogical and assessment innovations.

The New Basics Project being trialed follows Bernstein (1990) in seeking to align curriculum, assessment and pedagogies (Lingard et al. 2002). Within the context of Education Queensland's reform agenda, the new basics are 'clusters, families or groups of practices that are essential for survival in the worlds that students have to deal with' (Education Queensland 2000: 3). This curriculum dimension aims to improve student outcomes through a focus upon:

*   Life pathways and social futures (who am I and where am I going?);
*   Multiliteracies and communications media (how do I make sense of and communicate with the world?);
*   Active citizenship (what are my rights and responsibilities in communities, cultures and economies?);
*   Environments and technologies (how do I describe, analyse and shape the world around me?).

The dimensions have been developed in response to postmodern shifts in identities, technologies, work places, economies and communities as outlined in Chapter 1.

Rich tasks are the outward and visible assessment practices aligned to student engagement with the new basics. They are the assessable and reportable outcomes of a 3-year curriculum plan that prepares students for the challenges of life in 'new times'. The tasks require students to display their understandings, knowledge and skills through performances in transdisciplinary activities that have an obvious connection to the wider world. It has been claimed that learning experiences can be more intellectually demanding, and more relevant to the students' lives, interests and needs, when teachers and students can focus upon fewer tasks (Lingard 2000).

The new basics informed the development of a number of integrated tasks to be undertaken by students by the completion of years three, six and nine. While integrating a number of traditional subject areas with physical education has a precedence (see, for example, Gallahue *et al.* 1972; Housner 2000), the rich tasks are intended to be provide transdisciplinary assessment tasks that engage students in contemporary issues. For example, from years one to three, rich tasks will require students to create a web page, plan a travel itinerary, and develop a personal health plan. However, each task is designed to give teachers and students freedom to adapt the task to their own interests and contexts and encourages teachers to be creative and collaborative. For physical education, the rich tasks provide avenues for:

- physical educators to work alongside their 'classroom' colleagues;
- physical activity to become a central medium for student learning;
- physical education knowledge and skills to become embedded in how students think about their worlds (see, for example, Housner 2000).

The rich tasks are integral to Education Queensland's (2000: 1) 'attempt to empower and encourage teachers, unclutter the curriculum, up the ante intellectually, deliver fewer alienated students, prepare students for a future in an uncertain world, and position the classroom within the global village'. This discourse is consistent with postmodern perspectives that recognise the inevitability of change replete with errors, chaos and uncertainty, and the importance of students becoming knowledge producers rather than consumers (Fullan 2001). According to Doll (1989: 250), a 'postmodern curriculum will accept the student's ability to organize, construct and structure'. One of the dilemmas which faced our innovation was that the structures and systems of schools, together with students' expectations of what is 'real' schooling, were not necessarily consistent with postmodern agendas for what, where and how learning may occur (Macdonald 2003). Therefore, a challenge for teachers wishing to work with an integrated curricula is likely to be the need to appraise and alter some of the embedded schooling structures, such as the timetable or room allocations to provide the flexibility and collegiality required.

The fieldwork experience

I joined the teaching staff of Spender State High School (SSHS) for one school term (10 weeks). The school is a co-educational state secondary school situated in a relatively high socio-economic neighbourhood. It has approximately 1200 students and ninety teaching staff with six staff in the HPE department. As a long-standing and high achieving school, Spender was successful in its nomination to be a trial school for the New Basics Project. I had approached Spender as a teacher/researcher on the basis of my relationship with the school and its staff, its proximity to the university, and its involvement in curriculum renewal. My brief was to team teach two units in years eight and nine with Gill (an experienced HPE teacher, who had recently returned to the profession).

Taking into account the current lower secondary curriculum, available resources and facilities, and student interest, it was concluded that the year eight class would benefit from working with content related to the Olympic Games. Thus, it was decided to shape the unit around a years four to six rich task focusing upon a celebratory event. The task read:

> Students will show that they are able to work in a team to plan, organise and present a celebratory event or artistic event or festival to mark an occasion of significance within the school or within a particular local community.

These rich tasks were to be taught and assessed predominantly through two HPE lessons per week for one term, while also trying as much as possible to coordinate with other departments.

The task culminated in our year eight HPE class managing a mini-Olympics comprising a 'march past' of 'teams' and opening ceremony, a series of student-created games, and a closing ceremony. Lead-up learning experiences included a review of issues surrounding the Olympic Games, promotional activities, budgeting, games-making, and preparing a competition schedule and scoring system. On the day of the mini-Olympics, the class was responsible for organising the timing and flow of activities, equipment, briefing competitors, scoring, first aid, photography and public announcements.

Following the principles of ethnography, throughout my teaching experience at Spender I gathered a range of qualitative data from colleagues and students, as well as keeping a reflective journal. Semi-formal interviews were recorded with the principal, HPE head of department, my HPE teaching partner, and student volunteers from the year eight class. Students also submitted anonymous written feedback at the end of the term. My journal attempted to capture rich descriptions and reflections of my planning, teaching and student responses, school culture and meetings, and informal conversations with students and colleagues. I also collected planning materials, school publications, photographs and student work samples. As will be discussed below, this foray into rich task territory, while modest in its length and breadth (primarily delivered through HPE), was highly instructive in terms of the complexity of educational reform oriented towards integrated learning.

Rich task implementation: a clash of discourses?

The research at Spender SHS had two purposes. First, I wanted to ascertain what sense the school community (in particular students and teachers) made of the new basics agenda. Second, I was interested in how the school's organisational capacity (e.g. timetabling, room allocation, staff communication strategies) facilitated integrated learning.

The teachers' perspectives

My teaching partner and I were somewhat marginal to the system: Gill as a female in a contract position, newly returned to the teaching profession, and working with the 'low risk' years eight and nine programme; and I was a visitor. In some senses our time was not such a precious commodity, nor had we been party to the 'chronic revisioning' of curriculum and procedures as had many other staff at SSHS (Giddens 1991: 20). Nevertheless, to take on the trialing of rich tasks clearly intensified Gill's work on top of her other responsibilities, such as year eight coordination for HPE, school sport coordination, and athletics coaching. Gill commented:

> It did impact me greatly because it meant I was doing something different. Normally I would have been doing the same thing with all my classes for the year levels. For the year eight and year nine rich task classes I was doing something 'off line' which meant more work in preparation. . . . It was a big learning curve for me . . . [and] did create a lot of extra work.

Typically, secondary school staff are fragmented into what Hargreaves (1994) has called 'balkanised' communities, isolated physically and intellectually in their subjects/key learning areas as a legacy of disciplinary and bureaucratic control. Rich tasks, on the other hand, require integrated teams of teachers working collectively and, frequently, publicly. This balkanisation has been exacerbated by the competition between departments for staff, students, time and resources. In preparing to lead the year eight rich task, in the previous term Gill had:

> approached the other departments in the school but they already had their syllabus set or it was too difficult to change. The other difficulty is that, say, English was to come on board. I was given a list of eight different English teachers and told to go and see them all individually! Just the time constraints of trying to do that and trying to get them together in a meeting when I cannot get our own HPE staff together. . . . Music could have come on board and English with letter writing and with the mascot . . . and History. It would have been a very good cross-curricula task, but I still don't see how it could develop because of the liaison.
>
> (Gill, interview)

During the task planning I returned to the Art Department to seek some cooperation. The Art HOD wanted to know whose curriculum time would we use to make the Olympics banners? Who would pay for the materials? Where would the students do the art work, i.e. whose space? He only had limited 'spares' if the students needed any help and preferably could we send 'just four good kids.' As a consequence of these failed alliances, the rich task learning experiences were led by HPE staff only.

Given the scope of the rich task products (such as holding a mini-Olympics or a building design/model), there is pressure on teachers to ensure the product eventuates. As Gill reflected, rich tasks require:

> extra teaching staff because it is not like when you get something set up and running you can sort of settle into a bit of comfort mode because there will be constant adjustments and checking with other people and pulling it all together. The students couldn't be relied on to do that final pulling together. . . . Who was going to put their hand up and take over and make sure that it all happened?

Even amongst the HPE staff involved in the rich tasks the logistics of communication and coordination became very difficult in a crowded and busy staffroom. Gail concluded:

> You almost need one person who doesn't have a load that is just there as a coordinator to go around and liaise between all the departments, see where you are all up to, and share knowledge between all of them.

Clearly, as this experience unfolded, we were able to see how aspects of the school structures needed to change in order to optimise integrated learning.

The rich task process and product also makes teachers' work more public than it may normally be. They will be planning and teaching alongside colleagues from other disciplinary areas and students' products will also be subject to display and moderation, adding possibly new dimensions of surveillance to teachers' work. In speaking about the mini-Olympics, Gill said:

> We had a lot of feedback. I got four letters and four phone calls from other staff in the school saying how wonderful it was – which is unusual. Things like that don't happen. . . .

On that day, several other HPE and classroom teachers as well as the schools' deputy principal for curriculum were 'watching'. Conscious of this public 'product', Gill and I were very aware of the class moving ahead with its planning and of taking responsibility towards the end to get the tasks finished. While both Louis *et al.* (1996) and Lingard (2000) believe that deprivatisation of practice is essential for vibrant professional learning communities, rich tasks potentially increase teachers' sense of stress as their own and their students' work comes under scrutiny alongside the potential of teachers' work to be better appreciated. However, for professional learning communities to thrive, physical educators as with all teachers, need a willingness to plan, implement and assess learning experiences with colleagues and those in the wider community.

While, from one perspective, subject or discipline-based regimes can hold teachers accountable for rich task outcomes through this self and peer surveillance, from another, rich tasks challenge traditional disciplinary knowledge boundaries with which secondary specialists are comfortable. When engaging with their colleagues, secondary specialists need to be ready to relinquish their subject allegiance and position students' holistic learning as central (see, for example, Goodson 1993; Hargreaves 1994). How ready would most teachers be to do this? Research suggests that this may be particularly difficult for HPE teachers who frequently have a longstanding and strong commitment to the biophysical sciences, physical activity and sport (see for example, Macdonald and Glover 1997). Yet, teachers need to be ready to leave behind their often long-standing commitments to the primacy of particular subject specialisations, while also being ready to represent their specialisation in transdisciplinary planning and teaching if integration is to be a quality experience for students (see, for example, Relan and Kimpston 1993).

Another reason why it was very difficult to employ this form of inquiry-based pedagogy at Spender was the nature of the school structures and associated regimes of organisation and control that dominated our routine decision-making (King 1995). Where will my lesson be? What equipment will be free? Will the students be there on time? What can be contained to 30 minutes? How can the students' work be shaped to progress towards the stated learning outcomes? Can I change the class routine given the administration demands of such a change? Can I find any time to liaise with my teaching partners? These issues became impediments to our reform. In her treatise on the right to learn, Darling-Hammond (1997) emphasises the centrality of learning in school-based decision-making and the necessity of flexibility in the curriculum, teachers' work, and material resources to support this goal rather than have learning constrained by these factors. However, once such factors have been attended to, as physical educators we could see the potential for rich tasks to enrich our work and student learning.

Student learning

The students in year eight responded well to having a 'real' and substantial task that they were working towards over an extended period of time, and the intrinsic reward of finishing with a 'product'. They also greatly appreciated the space for negotiation, for example, deciding what activities they could work on in class time and making their own games, and they appreciated learning with reduced subject boundaries.

While the students also valued having some decision-making responsibilities in that, 'Making decisions without teachers was good', they were concerned (as were their teachers!) about their self-directed group work. There was an issue of dividing up the subtasks so that each self-selected group could move ahead on their planning. However, these required different timelines, places, spaces and levels of teacher assistance.

WILL: I think that there were two or three groups that were actually working on the game and the other groups were sitting there waiting for something to do.

LIBBY: Some people were working on the Olympics day but even on the day some people didn't have jobs to do. It was pretty boring. . . . We sorted out these jobs that we were going to do, but we never ever ended up getting around to doing them.

This highlighted the challenges in doing a task for the first time and the complexity of managing multiple learning experiences.

The students felt that, 'there was too much theory and not enough prac . . . ' (Sharon). Given the rich task was led by HPE teachers in HPE time, the students had come to expect a majority of class time would be spent engaging in physical activity. Did Allan enjoy working towards the mini-Olympics last term? 'Yes and no. I enjoyed it because I was making the [Olympic] cauldron. No because we didn't have much prac.' This was typical of students' responses in a context where there was only the time from one subject area available in which to do the task. For those who felt they had a clear role in organising the event, that is responsibility for the cauldron, torch, making posters/advertising materials, doing the programme on the computers, constructing the scoreboard and so on, there was a sense of focus, responsibility and achievement.

LAUREN: I found it actually a good way to learn because everyone had the one thing to work on and then they didn't have to think about other things. Like they had the mini-Olympics and they didn't have to worry about how they were going [in sport]. . . . It was like a team thing that we all worked together on.

However, the overwhelming message was that to only have two lessons of 'prac' per week on average was a loss of 'real' HPE and the students felt deprived. As another student put it, 'I didn't like learning all the time. I wanted to do more prac'.

The complex demands of a task to be completed in a relatively short timeframe meant a loss of time devoted to physical activity and, furthermore, contributed to a diminution in the quality of the learning when the students' and teachers' time was devoted to managing the learning experiences rather than promoting a deep understanding. My diary recording mid-unit read, 'I am concerned that students are learning little about planning a community event . . . they have simply relied on their ideas for it'.

While wanting to promote student-centred pedagogies, Gill and I felt that we needed to have a mechanism that was effective in keeping ourselves and the students directed towards similar outcomes across classes, hence we created a student booklet for each task, a retreat to the familiar control of student learning. The booklets contained a range of background materials to address learning in areas, such as group work, Olympic education, games making, event promotion, and creating speadsheets. The booklets provided an anchor for students' progress, which was a positive contribution, but did little to enhance any deep understanding and generated the added tension of keeping track of the booklets.

Where students had choices and freedom, their preferences at times reflected stereotypical behaviours that were contrary to an inclusive pedagogy. For example, the boys tended to take over all the tasks that were oriented to equipment and computers, while the girls opted to do the 'creative' tasks associated with promotion and media. Thus, there needs to be time for students to reflect on who is in their group, how it can work cooperatively, and to challenge the taken-for-granted decisions made when students self-manage their learning – a fine balance between a pedagogy that allows for student direction and a pedagogy that is inclusive in terms of its outcomes.

Conclusion

What did we learn about introducing an integrated curriculum experience into a subject-based schooling context? Physical education is well placed to contribute to the inquiry-based content and pedagogies that are rewarding for the students. To do so, integrated tasks require school spaces that facilitate regular and ongoing teacher interaction, rather than 'bunkered' departmental staff rooms, and allocated time for teacher planning and monitoring meetings. During implementation of the tasks, teachers and students also need the flexible use of time and space in ways that challenge traditional conceptions of schooling. Given the intentions of the rich tasks, students needed to be able to access a variety of spaces at short notice, and store their ongoing project work in a safe space. For example, in the year eight unit in any one lesson students needed to access computers, paints, sporting equipment and the school oval. On occasions they needed time beyond the allocated 'lesson'. Although modest in their scope, our rich task implementation highlighted how important it is to have flexibility in the use of school time and space.

The following conclusions are offered from a teacher's perspective with respect to organisational issues to facilitate implementation of an integrated curricula:

- a lengthy planning phase (e.g. 12 months);
- an interdisciplinary planning team with ample release time;
- dedicated timetable space for task implementation (e.g. every afternoon);
- a dedicated budget for each task;
- a dedicated space for the storage of task-related materials;
- professional development of teachers to ensure they have contemporary content knowledge of their learning area alongside with familiarity of content across the curriculum.

The richness of the innovation was shaped substantially by students':

- sense of what knowledge was appropriate;
- self-management of their individual or group's contribution to the task (i.e.

to what extent did the students cooperate in their use of time, space and resources?);

• commitment to the impending public display or production of their artefact.

Therefore, a good deal of time needs to be spent prior to the use of this type of approach, explaining to students what it will entail and why. In turn, this study has left us wondering what may have occurred in this learning space if the young people had negotiated their own problem to be addressed, an often promoted principle of the integrated curriculum model (Beane 1993). How would this have played out in terms of students' engagement and enjoyment, the cooperation of teachers to assist them in their inquiries, the resources they drew upon, and their inter- and intragroup collaboration?

Curriculum integration may not always be a good idea. Brophy and Alleman (1993), along with others (see, for example, Relan and Kimpston 1993) suggest that some tasks lack educational value, are strange, difficult or even impossible to achieve, and can disrupt the accomplishment of major goals in disciplines or subjects. Yet, integrated tasks can be engrossing and enriching, and with the required support of the school's structures, organisation and resources, physical education can make a substantial contribution to them.

Acknowledgement

This chapter has been adapted from D. Macdonald (2003) 'Rich task implementation: modernism meets postmodernism', *Discourse* 24(2): 247–62.

References

Beane, J. (1993) 'Problems and possibilities for an integrative curriculum', in R. Fogarty (ed.) *Integrating the Curricula*, Melbourne: Hawker Brownlow Education.

Beare, H. (2001) *Creating the Future School*, London: Routledge Falmer.

Bernstein, B. (1990) *Class, Codes and Control, Volume IV: The Structuring of Pedagogic Discourse*, London: Routledge.

Biggs, J. (1999) *Teaching for Quality Learning at University*, Buckingham: Society for Research into Higher Education and Open University Press.

Brophy, J. and Alleman, J. (1993) 'A caveat: curriculum integration isn't always a good idea', in R. Fogarty (ed.) *Integrating the Curricula*, Melbourne: Hawker Brownlow Education.

Darling-Hammond, L. (1997) *The Right to Learn*, San Fransisco: Jossey Bass.

Doll, W. (1989) 'Foundations for a post-modern curriculum', *Journal of Curriculum Studies* 21(3): 243–53.

Education Queensland (2000) *New Basics: Theory into Practice*, Brisbane: Education Queensland (see also the EQ web site: http://education.qld.gov.au/corporate/framework).

Fullan, M. (2001) *The New Meaning of Educational Change*, New York: Teachers College Press.

Gallahue, D., Werner, P. and Luedke, G. (1972) *A Conceptual Approach to Moving and Learning*, New York: John Wiley and Sons.

Gardner, H. (1993) *Multiple Intelligences: The Theory in Practice*, New York: Basic Books.

Giddens, A. (1991) *Modernity and Self-identity*, Stanford: Stanford University Press.

Goodson, I. (1993) *School Subjects and Curriculum Change*, London: Falmer Press.

Hargreaves, A. (1994) *Changing Teachers, Changing Times*, London: Cassell.

Hiebert, J., Carpenter, T., Fennema, E., Fuson, K., Human, P., Murray, H., Olivier, A. and Wearne, D. (1999) 'Problem-solving as a basis for reform in curriculum and instruction: the case of mathematics', in P. Murphy (ed.) *Learners, Learning and Assessment*, London: Paul Chapman Publishing.

Housner, L. (ed.) (2000) *Integrated Physical Education: A Guide for the Elementary Classroom Teacher*, Morgantown, WA: Fitness Information Technology Inc.

Jackson, A. and David, G. (2000) *Turning Points 2000: Educating Adolescents for the 21st Century*, New York: Teachers College Press.

King, B. (1995) 'Disciplining teachers', *Education and Society* 13(2): 15–29.

Lingard, R. (2000) 'Aligning the message systems', *Independent Education* (October): 24–6.

Lingard, R., Hayes, D. and Mills, M. (2002) 'Developments in school-based management: the specific case of Queensland', *Journal of Educational Administration* 42(1): 6–30.

Louis, K., Kruse, D. and Marks, H. (1996) 'Schoolwide professional community', in F. Newmann and Associates (eds) *Authentic Achievement Restructuring Schools for Intellectual Quality*, San Francisco: Jossey-Bass.

Macdonald, D. (2003) 'Curriculum change and the postmodern world: is the school curriculum reform project an anachronism?' *Journal of Curriculum Studies* 35(2): 139–49.

Macdonald, D. and Glover, S. (1997) 'Subject matter boundaries and curriculum change in the Health and Physical Education key learning area', *Curriculum Perspectives* 17(1): 23–30.

Macdonald, D. and Isaacs, G. (2001) 'Developing a professional identity through problem-based learning', *Teaching Education Journal* 12(3): 315–34.

Post, T., Ellis, A., Humphreys, A. and Buggey, L. (1997) *Interdisciplinary Approaches to Curriculum*, Upper Saddle River, NJ: Prentice Hall.

Relan, A. and Kimpston, R. (1993) 'Curriculum integration: a critical analysis of practical and conceptual issues', in R. Fogarty (ed.) *Integrating the Curricula*, Melbourne: Hawker Brownlow Education.

School of Education. (2001) *School Reform Longitudinal Study: Final Report*, Brisbane: University of Queensland.

Savin-Baden, M. (2000) *Problem-based Learning in Higher Education: Untold Stories*, Buckingham: Society for Research into Higher Education and Open University Press.

Young, M. (1998) *The Curriculum of the Future*, London: Falmer.

Chapter 10

Negotiating the curriculum

Challenging the social relationships in teaching

Trish Glasby and Doune Macdonald

Consider these six questions as the basis for interrogating the balance of responsibility and involvement between teachers and students within the teaching and learning cycle:

- Who decides what is to be taught and learned, and on what basis are such decisions made?
- Who determines the starting point of the teaching, and on what evidence?
- Who decides how the learning is to be organized: what teaching and learning methods are to be employed?
- Who provides, describes and exemplifies the criteria for success in this learning, when is this done and how?
- Who is responsible for the assessment: when and how is it done?
- Who records the outcomes: where, when and for what purpose?

(Lambert and Lines 2000: 126)

If the answers are 'the teacher' then it follows that there is little inquiry-based pedagogy in this 'classroom'. Negotiation of decisions surrounding what, when, where, how and why, in a teaching/learning relationship are pivotal to student-centred inquiry. Such negotiations challenge the notion that it is the sole responsibility of the teacher to determine the nature of the teaching and learning process. They also negate any 'one-size-fits-all' understanding of each learning space. These questions can be used as a framework within which diverse entry points for negotiating the curriculum and assessment can be identified. They also serve to introduce the focus of this chapter.

Teachers need to be thinking about and planning for the opportunities which will enable students greater involvement in their learning. As discussions about changes to schooling gather momentum (Beare 2001; Braggett *et al.* 1999; George and Shewey 1994), so, too, do the number of solutions that are offered in response to the perceived needs of young people that are unattended in more traditional schooling structures. When we hear such terms as 'integrated curricula', 'authentic assessment' and 'negotiated curriculum', we need to appreciate that each of these represents a specific set of actions aimed at (re)connecting young people to schools and learning.

While transformations of some structures of schooling (e.g. middle school campuses, dissolution of bounded subjects) are fundamental to the notion of school and curriculum renewal, Boomer *et al.* (1992) argue that the best opportunities for maximising learning emerge from teachers and students coming together to negotiate the curriculum. Such negotiation should not be limited to 'what' is to be learnt; a tokenistic gesture that merely offers students choice in the games that are played or in the activities in which they participate. To work more credibly with students in ways that genuinely focus on (re)engaging them in their learning, physical education must also involve them in the practices of how learning can occur, as well as assessment of their progress and outcomes. Students need to be provided with opportunities not only to make decisions about 'what' they learn, but also how to demonstrate that learning has occurred and how it will be judged.

This chapter will consist of four sections. The first three will consider key questions:

- Why negotiate?
- On what can we negotiate?
- In which ways can we negotiate?

The final section of the chapter will consider the challenges and limitations of negotiating the curriculum and its assessment.

Why negotiate?

To engage in negotiation is to 'confer with others in order to reach a compromise or agreement' (*The Australian Concise Oxford Dictionary* 2001: 896). Traditionally, power relations between teacher and students privilege the unilateral decisions of the teacher yet in 'new times' many educators argue that young people's futures are dependent upon negotiated schooling experiences (e.g. Beare 2001). Didactic power is purposively disrupted when students are given a greater or equal say in what and how they wish to learn and how they wish that learning to be assessed. A great deal of our work as teachers revolves around the ways in which knowledge is presented, received, shared, controlled, understood or misunderstood by students and by teachers themselves. Edwards and Mercer (1987: 60) suggest that at times 'teachers willingly restrict access to educational knowledge [in order to] maintain more control over the process of education and hence their class. They [teachers] believe a good teacher should not make everything explicit'.

As consequence of teacher control, students may fail to develop skills in, and appreciation for, meaningful democratic participation. Through the inclusion of students in negotiation from the classroom through to the whole school level, they can 'experience the change process, learn the skills of solving problems, of communication in groups, of leadership and membership' (Dalin 1998: 1065). As Darling-Hammond explains:

For developing adolescents who need both autonomy and affiliation, the opportunity to be heard and to be taken seriously is a major incentive to commit to the school environment. . . . Incentives and structures that take account of students' needs to be cared for and to participate in shaping their own work are as important as those that take account of teachers' needs for knowledge, information, and authority in managing their work. Through genuine negotiation across processes, content and assessment, students gain a sense of power and control that is positive and engaging.

(Darling-Hammond 1997: 175–6)

Ideas about negotiation are not new within the physical education and physical education teacher education literature (Kirk 1986; Macdonald 2002; Tinning 1997) where they have been positioned within writing on critical pedagogy and its underpinning concepts of social justice, empowerment and student voice. Macdonald (2002: 171) argues that 'if a critical pedagogy is adopted, then this is said to represent a significant shift from a pedagogy characterized by the transmission of existing knowledge to a pedagogy concerned with the production of knowledge and socially just outcomes'. In other words, a critical pedagogue rethinks the way that knowledge is regarded and the part that they as a teacher (and their school) play in its construction, contestation and distribution. Anecdotally we know that physical educators frequently negotiate when selecting, for example, what game will be played or what 'position' a student might play in. Both research and practice highlight the potential of negotiation within physical education curriculum and assessment and the opportunities that can be created for students to share in substantial decision-making and communication processes associated with their learning. More specifically, negotiation can promote 'successful learning', learning that requires the teacher to value difference, scope, variety, diversity, inclusivity and change through:

- understanding the heterogeneity of the class;
- approaching learning as an active process; and
- valuing students' knowledge and interests.

Understanding heterogeneity

The first premise for successful learning requires that the teacher recognise the heterogeneous nature of physical education classes. The subject does not lend itself to the creation of a learning environment in which all can succeed if all students are expected to undertake the same tasks, in the same way, at the same time. For a culture of success, teachers must move their practices away from 'one-size-fits-all' learning experiences that deny many students access to the serendipitous aspects of learning and that set the stage for students to underachieve or fail (Darling-Hammond). In order to progress the learning of all students, differentiated learning methods and experiences will need to play a central role in our teaching.

If we take into consideration differences in, for example, culture, skills, maturity, body shape, expectations, knowledge and experiences, it is unrealistic to expect one teacher to plan separate work for each pupil. It is however possible to negotiate a range of learning tasks or outcomes that address the different needs of students and to encourage students to have a role in determining their progress across those outcomes.

Learning as an active process

A second premise upon which successful learning is based is that learning is an 'active process' as discussed in Chapter 2. Understanding learning as a process of active meaning making moves teachers towards a 'student-centred' approach to teaching (Edwards and Mercer 1987). Further, if learning is predicated on what might be characterised as a Vygotskian (1962) model, then 'guided discovery' learning is encouraged through children solving 'practical tasks with the help of their speech as well as their eyes and hands' (Vygotsky 1978: 26). Vygotsky argued that, 'the role of communication, social interaction and instruction in scaffolding thinking and cognitive development is crucial' (Lambert and Lines 2000: 236). An inextricable relationship between cognition, social understanding and social position is developed. Learners need the opportunity to construct meaning for themselves (e.g. can I have more time to experiment with changing this angle of release to improve my throw? Could we look at why there are no girls in our local skate park?). The ensuing learning is likely to be more effective where students are actively involved with new materials/knowledge through critical thinking, discussion and an awareness of their own learning strategies following teacher–student and/or student–student negotiation. Teachers have the opportunity to lead students to new levels of conceptual understanding through their daily conversations, interactions and negotiations.

Valuing students' knowledge and interests

Third, what teachers see as the 'core of knowings' that are essential for all students may not coincide with what the students' value. Through the media and a broad range of life experiences students bring to the teaching/learning relationship some clear ideas of what should be valued if successful learning is to occur. How often do teachers encourage students to pursue knowledge that the teachers see as interesting and relevant such as the ubiquitous athletics unit leading into the school athletics carnival? Recently, the second author asked a year nine class what activities they would like to pursue in a unit and they chose indoor rock climbing, aerobics, judo and walking after some negotiation amongst each other (none of which were programmed for that term). In following the students' requests, throughout the unit there was 100 per cent attendance and participation. The assessment literature (Torrance and Pryor 2001; Weeden et al. 2002) also highlights that student learning improves when students are given the opportunity to develop their own learning goals and participate in self-assessment. Teaching as such should be facilitative, interventionist and at every opportunity, involve the students in negotiating their own pathway through their learning. To do so, their planning needs to be flexible and complex reflecting the positive or negative experiences of students in their interactions with the curriculum and assessment.

How physical educators think about successful learning will impact on whether they are comfortable negotiating the curriculum. Where negotiation is valued as integral to learning, the classroom relationships change. Teachers come to know more about their students and this has repercussions for the students' sense of well-being (Glover *et al.* 1998) and, in turn, their sense of achievement.

On what can we negotiate?

In the discussion on 'why negotiate', an argument was made for a breadth of negotiation around content, pedagogy and assessment. The scope of negotiation as discussed below will be mediated, however, by such things as the degree of flexibility of the curriculum and assessment, and students' and teachers' expectations of their role and relationships.

Content of the curriculum and assessment

Traditionally, the way in which the curriculum is constructed suggests a preferred linear approach that sequences 'knowledge' from the simple to the complex. However, the international shift to an outcomes approach to education emphasises the end products or outputs of an education process leaving the pathways towards the outcomes open to negotiation. Because the outcomes, as suggested in one Australian state, delineate 'what students know and are able to do as a result of planned learning experiences' (Queensland School Curriculum Council 1999: 9), they should be made explicit to all concerned in the education process. Having done so, within the limitations of mandated syllabuses, teachers and students can share in curricular decisions. Ways of thinking about negotiation are now described using the Queensland syllabus as a backdrop.

The following are examples of two conceptually sequenced outcomes from the 'Developing Concepts and Skills for Physical Activity' strand of the Queensland (1999) *Health and Physical Education Years 1 to 10 Syllabus*. These outcomes, which are drawn from levels 5 and 6, would typically be demonstrated by 14- or 15-year-old students.

5.2   Students demonstrate a range of tactics and strategies to achieve an identified goal in games, sports or other physical activities.
6.2   Students select and implement individual or group tactics and strategies in games, sports or other physical activities to respond to environmental conditions or opposing players.

The flexibility of an outcomes-based approach enables teachers and students to negotiate the content implicit within each outcome statement, the order in which it may be covered, and the depth to which work should be performed. The following two questions shape the possibilities for how the learning experiences that elaborate these outcomes could be designed:

*   What does a student need to demonstrate to be judged as at level 5?
*   What additional knowledge and skill does a student need to demonstrate to be judged as at level six?

In this mix of content possibilities and cognitive and physical expectations, what can be negotiated? To follow is a list of possible dimensions for negotiation in the context of outcomes-based education.

*   The range of tactics and strategies to be demonstrated within, for example, volleyball – How many? What are they? What tactics and strategies differentiate the two levels?
*   The range of tactics and strategies to be demonstrated across, for example, volleyball, tennis and touch football – How many? What are they?
*   The individual or group nature of different tactics and strategies – What balance of individual or group strategies is required to be demonstrated? What role does team work play? Will I work in the one team for the entire unit of work? What happens if I am not on a 'good' team? Will I be disadvantaged if my team always loses?
*   The goal students identify as appropriate for themselves – What might this look like? Will girls select the same goal as will boys? Does the goal have to be about winning? What about consistent effort and participation? Could it be that as a whole class we will select the goal? Can each student have a different goal?
*   The level that students identify as appropriate for themselves – How can I self-assess? On what criteria and standards will I be assessed? Can these be developed by consensus by the class? When will I be given feedback to assist my learning? How many opportunities will I be given to demonstrate that I can consistently demonstrate the outcome for which I am aiming? How will 'responding to environmental conditions' be interpreted across diverse activities such as volleyball, rock climbing or swimming? If our activities are not team-oriented, how will I demonstrate capability in defense and attack?

Together, the teacher and students also should consider the assessment process. What task or tasks would the students like to contribute towards their assessment? Here the students might prefer a particular balance written, oral or performance used formatively or summatively. Might students have the opportunity to resubmit or repeat a task and what could be the submission dates? Students can also be offered the opportunity to decide whether the final product will be presented as an individual piece of work or a collaborative piece. What balance of the grading might be individual or group and who will do the grading? Might peers assist with assessment?

The example of outcomes as a basis for negotiation reminds us that some curriculum approaches are more amenable to negotiation than others. Where there is a tightly mandated scope and sequence of the curriculum in conjunction with external exams, there is minimal space for negotiating content and assessment although there may be opportunities created for negotiation of teaching and learning approaches.

Approaches to teaching and learning

The possibilities for negotiation are enhanced when physical educators attempt to accommodate the various ways in which students learn. As such, planning needs to reflect learning opportunities that are social and collaborative, that demand oral and group work, that require active engagement with ideas and that require problem-solving and risk-taking. Further, planning and resources need to support the different styles of teaching and learning and how these influence 'how' students learn and how those preferences for learning in particular ways affects their learning behaviours (Capel *et al.* 1999).

If physical educators are adaptable and ready to draw on a range of student-centred teaching styles (Joyce *et al.* 1997; Mosston and Ashworth 1994), they may be able to assist students to, for example:

- select a number of tasks, design task cards or stations, and decide upon when and how they will move through the tasks;
- work with a partner in a reciprocal teaching programme;
- write an individual programme;
- frame questions and choose resources that will help them discover and reflect upon solutions to their challenge.

While providing a robust framework for ways towards encouraging teachers to negotiate with their students, Mosston and Ashworth's framework can be enriched by overlaying an understanding of multiple intelligences.

Gardner's (1987, 1999) work has been highly influential in offering new views on intelligence and the ways in which students can demonstrate their intelligences through their work. He proposes eight different intelligences (linguistic, logical–mathematical, spatial, bodily–kinesthetic, musical, interpersonal, intrapersonal and naturalist) to account for a broader range of human potential. While all students possess each intelligence, they will be particularly strong in one or two. With respect to inquiry-based pedagogies, the physical educator's task it to work with students to recognise their strengths and create teaching-learning processes that build upon these. Gardner's work encourages teachers to include a wide variety of possibilities that reflects each intelligence in each unit of work around which students can negotiate; for example, poems, conferences, deductive and inductive reasoning, concept maps, physical demonstrations, playing music, interviewing, filming, cooperative learning, team games, reflecting and field trips.

The following outcomes are provided as examples of the possibilities for different learning experiences, so students can negotiate to work with preferred intelligences. The outcomes are examples of levels 4 and 5 from the strand 'Promoting the Health of Individuals and Communities' from the Queensland (1999) *Health and Physical Education Years 1 to 10 Syllabus*.

4.2   Students develop and implement strategies for optimizing personal diet based on identified nutritional needs for growth, energy and health.

5.2   Students devise and implement for themselves and others health-promoting strategies which recognise the influence of a range of factors on personal dietary behaviours, now and in the future.

Several intelligences may be recognised in the following learning experiences:

Logical–mathematical intelligence:
•   Investigate a nutritional issue and report on your findings.
•   Compare healthy and unhealthy nutritional behaviours and note the factors that facilitate or constrain these behaviours.
•   Discuss, evaluate and critique dietary guidelines.
•   Survey the popularity of different snacks and reasons why students eat these snacks (e.g. cost, availability, advertising, taste).
•   Analyse and evaluate the sugar, fat and fibre content of popular snacks, and research the health implications of having a diet high in fat and sugar and low in fibre.

Verbal–linguistic intelligence:
•   Take part in a debate or write a poem on the relationship of snacking to physical, social and mental health.
•   Keep a logbook of progress towards goals, noting relevant social, economic, physical and emotional factors.

Bodily–kinesthetic intelligence:
•   Make your own snacks and compare them to commercially prepared ones, for example, hamburgers.
•   Create a collage of advertising images of snacks and explain the advertising techniques that are used to sell snacks.
•   Teaching for successful learning would seek to introduce students to these possible learning experiences, and have the resources in place for multiple options to be taken up following negotiation.

Silver and Hanson (1998) argue that by limiting opportunities for learning to the more traditionally focused verbal–linguistic and logical–mathematical intelligences, many students are denied different ways of thinking and acquiring knowledge and skills. The consideration of teaching–learning styles and multiple intelligences encourages teachers to be more flexible in the repertoire of learning experiences available for their students and how they wish to demonstrate that learning.

In what ways can we negotiate the curriculum?

In response to the question, 'on what can we negotiate?', we have introduced an array of questions and challenges for teachers and students inviting negotiation on unit topics, learning experiences and assessment, to meet students' needs, interests and preferred intelligences. Clearly negotiation is likely to be a complex and time-consuming process. How might teachers approach it? Beane (1993) suggests that there are four key questions that students can ask to begin this process:

- What do we already know? (e.g. about team games? biomechanics? physical activity and young people?)
- What do we want and need to find out?
- How will we go about finding out the information? (e.g. alone? in groups? research? physical engagement?)
- What are the findings, what have we learnt, who will we show and for whom are we doing the work, and where next? (e.g. what will we show for assessment? when? to whom? for what contribution?)

There are many ways, a student or a class can enter into the negotiation process. One way of engaging students in these questions can be the following:

- students form into small groups ensuring diversity;
- independently, each student notes responses to, for example, 'What do we know already?';
- the small group prioritises the groups' responses;
- each group nominates to the class their preferred content direction (or learning experiences, assessment process, etc.);
- the class then considers the possibilities taking account of their diversity, the time available, the demand upon resources, etc.;
- a cluster of learning pathways are identified.

(Adapted from Beane 1993)

To negotiate is not a one-off occurrence that happens at the start of a programme or unit. Rather, negotiation is in itself an ongoing process that is demanding upon teachers in terms of planning and monitoring. Teachers will need to think through what are the constraints or limits within the negotiation process such as the time, space and breadth of resources available that will impact upon the direction of the negotiation. They will also have to assist students to frame the project or performance as it unfolds through constant questions, discussions and collaborative decision-making to ensure intellectual rigour and that students move beyond the taken-for-granted. The teacher should monitor that all students have a voice in the negotiation and learning processes to ensure that the environment is supportive and inclusive. A tension for teachers is between the how they see their role and the assistance that students 'need' and keeping the negotiation process genuinely democratic.

These suggested processes and responsibilities place the student and their inquiries at the heart of the learning process and can act as the starting point for teachers and students to work cooperatively in negotiating units or lessons that meet the needs of young people. Thus far, the chapter has provided some ideas on why physical educators should negotiate, on what aspects of their practice can they negotiate, and in which ways they can negotiate. The final section of this chapter will consider the challenges and limitations of negotiating the curriculum and its assessment.

What are the challenges and limitations?

There are a number of key points to be made in any discussion about whether or not to negotiate within physical education. What one teacher sees as a challenge and therefore surmountable, another may perceive as a limitation. Within the everyday demands of the school, we suggest that time is an element that most negatively influences a teacher's decision to adopt a negotiated approach (e.g. Hargreaves 1994). To work in negotiated ways with students can take significant time, particularly if teachers want to try negotiating large issues such as the focus of units of work. Planning choices in learning experiences into a unit of work, then working with students in negotiated ways to complete one of these tasks, would require a great deal of energy on the teacher's part and a clear commitment to providing learning opportunities to suit all learners. In addition, the process of meeting the external demands and constraints of credentialing authorities can be extremely constraining and time consuming for teachers. Finding time to cover the curriculum in ways that are considered appropriate by the students and that meet the demands of these authorities can discourage teachers from working in creative and collaborative ways with students. Further, a negotiated curriculum that eventuates in several learning pathways in the one class can create, to an outsider, a sense of chaos as students have differing demands in where, how and what they will be working with in any one lesson. Colleagues and parents will need to be fully briefed on the negotiation process and its justifications.

As mentioned earlier in the chapter, some teachers may find the 'new role' of facilitator foreign and uncomfortable despite changes in schools that are occurring to accommodate new relationships between students and teachers. Teachers have to set aside their preferred topics, approaches and resources and listen to the students. They may feel they are 'sitting by' watching students 'waste time' and 'go up blind alleys'. Similarly, they may need to resist 'stepping in' to 'resolve' an impasse in order to maintain the integrity of the negotiation process.

Needless to say, students may also find the negotiation process challenging. With perhaps thousands of hours of schooling behind them in which they have 'practised' being compliant, 'being told' and being managed, to have to share in this responsibility can be unwelcome. They too can become frustrated with the democratic process in terms of its time and co-operation (Apple and Beane 1999). To have no definitive product may also generate a sense of insecurity as students frequently want to know, 'is this right?' They may also find the array of assessment products and arrangements an issue as they strive for comparability with their colleagues. Thus, as with colleagues and parents, it is particularly important that students are fully briefed on why negotiation is being introduced and how they might expect to feel as the process evolves.

Conclusion

As the linear, age-related, subject-based approaches to curriculum development and implementation are increasingly challenged, so too will be the ways in which educators assist students to learn. There will be an increased emphasis on working jointly with others in a team on joint problem solving. Students will need to acquire expert skills in an increasingly networked curriculum (subject boundaries dissolved/knowledge acquired through information technologies) applied through effective learning teams and alliances. Their engagement in their own learning will increase and they will need to become increasingly responsible for asking significant questions and being able to provide detailed evidence about their own levels of performance. Experiences and skills in negotiation will become particularly important as schooling increasingly takes place outside the traditional geographically bounded space called school (Macdonald 2003).

This chapter unashamedly paints the need for negotiation with our students in a positive light despite the challenges outlined above. If schools are for and about students, then the way forward in how educators (teachers, parents, curriculum writers, coaches, etc.) work with students is clear. Physical education practices need to adopt a student-centred negotiated approach to teaching and learning.

References

Apple, M. and Beane, J. (1999) 'Lessons from democratic schools', in M. Apple and J. Beane (eds) *Democratic Schools*, Buckingham: Open University Press.
The Australian Concise Oxford Dictionary (2001), Oxford: Oxford University Press.
Beane, J.A. (1993) *A Middle School Curriculum: From Rhetoric to Reality*, Ohio: National Middle School Association.
Beare, H. (2001) *Creating the Future School*, London: Routledge Falmer.
Braggett, E., Morris, G. and Day, A. (1999) *Reforming the Middle Years of Schooling*, Australia: Hawker Brownlow Education.

Boomer, G., Lester, N., Onore, C. and Cook, J. (1992) *Negotiating the Curriculum: Educating for the 21st Century*, London: Falmer Press.

Capel, S., Leask, M. and Turner, T. (1999) *Learning to Teach in the Secondary School: A Companion to School Experience*, London: Routledge.

Dalin, P. (1998) 'Developing the twenty-first century school: a challenge to reformers', in A. Hargreaves *et al.* (eds), *International Handbook of Educational Change*, Dordrecht: Kluwer Academic Publications.

Darling-Hammond, L. (1997) *The Right to Learn*, San Fransisco: Jossey-Bass.

Edwards, D. and Mercer, N. (1987) *Common Knowledge: The Development of Understanding in the Classroom*, London: Routledge.

Gardner, H. (1987) *Frames of Mind: The Theory of Multiple Intelligences*, New York: Basic Books.

Gardner, H. (1999) *Intelligence Reframed: Multiple Intelligences for the 21st Century*, New York: Basic Books.

George, P.S. and Shewey, C. (1994) *New Evidence for the Middle School*, Columbus, OH: National Middle School Association.

Glover, S., Burns, J., Butler, H. and Patton, G. (1998) 'Social environments and the emotional wellbeing of young people', *Family Matters* 49: 11–16.

Hargreaves, A. (1994) *Changing Teachers, Changing Times: Teachers' Work and Culture in the Postmodern Age*, London: Cassell.

Joyce, B., Calhoun, E. and Hopkins, D. (1997) *Models of Learning – Tools for Teaching*, Buckingham: Open University Press.

Kirk, D. (1986) 'A critical pedagogy for teacher education: toward an inquiry-oriented approach', *Journal of Teaching in Physical Education* 5: 230–46.

Lambert, D. and Lines, D. (2000) *Understanding Assessment: Purposes, Perceptions, Practice*, London: RoutledgeFalmer.

Macdonald, D. (2002) 'Critical pedagogy: what might it look like and why does it matter', in A. Laker (ed.) *The Sociology of Sport and Physical Education: An Introductory Reader*, London: RoutledgeFalmer.

Macdonald, D. (2003) 'Curriculum change and the postmodern world: is the school curriculum reform project an anachronism?', *Journal of Curriculum Studies* 35(2): 139–49.

Mosston, M. and Ashworth, S. (1994) *Teaching Physical Education* (4th edn), Columbus, OH: C.E. Merrill.

Queensland School Curriculum Council (1999) *Health and Physical Education: Years 1 to 10 Syllabus*, Queensland: Publishing Services, Education Queensland.

Silver, H.F. and Hanson, J.R. (1998) *Learning Styles and Strategies*, Woodbridge, NJ: The Thoughtful Education Press.

Tinning, R. (1997) *Pedagogies for Physical Education: Pauline's Story*, Victoria: Deakin University.

Torrance, H. and Pryor, J. (2001) 'Developing formative assessment in the classroom; using action research to explore and modify theory', *British Educational Research Journal* 27(5): 615–31.

Vygotsky, L.S. (1962) *Thought and Language*, Cambridge, MA: MIT Press.

Vygotsky, L.S. (1978) *Mind in Society: The Developmental of Higher Psychological Processes*, London: Harvard University Press.

Weeden, P., Winter, J. and Broadfoot, P. (2002) *Assessment: What's In It For Schools?* London: RoutledgeFalmer.

Part III

Critical inquiry and problem-solving in the senior years of schooling

Chapter 11

Reflective practices in teaching and coaching

Using reflective journals to enhance performance

Cliff Mallett

One of the major aims for many athletes in competitive sport is the pursuit of excellence. Optimising sports performance is a complex problem-solving exercise that relies heavily upon a successful working relationship between the coach and the athlete. This is no different to stressing the importance of a healthy relationship between teacher and student in schools. Effective instruction and learning is dependent on the instructor having appropriate knowledge of the sport and pedagogical practices (Shulman 1986).

The purpose of this chapter is to outline the use of a specific pedagogical strategy, a reflective journal in a physical education/sporting context that facilitates problem-solving skills consistent with constructivist approaches to effective instruction and learning. The chapter comprises two sections. The first section briefly outlines the rationale that underpins the use of a reflective journal and in the second section, a working example of applying the theory to practice is discussed. However, before I embark on the 'what' and 'how' of the strategy, I want to draw your attention to the 'why'.

In recent times, as the standard of performance improves in many sports, the search for even higher performances has necessitated alternative views of how this can be achieved. The development of *Teaching Games for Understanding* (TGfU) by Bunker and Thorpe (1982) was in direct response to exploring alternative approaches to teaching and coaching in the pursuit of excellence (see Chapter 3 in this volume for a further discussion of this approach). Underpinned by the notion of the 'intelligent performer', TGfU emphasises the cognitive domain over the psychomotor domain, which was uncharacteristic of traditional pedagogical practices. The emphasis of one domain over another may depend upon the requirements of the sport and in some cases the specific playing positions. Nevertheless I support the argument that the facilitation of 'intelligent performance' requires the teacher and/or coach to consider more than the psychomotor domain (Cassidy and Jones 2002). The issue at hand is that if coaches want their athletes to be 'thinking players', then it is imperative that strong consideration should be given to their own pedagogical practices. Reproductive pedagogies are commonplace in coaching, partly because coaches tend to coach they way in which they were coached. However, if athletes are to develop appropriate thinking skills and take personal responsibility for their performance, and part responsibility for their preparation for performance, then I argue that reproductive pedagogies are inappropriate. I contend that pedagogies that emphasise higher order thinking (that is, the ability to analyse, synthesise and evaluate information) will promote problem-solving skills that are key to 'intelligent performance'.

The what and why of reflection

Optimal performance in teaching, coaching and in the sporting arena can be thought of as a problem-solving exercise. The challenge is to find the means through which to produce the optimal performance. There may be several means through which to facilitate performance, however, the basic problem is: 'How can I get a superior result?' Consciously attending to how performance can be improved is one avenue of reflection. The process of reflection is an important tool for empowering the individual to improve their practice. Systematic reflection can also be motivational. The performer is motivated by the perception that they are in control and can influence their future behaviour/performance. For change to occur, data collection is required followed by an analysis of that data with the intention of using the information to improve performance. Intelligent performance requires the performer to reflect on action and consider alternatives to solve the problem of enhancing performance.

Many scholars and practitioners have defined the term 'reflection' in different ways, hence it is important from the outset to define the term within the context of this chapter. Essentially, reflection is a conscious or intentional analysis of behaviour or performance in which the person responds to questions, some of which are pre-determined, about their practice (Tinning *et al.* 2001). In addition to a conscious analysis of behaviour, the reflective process includes consideration of the consequences of that analysis. In other words, what changes might occur as a result of that analysis? Reflection can take several forms. The different types of reflection are contingent on the outcomes required and the type of questions to which they respond.

Van Manen (1977) has been one of the most influential writers on reflection. He distinguishes between three major hierarchical levels or forms of reflection: technical, practical and critical. He defines the most elementary form of reflection, 'technical reflection', in terms of the production of instrumental outcomes from the application of existing knowledge. Technical reflection 'takes the social contexts for granted . . . [the] primary focus is on resolving the concerns of the practitioner' (Kidman and Carlson 1998: 102). An example of technical reflection would be a situation where a teacher analyses his performance in terms of how much time on task was devoted by students to physical activity during a physical education lesson or coaching session. In other words, technical reflection is concerned with using existing knowledge to reach some instrumental outcome or goal (e.g. sporting performance). Tinning (1995) points out that Van Manen's definition of technical reflection is similar to Grimmette *et al.*'s (1987) first category of reflective teaching in which applied practice or action is influenced by empirical findings. Tinning (1995: 27) comments that this type of reflection 'essentially represents thoughtfulness about action'.

'Practical reflection' is the next level of reflectivity in the hierarchy and is concerned with thoughtful analysis of the theoretical underpinnings of practice, that is, connecting theory and practice (praxis). Tinning (1995: 26) defines practical reflection as 'a form of contemplative inquiry that involves clarifying the assumptions underpinning practical actions. It is concerned with moral, ethical and value considerations in that all actions are linked with value commitments.' In ways that are similar to Van Manen's notion of practical reflection, Grimmette *et al.* define their second category of reflection in terms of the thoughtful consideration of the knowledge which underpins practice. In this sense, 'reflection is essentially a deliberation among choices of competing versions of good teaching [or coaching]' (Tinning 1995: 27). For example, a coach might consider which of various methods is most appropriate for teaching the dribble to a novice group of players, or whether a skill should be taught in isolation or in a game context.

In Van Manen's hierarchy of reflectivity, the final and highest level of reflection is 'critical reflection'. This third level of reflectivity considers the 'political' or ideological dimensions that will influence practice (e.g. gender equity issues). This requires an analysis of the social and cultural context and challenging the taken-for-granted assumptions that underpin behaviour/performance. 'Other spheres of knowledge emerge from the argument that reflectivity should lead practitioners to question their practices, particularly in connection with equity and social issues' (Kidman and Carlson 1998: 102). This last form of reflection has some parallels with the third categorisation of reflection proposed by Grimmette *et al.*, in which new understandings of previously taken-for-granted assumptions about practice are developed. For example, a coach might ask a critical friend to collect data about how many times she speaks to each of the players in a mixed team and what kinds of feedback she provides. Further reflection might be directed at considering the consequences of her behaviour for those being coached.

All forms of reflection should be valued and encouraged (Hellison and Templin 1991), not only by teachers, but students can also be involved in and benefit from reflection in all its forms. This chapter, however, focuses on 'technical reflection', as an important form of reflection which can meet the needs of students and elite athletes who are primarily focused on improving their performance. It reports on work which took up the challenge of encouraging senior school students and elite athletes to develop the skills required for technical reflection and to practise these in ways which would improve their performance.

Donald Schon (1983) makes the important distinction between 'reflection-in-action' and 'reflection-on-action'. Reflection-in-action is the process of engaging in reflection, or analysis of the situation, during the activity itself and responding to that reflection during the activity. For example, changing the lesson or the training session to accommodate more recent information about the performance, such as the students'/athletes' unexpected response to a task, would constitute reflection-in-action. Reflection-on-action is concerned with analysing, synthesising and evaluating information post-performance. The use of reflective journals and training diaries to record post-performance evaluation/reflection is a useful means of developing the ability to self-reflect in this way. Reflection is a skill that requires first, a conceptual understanding of the nature of reflection, as well as establishing a formal process of reflection. The ability to self-reflect requires both structured guidance from teachers and coaches, as well as regular practice with constructive feedback.

Some studies (e.g. Gore and Bartlett 1988), provide examples of the systematic use of a reflective journal to assist students and athletes work strategically towards completion of a set task. As a strategy it has provided a focus that has prompted students and athletes to find solutions to an identified problem or set target (e.g. performance standard, technical excellence). The strategy enables the student to think beyond the outcome and actively work on the process of achieving the desired outcome (Carlson 2002). In other words, the students/athletes work hard towards creating their own blueprint for success.

What is a reflective journal?

The following discussion highlights how I have used technical reflection to monitor and enhance performance. In particular, I demonstrate the means through which a teacher or coach can guide students and athletes as they constructively analyse performance through the use of reflective journals. Such an approach follows the principles of constructivist learning discussed in Chapter 2 of this volume. As students analyse their performance and reflect on how it might be improved they are able to take greater control over their own learning. In a broader sense, they construct new understandings as they interpret 'new' information in the context of 'old' or 'established' information.

A reflective journal gives direction by providing a useful process through which to reflect about what happened in a lesson or training session or during a performance. In the main it includes descriptive notes about actions, but students/ athletes should be encouraged to write more personal accounts of connections between theory and practice, including feelings. What we know about something will depend on the questions we ask of it (Postman 1989). In this regard the role of the teacher/coach is critical. To facilitate increasingly more sophisticated or insightful reflections on an individual's thoughts, feelings and behaviours, the instructor should provide appropriate guidance focusing on important questions that enable the student/athlete to demonstrate higher order thinking.

Creating a reflective journal

In a unit, track and field (taught as part of the senior physical education subject in Queensland secondary schools), students are required to select the event which they believe is most appropriate for themselves. It is an important feature of the unit that they make this decision and that the decision is based on explicit criteria. Providing students with the choice in which event/s to develop their performance assists in the promotion of self-determination; students are more likely to feel that they have some choice in the decision-making process and subsequently more autonomy (Deci and Ryan 1985). This is consistent with the notion of independent learning. The students in the preamble to their journal justify why they chose the event. The criteria may include pre-test results or the use of fitness indices, or a positive previous experience. Once the students select their event, they spend time developing a training schedule. The development of a training schedule involves library research, as well as opportunities for students to work co-operatively to design an appropriate schedule. A common problem is teachers' expectations that students can manage information from several of the major knowledge areas within exercise science (e.g. skill acquisition, biomechanics, exercise physiology, sport psychology); this is a complex task and one with which many students struggle. It is generally more useful to suggest that students focus their attention on one knowledge discipline at a time within exercise science; their choice however needs to be defended. For example, their training schedule and training diary might primarily focus on sport psychology because the student can argue that this knowledge will provide the best opportunity for improvement.

Reflective journals can be used in several contexts. In addition to that described in this chapter, in the world of elite sport, athletes can be encouraged to write reflective notes about their training, competition and day-to-day living. The purpose is for athletes to be aware of their thoughts and feelings and to record these, because behaviour change is only possible if athletes are first aware of their thoughts and feelings.

A good quality journal might include the following:

- A general description of what took place (i.e. recall content);
- Analysis of what was done (i) in general terms (ii) makes connections with the basic concepts within exercise science;
- Synthesis and evaluation of ideas – the inclusion of the training program design (and justification) and in particular subsequent changes as a consequence of 'new' knowledge;
- A good reflective journal goes beyond mere description. There is demonstration of clear links between theoretical concepts and reflections of what was experienced (i.e. praxis).

Reflection on a training session

As students complete their contract for the 'track and field' unit they use their reflective journal to record their thoughts, feelings and behaviours on a daily basis. The journal may include the following features:

- Targets/performance goals (e.g. physical, technical, psychological goals).
- An overall plan for the duration of the task (competitive season; length of unit). It is preferable that the athlete/student engages in this process alongside the coach/teacher because it provides the individual with a sense of ownership of the document ('blueprint for success').

For each day the athlete/student enters information about the day's training and responds to some general questions with provision for additional comments. Some of the questions to which the students respond are:

- What is the purpose of the session?
- What training was prescribed?
- What was completed?
- If some training was not completed, outline why not.
- Did the training reflect the purpose of the session (e.g. was the training appropriate for what you wanted to achieve)? If yes, outline an example. If no, what would you change for next time and why?
- What did you learn about yourself from this session?
- Can you make connections between the training session and some of the theory that you have been learning in class (e.g. exercise physiology, skill acquisition, biomechanics)?

The role of the teacher/coach is to facilitate learning, as opposed to transmitting their knowledge to a passive learner. Although students are encouraged to ask themselves relevant questions, experience has shown that many students struggle with the type of questions to ask. For many students, to write a description of the action that took place is a reasonable request. For students to think more deeply, however, requires more insightful questions to be considered. The majority of students generally require some assistance in choosing questions which will help them to demonstrate higher order thinking. The role of the teacher is to guide an appropriate line of thinking that over time will assist students to go beyond pure description. For example a dialogue between teacher (T) and student (S) might sound like:

T: Compare that start with the previous start. What was different?
S: The second start was better.
T: What specifically was better about the second start?
S: I felt the second start was faster. I think I snapped off the blocks better.
T: Why do you think that you snapped off the blocks faster? What did you do differently?
S: I put more pressure onto the block with my feet in the 'set' position.
T: Can you tell me why that caused you to get a better push off the blocks?
S: Greater force.
T: Yes, you are on the right track. Do you remember Newton's laws of motion?

s: Yes.

T: Which of his three laws of motion do you think is most relevant to what you found out in the second start?

s: His second law, force is equal to mass times acceleration.

T: What does that particular law mean in the context of the block start in sprinting?

s: The greater the force that I apply to the blocks the faster I will snap off the blocks.

T: That is correct! Well done! It would be useful to make a note of that in your journal. For the future also consider what you can do to increase the force that you can apply to the blocks. Think about that question and what are the implications. We can discuss some of your ideas next lesson.

Weekly summary

At the completion of each week, the students are required to reflect on their week and make a summary of the work they have completed using the following questions as a guide:

- Did you achieve your performance targets/goals this week? If not, why not? If so, what specifically did you find useful? How do you know this?
- Was the schedule too demanding for you? If so, how do you know this? What changes do you suggest? Why?

Mid-term summary/final summary

The main focus of the mid-term and final summary is to encourage students to examine the daily entries and weekly summaries in an attempt to identify patterns that might emerge from the data collected. Guiding questions could include:

- What have your most significant improvements been to date? Were these expected? Why or why not?
- Reflect on the progress that has been made (e.g. What has changed? What do you think caused that change? How do you know that?)
- If you were to redesign your unit what amendments would you make? Why?
- To what extent does what I experienced match what the theory says? Give an example to illustrate your point. For example, within the discipline of exercise physiology, consider training intensities, recoveries, volume and the overall training stress.

Assessment

In physical education contexts where reflective journals are used, it may contribute to the assessment process. The assessment should be concerned with the demonstration of higher-order thinking. Purely descriptive passages will be commonplace, however the students who demonstrate the ability to analyse, synthesise and evaluate information will make appropriate connections between the theory (e.g. exercise science) and the practice. For example, a student may experiment with various starting positions for the 100-m sprint, in order to develop the most appropriate start. Feedback from several sources, including an analysis of video footage, relevant literature, task sheets and additional feedback from other students and/or the teacher, will provide the student with ample opportunities to make an informed decision as to the best starting position for them. The important consideration for assessment is their ability to justify their decision as to why they chose that particular starting position. For example, in a reflective journal I would be looking for comments similar to those presented in Figure 11.2. The use of several assessment strategies to enable students to demonstrate their thinking caters for several learning styles (group discussion, one-on-one chats, written report). However, assessment should focus on the written entries in the reflective journal, which can be combined with verbal discussions with the student throughout the course to clarify their understandings and feelings. It is important for the teacher to record the discussions with students as evidence of how the students are processing the information.

The following excerpts are from a reflective journal of an international athlete at different stages in the process. The quality of the reflection presented in Figure 11.2 shows an improvement upon that presented in Figure 11.1. The quotes demonstrate the different types of reflective comments that are sought in a journal.

The comments in Figure 11.1 are descriptive and do not demonstrate higher-order thinking. Although the type of information presented in Figure 11.1 is acceptable, further questioning by the teacher/coach should guide the student/athlete to analyse the session in greater depth. The journal entry that is presented in Figure 11.2, shows a greater depth of analysis, providing the coach with a better understanding of what the athlete knows about their performance.

Monday 22 May 1995

THROWS – Mondays are not good days. I have to start worrying about not fouling. I have to get speed and keep up at start, don't drop on left leg. Don't crab at end. Nothing is going right at the moment.

AFTERNOON, WEIGHTS
[an outline follows of the weights programmes for the Snatch, Bench, Squats, Lunge}
Comments are written in relation to the
Snatch: Tech(nique) not the best
Bench: Everything is getting easier
Squats and Lunge: Dropping down to one session per day

Figure 11.1 A journal entry demonstrating mostly description with some analysis

Thursday 23 January 1997

THROWS
ALMOST seems to be the best word to describe me and my technique at the moment. I was almost in tears today because my technique was almost there. My gosh it is so frustrating to be almost catching the movement.
I feel the problem is in the middle, my arm is already caught the rest of my legs. I do not feel a pull of any sorts on my arm. Feel placement has improved and I feel I turn with my right.
What can I do?
I am constantly thinking about turning, squeezing, pushing, pulling , blocking, relaxing, but my arm is still catching me.

Figure 11.2 A journal entry demonstrating some analysis at both technical and psychological levels

What has been said about reflective journals?

Committing thoughts and feelings to writing can provide a rich source of information that prompts further discussion. The opportunity for others to 'see things from your perspective [provides] an extremely rich source of feedback' (Sykes 1995: 188). The following quote highlights the significant role of the teacher and coach in the effective use of training diaries and reflective journals.

> To me, journalling is like mining for minerals. These minerals are found in ore that lie deep beneath the earth. It takes courage and determination to go down a dark mineshaft to search for it. Once found it must be crushed, sifted and treated to allow the precious metal to be extracted. This process is costly and time consuming, but once finished can be very rewarding in its worth. I find myself with a mind full of ore, some still buried, some on the surface that needs to be crushed and sifted. Even after this is done I might not realise its worth. Hopefully this will come in time.
> (Taken from a student journal, Sykes 1995: 190)

In recent times there has been considerable research examining the various forms of reflection and the benefits of reflection in pre-service teaching programmes and in professional practice (e.g. Good and Whang 2002; Sykes 1995; Tsangaridou and O'Sullivan 1997). Tsangaridou and O'Sullivan (1997) found that the reflections of experienced teachers were situationally and contextually bound and that over time reflections that informed teachers' practices, influenced changes in the teachers' classroom practices and professional development.

Good and Whang (2002) examined the use of a written journal in reflecting, applying and questioning in an undergraduate educational psychology course. The participants in their study reported several benefits from using the reflective journal, including enhanced thinking skills, the ability to demonstrate and monitor progress, and opportunities to connect past personal events with future development (reflection) and provide moments for self-evaluation.

However, students engage with the reflective process differently. Gore and Bartlett (1988) identified three types of reflectors, namely, recalcitrant, acquiescent and committed reflectors. In their examination of the quality of reflection in a teacher education course, they found that the participants 'differed in terms of how they reflected and on what they reflected' (Gore and Bartlett 1988: 23). They defined 'recalcitrant reflectors' as those not committed to the process of reflection, probably because they did not see its relevance. The students in this group wrote descriptively and sporadically reflecting a high degree of amotivation towards the process. The largest group of reflectors fell into the category of 'acquiescent reflectors'. Similar to the recalcitrant reflectors, the acquiescent reflectors were motivated by instrumental outcomes (i.e. grades). In this regard their responses were driven by the need to please others. They participated not because they wanted to, but because they perceived they had to. Committed reflectors, on the other hand, were those who valued the importance of reflection and the intrinsic satisfaction associated with writing in their journals. They regularly entered data into their journals because they wanted to. Consequently, their reflections went beyond the technical level. Further to this Macdonald and Brooker (1999) in a similar context with physical education teacher education students, encountered so much resistance to a journalling task, that they chose to withdraw the task from the course assessment.

The use of reflective journals can, nevertheless, be the catalyst for healthy dialogue between the student/athlete and the instructor. This sharing of thoughts and ideas is consistent with Vygotskian principles, in which knowledge is co-constructed (McInerney and McInerney 2002). The role of teachers is to facilitate a line of thinking that attempts to make connections between what was experienced and what was taught. The teacher guides learning through appropriate questioning (i.e. scaffolding) that addresses the full range of Bloom's taxonomy of cognitive skills. The questions that are asked and ensuing discussion provides opportunities for students and athletes to enhance their thinking skills in a meaningful learning exercise. In this way, 'ore' is processed progressively into 'precious metal'.

What has been of tremendous utility for the students/athletes undertaking the track and field unit, in terms of both learning and improved performance has been that they can engage in a 'real life' situation and then reflect on that engagement. The reflective process has required methodical analysis, synthesis and evaluation of the information from both theoretical and applied sources. The activity was found to be authentic and thus meaningful which, in turn, promoted a sense of autonomy. The individual takes personal responsibility for the task/problem and perceives that s/he has control over his/her product/performance (i.e. outcome). The increase in personal control leads to increased motivation and positive consequences (e.g. self-efficacy, effort leads to rewards, perseverance). Subsequently, the use of a diary can facilitate healthy motivation towards student participation.

If assessment of reflective journals is to be used, it should focus on the process, as well as the performance. This also increases the perception that students have some control over the result. If they work hard and demonstrate the ability to analyse, synthesise and evaluate appropriate information to work through the problem they can expect to be rewarded for their efforts. The rewards can be both intrinsic (e.g. sense of accomplishment) and extrinsic (e.g. a good grade). The use of reflective journals can be motivational because it can increase both perceived competence and self-determination that in turn will facilitate adaptive forms of motivation (e.g. intrinsic motivation) (Deci and Ryan 1985).

Concluding ideas

This chapter has explained how the use of reflexive journals at a technical level can be an effective pedagogical strategy to develop basic skills of problem-solving, which in turn can assist in developing 'intelligent performers'. Reflective journals promote inquiry by prompting students to think about what they did, why they did it, and what they learned from it. For some students to use the journal to reflect beyond the technical may also be appropriate. For example, they could consider how their feelings about their body shape change or do not change as training continues and why the members of their multicultural team are not communicating with each other as well as they could. Such considerations can be just as pivotal to the progress of an athlete as technical questions. Good reflection whether it is technical, practical or critical, is shaped by inquiring questions, that is, the quality of reflection is contingent on the questions that are asked. Reflection is a skill and consequently requires appropriate practice and feedback (Senne and Rickard 2002). A good reflector will have developed an inquiring mind and respond to questions that invite them to go beyond mere description.

References

Bunker, D. and Thorpe, R. (1982) 'A model for the teaching of games in secondary schools', *The Bulletin of Physical Education* 18(1): 5–8.

Carlson, T. (2002) 'Pedagogies for coaches: a guide to help coaches find the critical edge in their coaching performance,' *Course Materials for Pedagogies for Coaches (HMST7236)*, Brisbane: University of Queensland.

Cassidy, T. and Jones, R. (2002) 'The social, cultural and pedagogical foundations of sports coaching', paper presented at the International Association for Physical Education in Higher Education, Spain, 22–25 October.

Deci, E.L. and Ryan, R.M. (1985) *Intrinsic Motivation and Self-Determination in Human Behaviour*, New York: Plenum Press.

Good, J.M. and Whang, P.A. (2002) 'Encouraging reflection in pre-service teachers through response journals', *The Teacher Educator* 37(4): 254–67.

Gore, J. and Bartlett, L. (1988) 'Pathways and barriers to reflective teaching in an initial teacher education program', *Research Grant Series* 4: 19–31.

Grimmette, P., Mackinnon, A. and Erickson, G. (1987) 'Studying reflective practice: a review of research', in *Working Conference on Reflective Teaching*, Texas: University of Houston

Hellison, D.R. and Templin, T.J. (1991) *A Reflective Approach to Teaching Physical Education*, Champaign, IL: Human Kinetics.

Kidman, L. and Carlson, T.B. (1998) 'An action research process to change coaching behaviours', *Avante* 4: 100–17.

Macdonald, D. and Brooker, R. (1999) 'Articulating a critical pedagogy in physical education teacher education', *Journal of Sport Pedagogy* 5(1): 51–64.

McInerney, D. and McInerneny, V. (2002) *Educational Psychology: Constructing Learning*, Sydney: Pearson.

Postman, N. (1989) *Conscientious Objections: Stirring Up Trouble About Language, Technology, and Education*, London: Heinemann.

Schon, D. (1983) *The Reflective Practitioner: How Professionals Think in Action*, New York: Basic Books.

Senne, T.A. and Rickard, G.L. (2002) 'Experiencing the portfolio process during the internship: a comparative analysis of two PETE portfolio models', *Journal of Teaching in Physical Education* 21(3): 309–36.

Shulman, L. (1986) 'Those who understand: knowledge growth in teaching', *Educational Researcher* (February): 4–14.

Sykes, H.J. (1995) 'Promises, possibilities and problems of reflective journals', in C. Paré (ed.) *Training of Teachers in Reflective Practice of Physical Education*, Trois-Rivieres, Quebec: Départment des Sciences de l'Activité Physique.

Tinning, R.I. (1995) 'We have ways of making you think, or do we? Reflections on "training" in reflective teaching', in C. Paré (ed.) *Training of Teachers in Reflective Practice of Physical Education*, Trois-Rivieres, Quebec: Départment des Sciences de l'Activité Physique.

Tinning, R. Macdonald, D., Wright, J. and Hickey, C. (2001) *Becoming a Physical Education Teacher: Contemporary and Enduring Issues*, Melbourne: Prentice-Hall.

Tsangaridou, N. and O'Sullivan, M. (1997) 'The role of reflection in shaping physical education teachers' educational values and practices', *Journal of Teaching in Physical Education* 17(1): 2–25.

Van Manen, M. (1977) 'Linking ways of knowing with ways of being practical', *Curriculum Inquiry* 6: 205–28.

Chapter 12

Biomechanical analyses in physical education

Ross H. Sanders

Introduction

'You need to get higher and to spin faster'. This was the advice I gave on countless occasions to high school physical education students performing front somersaults from a minitrampoline. Not once in my 7 years as a physical education teacher did I explain to the students how those goals could be achieved. I just assumed that having been told to 'get higher and spin faster' the students would comply with that instruction. Perhaps surprisingly, perhaps not, but at least interestingly in the context of this chapter, no student ever requested elaboration on the statement. That is, none of them ever said 'What should I do to get higher?' or 'How can I spin faster?' It seems that there was a lack of curiosity by both teacher and student as to how the goals of achieving greater height and spinning faster could be achieved.

Of course, curiosity is the essential precursor of the chain of processes involved in analysis of performance, effective instruction and learning. Curiosity is the progenitor of questions such as 'What should be done to get more height?' and 'What do I need to change to be able to spin faster?', that is, it leads us to inquire.

Ironically, when I taught school physical education in the late 1970s and early 1980s, I considered myself to be conscientious in identifying aspects of technique that could be improved and in giving useful information to the student. I expect that physical education has advanced since then and many syllabuses require students to, for example, undertake biomechanical analyses of their performances, and to devise, implement and evaluate training programmes.

In this chapter, I wish to discuss inquiry with respect to the application of the science of biomechanics to analysis of performance of motor skills. I see inquiry in the application of biomechanics as having two dimensions – depth and width. Thus, in the first section we will discuss 'thinking deeply' and in the second 'thinking laterally'.

Thinking deeply

When observing the performance of a skill we tend naturally to compare it against an image 'in the mind's eye' of a 'model' performance. This image of model performance has been developed from observation of performances of elite exponents of the task. There is no doubting the usefulness of this process. However, we must bear in mind two concerns. First, the model image by itself provides no direct and overt information about how the movement was produced. It is purely a description of the result of the performer's efforts.

To find explanations for the resulting movement we need to think deeply. Like a detective solving a crime mystery we need to gather evidence from the observable characteristics to solve a puzzle. The explanation of the resultant performance of the motor skill lies in principles of mechanics. Thus, we need knowledge of basic mechanical principles and then to apply those to identify what is important in producing the desired movement characteristics. For example, we observe that elite discus throwers are typified by several characteristics that would be lacking in the early attempts of most physical education students. The elite discus throwers commence with considerable hip and knee flexion, they have several spins in the circle. They exhibit particular characteristics of sequencing in which the arm action seems to lag behind the rotation of the body and trunk rather than being in synchrony with it. Their hip and knee joints are extending near release, and the arm is moving upwards to release the discus at an angle near 45°. Of course we can break this movement pattern into parts and teach the release and spin separately before integrating them into the whole performance. We demonstrate the technique or provide other visual models of good performance. But how can the process of critical inquiry enhance the teaching process?

The answer lies in the relevant mechanical principles. The trunk and knee flexion and the spins in the circle are applying the principle that the amount of motion produced depends on the time over which forces are applied. These strategies maximise the time of applying the force and therefore the amount of motion generated. The pattern of sequencing the actions is related to the idea that motion can be transferred along a 'chain' of body segments (see, for example, Kreighbaum and Barthels 1981) to maximise the speed at the end of the chain. Motion is established in the large segments first, that is, the trunk, and then transferred in a sequential 'whip-like' pattern to the end of the rotating chain, that is, the hand holding the discus. The final extension of the joints is timed to assist in the upward motion of the arm and hand to approach the release angle that optimises the range of a projectile while maintaining a great speed of release. Inquiry about the underlying principles should assist students and teachers of physical education in identifying and understanding the 'critical features' of the technique. This provides a basis for identifying where the performance may be improved and in implementing desirable changes.

Rather than being a passive recipient of coaching, students develop insight and skill in answering questions, such as 'What can we do to increase the time of applying force to get our bodies moving?' and 'How can we transfer the motion of our bodies to the discus?' Through the development of the skills of critical inquiry, and its application through a systematic process, students are empowered to analyse performance of skills for themselves and to play a role in their own skill development. Further, they are developing some of the skills necessary for effective coaching of others.

Students' learning can be limited where they rely on purely descriptive accounts of how the skill should be performed. The texts and informational resources used to identify the important goals and technique characteristics when I was teaching in the late 1970s and early 1980s were often predominantly descriptive rather than explanatory. In particular, the scientific basis underpinning sound technique was elaborated rarely. The resources did not encourage the development of critical inquiry and its application. The process of applying science to identify the 'critical features' of technique is now developing but, as Lees (2002) has documented in his overview, remains at an embryonic stage.

One of the first formal attempts to establish procedures for analysing performance was by Hay and Reid (1982). To identify variables important to performance they developed a modelling approach in which mechanical variables contributing to the desired result were arranged in a hierarchical fashion with each variable in the hierarchy being determined by the variables in the level immediately below. The lowest level of the model comprises the body actions and postures that influence the mechanical variables, such as forces and torques. Thus, these models became known as 'deterministic models' following Hay and Reid (1988). The models are ideal for identifying the variables to be observed and analysed on a sound and mechanically correct basis and are used frequently by sports biomechanics researchers for this purpose. However, constructing the models is time-consuming and they are often difficult to develop. Consequently, this modelling method does not tend to be used by practitioners such as physical educators, students of physical education, sports participants and coaches.

A more practical approach for practitioners than deterministic models is to identify 'critical features' based on mechanical 'concepts' or 'principles'. The term 'critical features' came into popular use among sports biomechanists following the landmark paper by MacPherson (1990) entitled 'a systematic approach to skill analysis'. Various authors have produced lists of principles that can assist in identifying these 'critical features' to be observed in the performance of a motor skill. By listing fifty-three principles Bunn (1955, 1972) was a pioneer in this approach. Other sets of principles include those of Northrip *et al.* (1974), Norman (1975), Cooper and Glassow (1976), Bober (1981), Hochmuth (1984), Sanders and Wilson (1991, 1992a, 1992b), Hudson (1995) and Bartlett (1999). Observation of the lists indicates that while they are all based on sound scientific rationale and the same physical laws, there is little commonality in the way the ideas are expressed. There remains a need to produce a set of principles that can be applied universally. This would aid greatly in establishing a common 'language' that facilitates interchange of knowledge and ideas among sports scientists, teachers and coaches and to act as a catalyst in establishing a consistent approach to analysing and improving performance of skills.

The following project, based on the 'principles approach', is designed to develop analytical and coaching ability of first year university students in Physical

Education and Sports Science degrees. It would also be highly suitable for students in the advanced physical education courses in high schools, as well as practising physical educators and coaches.

For a sport skill of your choice:

1   Identify the biomechanics principles that apply to the skill.
2   Based on those biomechanical principles identify the 'critical features' of technique applying to the skill that should be observed and assessed.
3   Design a protocol to collect video data for subsequent analysis and feedback to athletes/players. Consider camera positions, lighting and background, subject attire, marking of subjects, etc. Make arrangements for data collection.
4   Collect video data and record details including subject name, date, critical features, camera details and pertinent information about the task. Allow space to comment on each trial in terms of the critical features and the degree of success of the attempt.
5   Qualitatively analyse the skill. There are several types of analysis from which you could choose for your assignment. Some examples are:

   a   Analysis of a novice or someone who has technique flaws that can be corrected. Their performance can be compared to that of elite performers or a model of sound technique. For this research design you only need to videotape a novice subject. If you wished an elite subject could also be videotaped from television, etc., to use as a comparison.
   b   Analysis of an elite performer. In this case the features of technique that distinguish this person's performance from that of a less elite player can be identified. For this research design you would only videotape the elite performer.
   c   Comparison of two performers of differing skill level. If using this design you would need to videotape two or more subjects of differing ability.
   d   Comparison of two or more techniques of performing a skill. For this design one or more subjects should be videotaped performing the skill with different techniques. A variation of this design is to have a subject perform the same skill a number of times and compare the successful performances with the unsuccessful ones.

6   Produce a written report that is readily understood by coaches and the athletes/players. This should include:

   a   An explanation of each critical feature. Establish the importance of each critical feature in terms of the relevant biomechanical principles.
   b   A description of the methods used to collect data. This should include:

      i   A description of the subjects (and comparison models), including their ages, background and experience in the skill.
      ii A description of data collection including camera positions, lighting, marking of subjects, shutter speeds, etc. A still picture of the set up

would be advantageous. The data collection methods should be justified in terms of the critical features that required observation.

c   Identify strengths and weaknesses of the performance.
d   Prioritise the areas where improvement can be made.
e   Outline the means by which improvements can be made. In doing so, identify and describe useful practice drills and activities.

The assignment generally follows a course in which basic biomechanical principles are taught with implications for sports performance identified, discussed, and exemplified across a wide range of sports skills. Students find the list of principles shown in the box adapted from Sanders and Wilson (1991, 1992a, 1992b) useful for analysis of land-based skills. However, students are encouraged to use other principles from other sources as appropriate.

The same exercise could be accomplished without recourse to the use of video cameras. However, using video cameras is highly desirable because it allows

---

Some biomechanical principles

The change in motion is dependent on the magnitude of the force and the time the force acts. Therefore, to maximise motion apply forces for as long as possible.

To reduce the magnitude of impact forces to avoid injury increase the time over which the motion is changed.

For accuracy, apply forces in the desired direction.

To optimise the change in motion position the body so that the necessary reaction forces can be generated.

When a large change in motion is required generate large reaction forces by using the large muscles of the body.

Control stability by changing the size of the base of support, moving the centre of mass with respect to the edge of the base of support, and changing the height of the centre of mass.

When projecting the body or an object use an appropriate angle of release, speed of release, and height of release to achieve the desired result.

In activities in which the human body is projected performance may be improved by redistributing the mass with respect to the centre of gravity.

To produce rotation, apply a force away from the axis of rotation.

Control the rate of rotation by redistributing mass with respect to the axis.

When using rotations to produce linear velocity use a radius and rate of rotation appropriate to the activity.

Skilled motion involves sequencing of segmental rotations. Therefore, coordinate the timing of contributions of body parts to optimise the result.

the observer to observe the skill many times, looking systematically at many aspects of performance in normal, slow and frame by frame, observing how the phases of the skill are linked and the interactions of the factors affecting performance. The use of video cameras is not only a great boon to the analysis of the particular performance and to learning about how the skill is performed, but the exercise emphasises the value of using video cameras on a routine basis in the coaching process. Further information on the use of video cameras in analysing skills and 'tips' for successful recording are presented by Sanders (1996).

Rapid advances in digital video, computer memory and speed have led to the development of affordable software packages that allow capture and display of multiple images. These systems are ideal for comparison of performances, for example, between an elite model and a person you are coaching, or between performances of the same person. A good example is the 'Quintic' system. In addition to being able to play multiple images in synchrony at normal, slow or frame by frame, one is able to highlight critical features using drawing tools and to measure simple variables such as joint angles and positions of body segments, speeds and accelerations of body parts and projected objects and the timing of segmental contributions. Thus, practitioners can easily conduct quantitative analysis to obtain data on which objective comparisons of performance can be based. For example, a high jump coach could show the differences in postures at take-off in successful and unsuccessful jumps and in the timing of the arm and leg actions prior to take-off. Students of physical education, teachers and coaches now have tremendous aids that can stimulate and foster critical thinking to improve effectiveness of analysing and improving performance. Further, they are readily available and affordable! Figure 12.1 shows how drawing tools can be used in these systems to assist in the processes of analysis and instruction.

Thinking laterally

In the first paragraph of 'Thinking deeply' I stated that there were two main concerns with respect to using descriptions of elite performances as benchmarks that can serve as comparisons for the individuals we coach. The first concern was that the model image by itself provides no direct and overt information about how the movement was produced. It is purely a description of the result of the performer's efforts. In the discussion that followed it was shown that rather than being preoccupied with the observable features of the skill we should identify 'critical features' of performance based on a scientific rationale. A 'principles-based' approach to that task was described.

The second concern is that models of elite performance may be appropriate only for elite performers. Thus, we need to think laterally as well as deeply in applying principles to optimise performance. In particular, we need to recognise that the relative importance of principles may change with learning, ability and individual characteristics. Concomitantly, the critical features of the skill may change or have different priority. Further, just as different routes may be taken to

Figure 12.1 An example of the ways in which digital video and computer graphics can be used to aid the analysis and instructional process (figure supplied by Quintic Consultancy Limited www.quintic.com/sportscoach-sci)

reach the peak of a mountain, a desired peak in performance may be achieved in different ways. In fact, we may reach a peak on an entirely different mountain!

Unfortunately, we have limited background knowledge with respect to sub-elite performance. Texts and many sports science journals commonly describe the characteristics of elite performance with scant attention to the process of skill development towards those levels of performance. Thus, the onus is on practitioners, such as physical education students, teachers and coaches to think laterally when analysing and correcting performance of skills. For example, we observe that elite golfers have large ranges of motion of many segments to generate great club-head speed and distance in their shots. This involves rotation of body parts about various axes. We may observe great rotation of the trunk. Accordingly, we could advise a high handicap golfer to 'throw the body' into the task with large increases in the range of motion of segments that are not yet contributing as much as they could. But is this what the golfer needs if he/she is still having difficulty controlling the accuracy of the shot? It may be better to encourage them to have less trunk rotation and to apply principles with a view to increasing accuracy and consistency rather than distance. Elite golfers are so practised and so skilled that they can control the direction of their shots despite the complex sequence and large range of rotations. For high handicap players the priority is to increase accuracy so that they can stay on the fairway rather than spending their time in frustrating hunts for lost balls. Clearly, we need to apply principles in a manner and with a priority that is appropriate to the level of the performer.

Just as sports science has been somewhat slow with respect to providing knowledge that takes into account different performance levels and the process of moving towards elite performance, it has also been slow also in taking into account individual differences. We tend to assume that what constitutes an appropriate movement pattern for one elite individual will be successful for others. The work by Veronique Colman and Ulrik Persyn over more than a decade is pioneering and exemplary with respect to considering individual differences in analysing and advising breaststroke swimmers (Colman and Persyn 1993, 2003; Colman et al. 1998). Their research has indicated that the style of breaststroke that should be adopted to optimise performance depends on individual characteristics of the swimmer such as strength, flexibility and anthropometric characteristics. Their analyses of breaststroke swimmers, and the subsequent advice, are strongly influenced by the data they collect on the individual characteristics of the swimmer. Despite the obvious wisdom of such an approach, sports scientists have been slow to use similar approaches routinely, although the concept is being applied increasingly in the area of talent identification.

We are all aware that different sports people perform the same skill in different ways and yet with equivalent success. The swings of elite golfers look different. This does not necessarily mean that they are applying different principles but may be finding different ways to apply them or may be applying them to different extents. When Janet Evans 'burst on to the scene' and became unbeatable in 800 m freestyle, biomechanists and coaches needed to reassess what constitutes good technique. Her arm recovery with an extended elbow was not 'textbook' and seemed contrary to the idea that a bent elbow allows a faster and more energy efficient recovery by reducing the moment of inertia of the limbs with respect to the shoulder axis. However, while it may not yet be known for sure, it may be that Janet found the 'peak of the mountain' by preferentially applying the principle of 'continuity of movement'. By recovering the arm with the elbow extended she may have saved physiological energy by 'rounding out the motion' so that the existing motion was transferred smoothly from one phase to the next, like saving petrol when driving by avoiding rapid accelerations and braking.

Thus, to improve skills we need to think laterally to avoid unnecessary constraints and to search for peak performance by applying principles in creative ways that suit our own characteristics or the characteristics of those whom we analyse and assist. We should attempt to change the technique only when violation of principles is clearly limiting or adversely affecting performance.

Another way of thinking laterally is to analyse performance with a view to identifying 'what is right' and 'what works', rather than merely 'what is wrong' and 'what doesn't work'. For example, many of us can play great shots in golf. The problem is we don't play them often enough! Part of the problem of not playing them often enough is that we don't know what it is that we do when we do it well. Therefore, analysing good performance can be as important as analysing poor performance. Further, rather than comparing against a perceived model of correctness such as an elite player, it may be more advantageous to compare one's performances against one's good performances. What is it that differs when the shot is poor? That is, what goes wrong? What is it that leads to inconsistency in the outcome? Keeping a video record of good performances is very important. Even when playing well, there may be a time in the future when form is lost. What has changed? If one has anticipated a loss of form and kept a video library then the recent performances can be compared to the good ones in the past. Whatever fault has 'crept in' can be identified. Strategies can then be implemented to correct or improve the performance. A video comparison system, such as the Quintic system, is perfect for this purpose.

Sources of knowledge for critical inquiry

Curiosity and the desire to think deeply and laterally are important prerequisites to analysis of motor skills and to effective learning. However, we also need sources of factual information. An important caveat in seeking sources of information is that there is much more not known than known. Further, much information presented as scientific fact is, in fact, fallacy. Thus, inquiry requires independence of thought and creative problem-solving rather than blind acceptance of the written or spoken word.

It is easy to become 'blinkered' by accepting too readily ideas that seem logical but have not yet been adequately tested or proven. A good example is the idea that good swimmers 'scull' and generate propulsive forces by lift rather than drag. This concept was accepted by swimming scientists and coaches for a prolonged period since the early 1960s, but is now being seriously questioned (see, for example, Sanders 1998 for a discussion of the issue). Another example is the assumption that the golf swing is, or should be, planar. That is, that the arms and/or hands and/or clubface move in a plane in the desired direction of the shot throughout the downswing. A clever study by Coleman and Rankin (2003) has shown recently that the swings of golfers across a range of handicaps do not conform to this idea and, importantly, elite golfers have very nonplanar downswings regardless of whether the plane is defined with respect to a set of body points involving the upper body and hands or whether the plane refers to the path of the hands or clubface.

Thus, inquiry incorporates an ability and willingness to challenge rather than accept 'conventional wisdom'. It is important to recognise that this process can be driven by practitioners rather than by sport science researchers. A good example is the application of new ideas in teaching swimming by Eduardo Ferre, a Brazilian physical education teacher and founder of an innovative learn to swim company, Swimming Nature Limited. His experience indicated that some children benefit from teaching elements of backstroke before freestyle. His methods encouraged me to think critically from a scientific perspective about why teaching backstroke before freestyle might be beneficial (Sanders 2000). In fact, it leads one to contemplate why we tend to become so entrenched in following conventional protocols and teaching progressions without challenge.

Thus, we can see that research by sports biomechanists can provide information to stimulate problem-solving among teachers, students and coaches and that, equally, practitioners can stimulate critical inquiry by sports biomechanists to generate knowledge that is useful. Notwithstanding the fact that involvement of practitioners is inadequate, much useful research is being conducted and new knowledge is being generated at a considerable rate. However, mechanisms of delivering this information have been inadequate. Further, the process of useful information 'filtering' down to sports participants, physical education students, teachers and coaches has been tortuous and slow.

While traditional sources of knowledge conveyance such as textbooks are useful, the latest findings can now be disseminated to practitioners very quickly and effectively using modern technologies such as the world wide web. A good example is the Coach Information Service (www.sportscoach-sci.com). This site features articles that elucidate in lay terms the implications and applications of research and encourages interaction among scientists and practitioners.

Conclusion

In this chapter, inquiry in the process of analysing and improving the performance of skills in physical education was discussed. It was proposed that physical educators and physical education students should engage interactively in analysing performance of skills and that both 'thinking deeply' and 'thinking laterally' are important. In doing so one should apply principles of biomechanics to identify 'critical features' to be observed. In assessing skills and planning strategies for improvement, one must consider individual differences among performers as well as ability levels. Modern technologies such as video cameras and video analysis systems can be a great aid to critical inquiry in analysing and improving performance. Sources of information provide a basis for sound skill assessment, as well as being stimuli for critical inquiry. Information should promote further critical thinking and exploration, rather than being regarded as irrefutable fact. Information based on recent research is available on the world wide web. Some of these sites also provide opportunities for interaction between sports scientists, physical educators, coaches and other sports practitioners.

References

Bartlett, R. (1999) *Sports Biomechanics: Reducing Injury and Improving Performance*, London: E and FN Spon.

Bober, T. (1981) 'Biomechanical aspects of sports techniques', in A. Morecki, A. Fidelus, K. Kedzior and A. Wit (eds) *Biomechanics VII-A*, Baltimore: University Park Press (pp. 501–10).

Bunn, J.W. (1955) *Scientific Principles of Coaching*, Englewood Cliffs, NJ: Prentice-Hall.

Bunn, J.W. (1972) *Scientific Principles of Coaching* (2nd edn), Englewood Cliffs, NJ: Prentice-Hall.

Colman, V. and Persyn, U. (1993) 'Trunk rotation, body waving and propulsion in breaststroke', *Journal of Human Movement Studies* 24: 169–89.

Colman, V., Persyn, U., Daly, D. and Stijnen, V. (1998) 'A comparison of the intra-cyclic velocity variation in breaststroke swimmers with flat and undulating styles', *Journal of Sports Sciences* 16: 653–65.

Colman, V. and Persyn, U. (2003) 'Kinesiology in the symmetrical swimming strokes: a methodological multimedia package for a bachelor and master degree', *Coaches Information Service-Swimming*: http://www.sportscoach-sci.com

Coleman, S. and Rankin, A. (2003) 'A three-dimensional examination of the planar nature of the golf swing', *Journal of Sport Science* (accepted).

Cooper, J.M. and Glassow, R.B. (1976) *Kinesiology* (4th edn), St Louis: Mosby.

Hay, J.G. and Reid, J.G. (1982) *Anatomy, Mechanics and Human Locomotion*, Englewood Cliffs, NJ: Prentice-Hall.

Hay, J.G. and Reid, J.G. (1988) *Anatomy, Mechanics and Human Locomotion* (2nd edn), Englewood Cliffs, NJ: Prentice-Hall.

Hockmuth G. (1984) *Biomechanics of Athletic Movement*, Berlin: Sportverlag.

Hudson, J.L. (1995) 'Core concepts in kinesiology', *Journal of Physical Education, Recreation and Dance* 66(5): 54–5, 59–60.

Kreighbaum, E. and Barthels, K.M. (1981) *Biomechanics: A Qualitative Approach for Studying Human Movement*, Minneapolis: Burgess.

Lees, A. (2002) 'Technique analysis in sports: a critical review', *Journal of Sports Sciences* 20: 813–28.

McPherson, M. (1990) 'A systematic approach to skill analysis', *Sports Science Periodical on Research Technology in Sport* 11(1): 1–10.

Norman, R.W. (1975) 'Biomechanics for the community coach', *Journal of Physical Education, Recreation and Dance* 46(3): 49–52.

Northrip, J.W., Logan, G.A. and McKinney, W.C. (1974) *Introduction to Biomechanical Analysis of Sport*, Dubuque, IA: W.C. Brown.

Sanders, R.H. and Wilson, B.D. (1991) 'Some biomechanical tips for better teaching and coaching, Part 1', *New Zealand Journal of Health, Physical Education, and Recreation* 23(4): 14–15.

Sanders, R.H. and Wilson, B.D. (1992a) 'Some biomechanical tips for better teaching and coaching, Part 2', *New Zealand Journal of Health, Physical Education, and Recreation* 24(1): 16–17.

Sanders, R.H. and Wilson, B.D. (1992b) 'Some biomechanical tips for better teaching and coaching, Part 3', *New Zealand Journal of Health, Physical Education, and Recreation* 24(2): 19–21.

Sanders, R.H. (1996) 'Sport biomechanics', in K.P. Hodge, A. McKenzie and G. Sleivert (eds) *Smart Training for Peak Performance: A Complete Sports Training Guide for Athletes*, Auckland: Reed Publishing (pp. 102–15).

Sanders, R.H. (2000) 'Which stroke should be taught first?' *Coaches Information Service-Golf*: http://www.sportscoach-sci.com.

Sanders, R.H. (1998) 'Lift or drag? Let's get skeptical about freestyle propulsion', *Sportscience Electronic Journal*. http//:sportsci.org. May–June, 1998.

Chapter 13

Desperately seeking certainty
Statistics, physical activity and critical inquiry

Michael Gard

Statistics are everywhere. We read them in advertisements for cosmetics ('get 40 per cent softer skin with brand X!'), breakfast cereals ('nine out of ten nutritionists recommend . . . ') and motor cars ('28 per cent more leg room than its nearest competitor'). Politicians quote them ad nauseam, while keeping a close idea on the mountains of data provided by polling companies that purport to reveal the thoughts of the 'average person'. The media's coverage of sport is awash with numbers and graphs of every imaginable kind. And 'experts' and 'commentators' throw them about (and, often, at each other) in order to 'prove' that their version of the 'truth' is the truest. Statistics are also a serious business. Government policies are (we hope at least sometimes) formulated according to the 'weight of evidence' and, as is often the case in many spheres of life, numbers seem to be considered the 'heaviest' of all forms of evidence. We might even say that numbers speak louder than words.

Statistics are both trivial and profound: while they are often produced, quoted and repeated just to fill in space, at other times they can tell us extremely significant things about the societies in which we live. Statistics are both certain and uncertain: they can create the impression of being precise and 'on top' of one's subject matter, while at the same time raising other questions for which we have no answer. Statistics can be both true and untrue: although on the surface a statistic might be a statement of a very particular numerical fact, it might actually conceal or obscure other 'facts' which tell a very different or even opposite story. And statistics can be both deadly boring and endlessly fascinating: I have endured a number of torturous introductory courses in statistics and swore never to utter the words '*t*-test' ever again, only to find later in my career that the intellectual tools I gained from these courses have helped me to analyse issues from a variety of different perspectives and to remind me that I never 'know it all'.

Amidst all this, one point remains central: in western societies numbers and statistics are often associated with science and, by extension, the explanatory power and credibility that people often associate with science. Simply by attaching a statistic to a truth claim seems to increase the likelihood that the truth claim will be believed. This is not always a bad thing. But sometimes statistics cause us to stop thinking and, in particular, thinking critically. It is as if we sometimes look at a graph or a statistic and see the end rather than the beginning of a story. This is not surprising since this is in part what statistics are designed to do, that is, to distil a lot of information down to a more easily digestible form and to provide answers. But what is lost in this distillation? What and who is hidden or excluded? And what are the dangers of not asking these questions?

By focusing on epidemiological data about people and physical activity, I want to suggest in this chapter that there is much to be gained from the study of statistics, both in terms of the development of students' critical thinking skills and in fostering what we might call a 'critical consciousness' about the societies in which students live, particularly the ways in which structural inequalities affect the health and physical activity of different social groups. In other words, I am making the argument that the development of a critical attitude towards statistics and information more generally should be a central goal of physical education. However, I want also to suggest that a 'critical attitude' is not simply the motivation and capacity to tell the difference between trustworthy and untrustworthy knowledge claims, but also entails an appreciation of the political nature of knowledge itself.

Epidemiology and people

Epidemiology is the branch of social science that attempts to quantify the 'incidence and distribution of diseases and illness in human populations' (Abercrombie *et al.* 1994: 146). The production of statistics about people and their behaviour is central to the practice of epidemiology and these statistics play a crucial part in shaping health policy. A clear example of where this kind of research has been extremely useful is in the development of public health strategies designed to contain the spread of HIV/AIDS in Australia.

In the last thirty years or so a great deal of research interest has been devoted to the relationship between physical activity, body weight, medical health and, in particular, cardiovascular disease, and it is for this reason that the study of levels of physical activity has become a legitimate object of medical research. But despite the efforts of literally hundreds of researchers, epidemiological research into people's participation in physical activity and the knowledge it has produced have remained controversial, as has the exact role physical activity plays in the prevention of cardiovascular disease and other illnesses. This is an important point to keep in mind because in this area of knowledge at least, no amount of numbers and statistics have been able to secure certainty. In fact, a respectable argument could be made to the effect that the generation of more and more statistics has produced far more questions than answers.

By way of illustration, this chapter focuses on *Physical Activity Patterns of Australian Adults: Results of the 1999 National Physical Activity Survey* (Armstrong *et al.* 2000), a report produced by the Australian Institute of Health and Welfare (AIHW). I have chosen this document for two reasons. First, this large report presents statistics on a wide range of aspects of physical activity and could make a useful object for study in schools. Second, one of the analytical strategies I will employ and advocate in this chapter is one in which different statistics are juxtaposed, a strategy the legitimacy of which relies on being able to compare 'apples with apples'. All of the statistics quoted in this chapter are derived from the same data set and therefore invite comparison.

The Armstrong *et al.* report contributes to the growing literature that claims that western populations are becoming more overweight and less physically active. For example, the report says that '(t)he average number of times each week people participated in walking, moderate and vigorous leisure-time physical activity declined between 1997 and 1999' (Armstrong *et al.* 2000: xiii) and suggests that levels of overweight and obesity in Australia may have risen slightly over the same short period. Indeed, there is much in the report that appears to conform to the general picture of Australian society, constantly repeated in the mass media, as increasingly lazy and gluttonous. While this is a view of Australia which has been accepted and endorsed by scientists, doctors and politicians alike, whether or not it is a helpful or accurate view is at least debatable.

To begin with, what are we to make of the report's claim that '88 per cent of people believe that their health could be improved by being generally more active' and that '92 per cent of people believe that health could be improved by participation in 30 minutes of moderate-intensity physical activity each day' (Armstrong *et al.* 2000: xiii)? This is an interesting statistic because a great deal of money has been spent on public education initiatives designed to inform people about the benefits of physical activity in the hope that they would result in people leading more active lives. On the one hand, then, these campaigns would seem to have been extremely successful since a vast majority of people appear to believe that there is a connection between physical activity and medical health. On the other hand, however, it raises doubts about the value of these campaigns if high levels of public awareness are not leading to high levels of physical activity. At this point some interesting questions present themselves. These are questions which students could be asked to consider: if knowledge about participation in physical activity does not necessarily lead to participation, what are the reasons for the apparent steady decline in physical activity levels? Is it, as we are often told, because we are a generally lazy bunch, or is the answer more complicated?

A great deal of the concern about population levels of physical activity has been directed at girls and women. It is now something of a cliché that girls lose interest in sport and vigorous physical activity as they enter and move through adolescence, a situation physical educators have sought to remedy in a number of ways, such as by introducing different forms of physical activity into the curriculum (for example, aerobics and 'power-walking') and by reverting to single-sex physical education lessons. With this in mind, consider Table 13.1 (Table 6.1 in the report).

The general picture emerging from these figures, which relate to adults rather than children, is that women are more likely to participate in lower intensity forms of physical activity (such as walking) than men, while also participating

Table 13.1 Sessions of physical activity in the previous week by sex (per cent), 1999

Physical activity	Men	Women	Persons
Walking			
Nil	31.5	24.1	27.8
1–2	17.7	19.3	18.5
3–4	16.6	20.5	18.6
5 or more	34.2	36.0	35.1
Total	100.0	100.0	100.0
Moderate-intensity[a]			
Nil	67.2	75.6	71.4
1–2	22.0	14.9	18.4
3–4	6.1	5.2	5.7
5 or more	4.7	4.3	4.5
Total	100.0	100.0	100.0
Vigorous-intensity[b]			
Nil	59.1	65.4	62.3
1–2	19.1	19.0	19.1
3–4	10.6	9.2	9.9
5 or more	11.1	6.4	8.7
Total	100.0	100.0	100.0
Vigorous-intensity gardening/yardwork			
Nil	54.0	60.5	57.3
1–2	32.8	30.0	31.4
3–4	7.3	5.4	6.3
5 or more	5.9	4.1	5.0
Total	100.0	100.0	100.0

Source: Armstrong et al. 2000.

Notes
Components may not add to totals due to rounding.
a Examples of moderate-intensity activities are gentle swimming, social tennis.
b Examples of vigorous-intensity activities are jogging, cycling, aerobics, competitive tennis.

in moderate and vigorous-intensity exercise less often than men. Do these figures confirm or dispute the idea that there is a problem with the amount of physical activity that females do? In other words, how should we interpret these statistics?

As the authors concede, '(t)he majority of the data in this report refer to leisure-time physical activity, which refers to an individual's discretionary time that is time left after completion of work, travelling, domestic chores and personal hygiene' (Armstrong et al. 2000: 12). As has often been the case in this kind of research, physical work done in the home is not considered worthy of inclusion in these statistics. But why should this be, particularly given that this kind of work has been, and remains, disproportionately 'women's work' in western societies? It is certainly true that people whose work in the home leaves them with insufficient time and/or energy for any 'discretionary' leisure-time physical activity would be considered 'sedentary' by this report.

At least two possible explanations for this apparent anomaly present themselves. First, as a society we have tended to undervalue housework. In the 1970s, feminists argued that 'housewives' should be paid by their wage-earning spouse for doing housework, a suggestion that was greeted with horror by many people. Second, there is a tendency for the term 'physical activity' to be equated with terms like 'sport' and 'exercise'. So although our bodies respond in roughly the same ways to different forms of physical stress, regardless of whether we are playing a game of tennis or vacuuming the house, it seems that not all forms of physical activity are treated equally. For example, people who do regular vigorous exercise (such as aerobics or jogging) or play competitive sport are often described as leading 'healthy lifestyles', and it is no coincidence that health campaigns designed to encourage people to be more active usually focus on these forms of activity. By contrast, it is extremely difficult to imagine anyone advocating housework as a means to improve medical health, even though it may be just as strenuous as many forms of recreational physical activity.

The point of this is not to advocate that people do more housework, but to begin to ask questions about the epidemiological data that we are given. The above table purports to tell us something about how physically active Australians are. But does it? Is it possible that this table says more about the ways in which we have to come to define a term like 'physical activity', and particularly the way people tend to equate it with sport and vigorous exercise, activities which continue to attract more men than women. A similar set of questions could easily be asked about the physical work that some people do at work – how is it possible that a report entitled *Physical Activity Patterns of Australian Adults* makes no attempt to measure work-related physical activity?

An even more striking example of the way narrow definitions of 'physical activity' can produce highly debatable research results can be found in Wright's (1997) critique of fundamental motor skill testing in New South Wales schools. As she points out, the government-sponsored 'bench-marking' survey of the mid-1990s was designed to produce a snapshot of the motor skill levels of New South Wales' schoolchildren. The report of the survey, released with a good deal of media attention, claimed that the general motor skill proficiency of school children was 'poor' and that girls performed even more poorly than boys. The report advocated programmes to address this situation, particularly the 'problem' with girls. But Wright reminds us that the battery of tests chosen for the survey was strongly biased towards sports such as soccer, rugby and cricket. While punting a ball was considered a sufficiently 'fundamental' skill to be included in the battery, tests to directly measure balance and the ability to move in time with a beat were not. Why, for example, might basic gymnastics and dance skills such as skipping or doing a handstand or a chassé not be included in a battery of 'fundamental' tests? In short, who decides what is 'fundamental'? While wanting to avoid the murky territory of conspiracy theories, I think the most likely explanation of this apparent bias towards traditionally male sports is to be found in the background of the researchers themselves. It has long been recognised that a background in competitive sports is the common denominator amongst many physical education and sports science teachers and researchers and it is probably not surprising that they tend to see activities that they enjoy doing as fundamental.

While this issue may seem relatively trivial, at its centre are significant questions about the information we receive on a daily basis as members of a globally connected and supposedly information-rich culture. In other words, an important part of making sense of information is the capacity to interrogate the motives and biases of the people generating the information in question. How might their motives and biases in intended or unintended ways shape their versions of 'the facts'? On the one hand, the issue of unintended bias has been one that has dogged the search for knowledge in all areas of scientific endeavour and is perhaps the single most important reason why so much research turns out to be of no long-term value. On the other hand, we live in an age of 'spin' in which the information and statistics we receive from governments, corporations and news outlets have been either massaged or deliberately invented for public consumption. Whenever students are presented with statistics that purport to prove something, we might profitably ask them to look into the circumstances and motivation of their production.

Another way in which we might interrogate epidemiological statistics is to place two different sets of statistics side by side. With the above statistics about physical activity in mind, let us look Table 13.2 (Table 5.4 in the report) which presents data on the body mass index (BMI) of respondents to the survey.

What are we to make of these figures which suggest that approximately 51 per cent of Australian men are overweight or obese compared with approximately 37 per cent of women, particularly in the light of the previous figures we saw which suggested females do less vigorous physical activity than men and 'exercise' less often than men? Before making a comment about this, it is important to remember that this BMI table refers to self-reported figures. In wanting to survey as many people as possible the researchers had to rely on respondents correctly reporting their own height and weight, the two measurements required to calculate a person's BMI. This raises the tricky question of whether either men or women are more likely to overestimate or underestimate their weight or height; in short, can these figures be trusted. In fact, this is a problem for all epidemiological and survey-based research, not just the current example. Therefore, before making judgements about the numbers presented, we (including students) could ask what reasons people might have for providing deliberately or inadvertently misleading answers. Although important, in the current example this is not a simple question to answer, although it is worth pointing out that these figures fairly closely match the results of 'first-hand' research into the levels of overweight and obesity in Australia and other western countries (Australian Bureau of Statistics 1995; Flegal 1999).

Table 13.2 BMI categories of survey respondents by age, sex, education level (per cent), 1999

	Underweight	Healthy weight	Overweight	Obese
Sex				
Men	1.7	46.9	39.5	11.9
Women	4.2	59.0	24.0	12.7
Persons	3.0	52.9	31.8	12.3
Age group (years)				
18–29	7.5	65.9	19.8	6.8
30–44	1.9	53.1	32.9	12.2
45–59	0.8	46.0	36.9	16.3
60–75	1.5	42.8	40.5	15.2
Education level				
Less than 12 years	2.5	46.9	35.5	15.2
HSC or equivalent	3.7	55.6	28.1	12.7
Tertiary	2.9	57.7	31.8	7.7

Source: Armstrong *et al.* 2000.

Notes
HSC, Higher School Certificate.

It is also worth remembering that while it is generally believed that women, on average, carry more body fat than men, no allowance is made for this in the calculation of BMI in this or most other studies. In other words, men and women are deemed overweight (BMI equal to or greater than 25.0 and less than 30.0) and obese (BMI greater than 30.0) using the same standards. Certainly if different (that is, higher) cut-off points were used to classify women as either overweight or obese then the difference between men and women would be even larger!

Questions of reliability aside, this table should force us to stop and think about the relationship between body weight and physical activity. Why is it that women as a group seem to be doing less physical 'exercise' than men while remaining considerably less prone to overweight and obesity? Of course, a number of potential answers to this question are possible. I would argue, however, that simply by posing this question, students are forced to ask other questions and to seek out other pieces of information. For example, do women eat less or differently to men? If so, why? Asking these questions may, in turn, open up other debates about the disproportionate cultural pressure on western women to be thin despite the fact that they already appear to be much thinner than men. Certainly there exists a large body of research which suggests that western women and girls are much more likely to be worried about their weight and/or to be dieting than men and boys (for example, see Chrisler 1996; O'Dea and Abraham 1999).

But there are more fundamental questions to be asked here. Given the apparently large gap between the levels of male and female obesity, is it defensible that most media and scientific comment on the issue seems to suggest that we are in the middle of a generalised obesity epidemic, one that is affecting everyone everywhere? In other words, if overweight and obesity are seen as a general problem, rather than one that affects some sections of the population more than others, is it possible that we might misdiagnose the problem and end up proposing solutions to problems which do not exist? The scientific and physical education literature is full of suggestions for making girls more active. Is the attention paid to girls and physical activity justified?

Perhaps an even more important dimension to discussions about physical activity, body weight and health is one that is often obscured amongst the general hysteria about the 'obesity epidemic', that of social class. What is apparent from the previous table is that people with less than 12 years of education were approximately twice as likely to be obese than people with a tertiary qualification? This difference becomes all the more significant when you consider that while the health risks of being merely overweight remain controversial, obesity and morbid (or extreme) obesity appear to be unequivocally bad for your health.

The over-representation of people from lower socio-economic bands within the ranks of the overweight and obese has been a consistent research finding both in Australia and other western countries (Paxton *et al*. 1994; Centre for Weight and Health 2001; Vescio *et al*. 2001; Wardle *et al*. 2002). In Table 13.3 (Table 6.7 in the report), the percentage of Australians achieving 'sufficient', 'insufficient' or no exercise each is estimated.

Table 13.3 Percentage of people achieving 'sufficient' time and sessions during the previous week by sex, age group and education level, 1999

	Sedentary	Insufficient	'Sufficient'[a]
Sex			
Men	14.6	38.3	47.1
Women	14.7	41.9	43.4
Persons	14.6	40.2	45.2
Age group (years)			
18–29	6.3	37.5	56.3
30–44	16.9	41.9	41.2
45–59	18.2	41.6	40.2
60–75	17.9	38.5	43.6
Education			
Less than 12 years	19.5	41.9	38.6
HSC or equivalent	12.5	40.5	47.0
Tertiary	10.9	36.8	52.3

Source: Armstrong *et al*. 2000.

Notes
HSC, Higher School Certificate.
a 'Sufficient' time and sessions is defined as 150 min (using the sum of walking, moderate activity and vigorous activity (weighted by two)) and five sessions of activity per week.

It is interesting to note that in this table the difference between males and females that we saw in the first table has virtually disappeared. Having combined all the different kinds of (discretionary) 'exercise' that people do, both high and low intensity, this table seems to conclude that women are almost as likely as men to get 'sufficient' physical activity for good health each week. This is a straightforward example of a 'problem', in this case the amount of physical activity females do, appearing or disappearing depending on the manner in which the statistics are grouped and presented. However, it is interesting to note that the summary of the report claims somewhat mysteriously that '(w)omen were 20 per cent less likely to achieve 'sufficient' physical activity compared with men' (Armstrong *et al.* 2000: xiv).

In this table the differences in people deemed to be doing 'sufficient' physical activity appear to be more pronounced with respect to age and level of education, generally accepted as an indicator of financial affluence. Once again, we might challenge students to interpret these figures. According to the table, the percentage of people with less than 12 years of education who are sedentary (19.5 per cent) is higher than the percentage of 60–75 year olds who are sedentary (17.9 per cent). This is also the case if we look at the percentage of people who do 'insufficient' physical activity (41.9 versus 38.5 per cent, respectively). I am also struck by the approximately 14 per cent difference between people with less than 12 years of education who do 'sufficient' physical activity (38.6 per cent) and those with a tertiary level education (52.3 per cent).

Of course, there is clearly scope for students to ask critical questions about how the authors of the report arrived at their definition of 'sufficient' physical activity. But if we accept this definition, consideration of these disparities across social class has the potential to open up a wide range of topics for further research and critical reflection. To begin, we might ask questions about the structural reasons for this difference. Is the expense of recreational physical activity (such as the fees for sports clubs and dance classes, the cost of sporting equipment, gym member- ships) a barrier to participation for some people? Or could it, as some have suggested, have something to do with the physical environments and conditions in which the poor live, such as high density housing and a lack of open green areas?

Of particular interest are what we might call cultural reasons for this difference, and it is here that we see some similarities to the situation with smoking. Although federal and state governments in Australia have substantially increased the cost of cigarettes over recent decades, smoking remains relatively popular amongst poorer people. And while anti-smoking campaigns have proven effective in getting middle-class people to quit, they appear to have been less successful the lower we go down the socio-economic scale. Are we witnessing a similar phenomenon when it comes to recreational or 'discretionary' physical activity? Has physical activity become a luxury? Has a slim body become a marker of socio-economic affluence, similar to fast cars and expensive clothes?

There certainly exists some anecdotal evidence that particular forms of physical activity, such as sport, play a much bigger part in the lives of middle-class families than it does for working-class people. And there has been a great deal of comment over the last 20 years about the connections between what has been called 'the fitness industry' (aerobics, private and corporate gyms and health clubs) and middle-class society. So, as well as thinking about the kinds of practical reasons why 'discretionary' physical activity might be more available to people with more money, students might also ask what physical activity means to different people. For example, is it possible that one of the ways in which poorer people differentiate themselves from richer people is to reject the middle class apparent preoccupation with body weight and physical fitness?

One way of answering this question would be to analyse the ways in which (conventionally) desirable bodies and 'healthy lifestyles' are constantly linked with affluence, 'stylish' urban living and the consumption of expensive fitness paraphernalia, such as shoes, lycra outfits and leisure wear. On a more straight-forward level, students can also be encouraged to look around at the world they inhabit. Where do they see 'fat' bodies? Where do they never see 'fat' bodies? I recall vividly a conversation I once had with a scientist who was trying to convince me that Australian society in general was becoming grossly overweight and that there was a particular problem with children. I replied that I spent a great deal of time in schools and rarely saw an obese child. Certainly, I argued, I found it impossible to accept her assertion that between 20 and 30 per cent of Australian children were either overweight or obese. The scientist replied, 'If you want to see obese children you just need to go down to your local shopping centre on a pension day, Thursday!' She paused for a moment and then changed the subject.

Desperately seeking certainty

It should be clear by now that the end point of the techniques I have just described may be somewhat disorientating and unsettling. By asking critical questions about the ways in which epidemiological data are compiled, by juxtaposing different sets of findings, and by moving beyond generalisations about 'society as a whole', there exists the obvious risk of a kind of intellectual vertigo where certainty about any knowledge claim becomes illusive. If all these old 'truths' about physical activity (such as claims that we are all getting fatter and lazier or that there is a bigger problem with females than there is with males) are rendered suspect, what is the truth? If not this, then what?

One answer to this concern would be to argue that moments of discomfort are a prerequisite for learning to occur. In this way, the teacher's role can be thought of as moving students from positions of certainty to uncertainty and then, perhaps, facilitating the formulation of answers and conclusions which students arrive at themselves. And as I have suggested above, one of the ways students might do this would be to look around them; look at the people they know, the culture they consume and the meanings people attach to things like body weight, physical activity and health. In my experience, the statistic that women are considerably less likely to be overweight or obese than men never fails to arouse the curiosity and even anger of at least some (particularly female) students, precisely because it contradicts their assumptions about who does and/or who should worry about their weight.

There is more at stake here, however, for both teachers and students. Perhaps my single most lasting memory of my own school teaching career, as well as watching practising and experienced physical/health education teachers in secondary schools, is that of students being asked to copy down lists; lists of the benefits of exercise, lists of the benefits of a 'healthy' or 'balanced' lifestyle, lists of the dangers of unsafe sex, alcohol, tobacco and other drugs, and lists of good food and bad food. There is perhaps no other school subject area that is so certain that it has the answers to what constitutes a 'good' or 'healthy' life than physical education. This certainty is so strong that it seems to lull us into believing that 'the facts' about exercise and health are so self-evident and compelling, that our job is simply to give students 'the facts'. Why spend time debating and researching 'the facts' when we already know what the truth is? And yet, unbeknownst to many, physical education's knowledge base is constantly shifting; for example, the idea that it is possible to be fat (in fact very fat) and fit and healthier than much skinnier people is currently quietly displacing old assumptions about the unavoidable perils of being overweight (for example, see Brodney et al. 2000).

In a similar vein, reports such as the one discussed in this chapter make no attempt to explain why physical activity and obesity appear to be linked to socio-economic class. This is perhaps not surprising since the researchers do not appear to have collected any data that could shed light on this association. The reasons for this relationship between physical activity, obesity and social class and the reasons that it is scarcely ever addressed in popular discussion about overweight and obesity are legitimate and important areas of critical inquiry for both teachers and students. The answers to these questions may not be so straightforward, but they do point towards classrooms where the copying of lists is no longer an option.

References

Abercrombie, N., Hill, S. and Turner, B.S. (1994) *The Penguin Dictionary of Sociology*, London: Penguin.

Armstrong, T., Bauman, A. and Davies, J. (2000) *Physical Activity Patterns of Australian Adults: Results of the 1999 National Physical Activity Survey*, Canberra: Australian Institute of Health and Welfare.

Australian Bureau of Statistics (1995) *National Health Survey*, Canberra: Australian Bureau of Statistics.

Brodney, S., Blair, S.N. and Lee, C.D. (2000) 'Is it possible to be overweight or obese and fit and healthy?', in C. Bouchard (ed.) *Physical Activity and Obesity*, Champaign, IL: Human Kinetics.

Center for Weight and Health (2001) *Pediatric Overweight: A Review of the Literature*, Berkely: University of California.

Chrisler, J.C. (1996) 'Politics and women's weight', *Feminism and Psychology* 6(2): 181–4.

Flegal, K.M. (1999) 'The obesity epidemic in children and adults: current evidence and research issues', *Medicine and Science in Sports and Exercise* 31(11): S509–14.

O'Dea, J.A. and Abraham, S. (1999) 'Onset of disordered eating attitudes and behaviors in early adolescence: interplay of pubertal status, gender, weight, and age', *Adolescence* 34 (winter): 671–9.

Paxton, S.J., Sculthorpe, A. and Gibbons, K. (1994) 'Weight-loss strategies and beliefs in high and low socioeconomic areas of Melbourne', *Australian Journal of Public Health* 18(4): 412–17.

Vescio, M.F., Smith, G.D. and Giampaoli S. (2001) 'Socio-economic position and cardiovascular risk factors in an Italian rural population', *European Journal of Epidemiology* 17(5): 449–59.

Wardle, J., Waller, J. and Jarvis, M.J. (2002) 'Sex differences in the association of socioeconomic status with obesity', *American Journal of Public Health* 92(8): 1299–304.

Wright, J. (1997) 'Fundamental motor skills testing as problematic practice: a feminist analysis', *The ACHPER Healthy Lifestyles Journal* 44(4): 18–20.

Chapter 14

Analysing sportsmedia texts

Developing resistant reading positions

Jan Wright

The American educator Darryl Siedentop includes in his definition of a physically educated person the capacity to be 'involved critically in the sport, fitness and leisure cultures of their nations' (in Tinning 2002: 338). David Kirk uses the term 'physical culture' to refer to the meanings, values and social practices concerned with the maintenance, representation and regulation of the body through institutionalised forms of physical activity such as sport, physical recreation, and exercise (Kirk 1997). He argues that in the process of their engagements with physical culture, young people do not merely 'participate' in physical activities, they are also consumers of the commercialised and commodified products of physical culture, ranging from foodstuffs, music, and sportswear to membership of exercise and sports clubs. These also include the cultural meanings and values associated with sport and physical activity as they are produced in a range of institutional sites, including schools, fitness clubs, sporting clubs, and most notably the mass media. It is through media coverage of sport and related activities and products that particular meanings and values associated with physical culture are produced and most widely disseminated both nationally and globally in contemporary societies. One important way, then, of being involved critically in sport, fitness and leisure cultures is to be able to recognise the ways particular meanings and values (ideologies) associated with sport and physical activity are produced and with what effects for the people who are participants in, and consumers of, these cultures.

Mediasport

As a social institution sport has the capacity to both challenge and reproduce dominant social values. While some aspects of sport and physical activity do challenge stereotypical values, for instance, women playing rugby league, young Asian women playing soccer (as fictionalised in the film *Bend It Like Beckham*) and young men choosing to become ballet dancers, this has often been through considerable struggle by those who would want to push the boundaries and bring about change. In general, however, sport and other forms of institutionalised physical activity (such as dance, aerobics, adventure education) tend to be more conservative institutions where stereotypes are reproduced rather than challenged. This is particularly the case in media coverage of sport, although again the possibilities for challenging dominant social values still remain.

There is now a considerable literature which demonstrates how media coverage of sport in different ways serves to construct mainstream values which often privilege white heterosexual middle-class men and marginalise female athletes, athletes of colour, gay and lesbian athletes, athletes with disabilities and so on (Burroughs *et al.* 1995; Kane 1996; Kinnick 1998; Lenskyj 1998; MacNeill 1998; Markula 2001; Mikosza and Phillips 1999; Pirinen 1997; Wilson 1997; Wright and Clarke 1999). Media research also demonstrates how advertising through its global promotion of sport-related products, such as brand name clothing and footwear, promotes particular versions of western values to young consumers in developed and developing countries worldwide. As McKay (1995) points out what these representations make invisible are the exploitative means by which much of the clothing and footwear has been produced by the poor in developing countries.

Media, fitness and the body

The analysis of media coverage of physical activity has expanded in the last few years from mediasport to also examine the ways in which fitness and leisure cultures are represented in the media and with what effects for those who watch television and film, and/or read newspapers, magazines and books. A quick glance at the 'Body and Soul' section of the *Sydney Morning Herald* (and the equivalent in most large circulation newspapers in English-speaking countries) or the front page of any magazine such as *Men's Health* and *Women's Fitness*, demonstrates the central messages about the body and the value of physical activity in maintaining a particular kind of body. Physical activity in this context is socially valued for its contribution to fitness, where fitness is indicated by a slim, toned body. While the ideal male body can show more visible evidence of muscularity, ideal female and male bodies demonstrate evidence of the considerable work done on the body to rid it of fat and shape it in specifically desirable ways.

Why do media representations matter?

To understand the argument that the ways in which the media represent sport and physical activity (or any aspect of 'reality' for that matter) actually have important implications for individuals and for the nature of our society, we need to go back to some theory about how cultures and individuals come to be as they are. Not surprisingly to do this we look to the work that has been developed in cultural studies and also critical literacy.

A starting point is the assumption that choices in language (or image, frames, camera angles, etc.) are not neutral but are motivated, not necessarily consciously, by particular social values or ways of thinking about the world; that is, meaning making needs to be understood as a social practice. Those who produce media texts (e.g. television coverage of sport, commentary and sports shows, newspaper, magazines articles, billboard advertising and even T-shirt inscriptions) do not only make choices about what sports are covered, but how they will be covered. These choices are made at all levels of the construction of an article or television show. For instance, writers, photographers, editors, directors and film-makers are constantly making choices about what points of view are represented by certain articles, headlines, quotes, photographs, camera angles, interviews, sections of interviews and so will select from all of the material available to them to construct a position, to dramatise an event, to tell a story.

By definition, the choices in the mainstream media are likely to be, by and large, those which support mainstream or dominant values or points of view, that is, what they assess to be the range of values acceptable to their readers. Depending on the newspaper, magazine, or television channel and their anticipated audience, these values can vary. For instance, in Australia, SBS, one of the national government-supported television channels has as its charter to 'deliver . . . multicultural and multilingual services that provide a credible source of international analysis for all Australians, reflect Australia's cultural diversity, and encourage a shared sense of belonging and harmony' (Special Broadcasting Service 2002: 1). SBS sport is thus more likely to carry a wider coverage of international sport and is the only channel in Australia that covers international soccer on a regular basis (this may seem strange to readers of this chapter in the UK, but in Australia, soccer is regarded as an ethnic minority sport). There is now a considerable body of literature which demonstrates how particular choices in language produce texts that help to build local and national identity (Brown 1998) that reinforce social and cultural stereotypes associated with race, ethnicity and gender and that reproduce dominant social ideals about what good citizens of particular societies should be like. This last happens particularly through the ways in which leading athletes are talked about as good role models and heroes; or if they behave in socially inappropriate ways as bad role models and as undeserving of their elite status.

The saying that people believe what they read is even more likely to be the case when it comes to what people see. As Bassett (1990: 2) points out, '[t]elevision creates images; it produces a reality in which particular knowledge, values and beliefs are constructed as natural, in ways that encourage the viewer to receive and uncritically accept the messages and meanings which it communicates'. The media then cannot only represent particular social values, it also serves to confirm and thus maintain them. If social values which are limiting or oppressive to individuals and to particular social groups are to change then consumers of media messages (i.e. readers and viewers) will need to be able to recognise how meanings are constructed and to make visible social values which are taken-for-granted because they are written down or incorporated into visual images. This does not necessarily mean that such values will be rejected, but rather they are available for scrutiny so that we can ask who they effect and in what ways.

How do we go about this?

If the meanings constructed in texts are ideological, how do we go about making these ideologies visible? The tools of textual analysis developed within the areas of critical literacy, critical discourse analysis, media literacy and cultural studies provide the means of critically analysing media texts to help make more visible the work they do in constructing social and cultural values. The following section will provide some examples of ways of working with the media from several of these positions.

As pointed out above, all media texts incorporate particular 'points of view' that are manifested in a variety of choices. In defining 'media literacy', the National Film Board of Canada provides the following questions to be asked about the work of the media in constructing meaning and reality. The first set of questions are those they suggest need to be asked at the point of production, but they are also useful questions to guide an analysis of a media product as well.

- What story will be told?
- From whose perspective will it be represented?
- How will it be filmed (camera placement, movement, framing)?
- How will it be edited?
- What sort of music will be used, if any?
- Whose voice will we hear?
- What will the intended message be?

To determine the point of view being presented they suggest asking:

- Who has created the images?
- Who is doing the speaking?
- Whose viewpoint is not heard?
- From whose perspective does the camera frame the events?
- Who owns the medium?
- What is our role as spectators in identifying with, or questioning what we see and hear?

(National Film Board of Canada, cited in Media Awareness
Network 2003: 1)

These questions can take us beyond the critical analysis of texts themselves to also ask questions about the contexts of their production. Elizabeth Thoman suggests that in exploring the deeper issues of media production we ask questions such as: For what purpose was the media product created? Who profits? Who loses? Who decides? (Thoman, cited in Media Awareness Network 2003).

Critical literacy and critical discourse analysis provide the tools to look closely at the language of written and spoken texts. These analytic tools provide the means to critically interrogate print, written and visual texts for the ways in which they both draw on particular social meanings to create texts and in doing so help to (re)produce and in some cases transform those meanings. As is the case for the media literacy approach described above, these ways of working with texts generally involve a scaffolded process, using a framework of questions, to interrogate the social meanings constructed in the text. Fairclough (1992, 1995) suggests a three-stage process to critical discourse analysis: description, interpretation and explanation. These stages are used below to structure a media analysis task that can be used with secondary or tertiary students.

By working with students in this way it both helps them to become more critical consumers of media texts as these are associated with physical activity and sport and also to more broadly develop the skills needed to resist and challenge the ways in which media texts would position their readers.

Working with students

It is rarely useful to tell or show students how media texts work to construct particular social values, particularly in many cases when these social values are very similar to those which they themselves currently hold. To see the world differently, as in most cases of critical inquiry, the students need to become 'active researchers in their worlds', interrogators of the taken-for-granted; that is, they need to be involved in raising questions, collecting data (description), coming to conclusions on the basis of their analysis of their data (interpretation) and explaining these in relation to other evidence of similar and different social and cultural patterns. In the case of media texts, they need to be helped to collect, explain, interpret and present their own data about media texts. There are many ways to do this and many resources in the field of critical literacy to assist with this task. In the first instance, it is about structuring tasks and asking 'thoughtful' questions to assist in the inquiry. What follows are some examples of tasks that I have developed over the years to work with tertiary students; they are equally applicable to secondary students, and those working in critical literacy use similar activities very successfully with primary students (e.g. Luke *et al.* 1994).

Description

One way of starting is to ask students to collect quantitative data about media coverage of particular sports and/or physical activities. The sources of coverage can vary from the broadest sweep – for instance, calculating television coverage of sports as a percentage of total television time and the coverage of particular sports as a percentage of all sports coverage, by using a television guide. A similar but more focused approach could be to collect the coverage of different kinds of sport in a television show, such as the *Wide World of Sport*. It is often useful to divide the collection of data from different media amongst different groups in the class, or different members of the class can take up different tasks related to the same media coverage. There are many different iterations of how the tasks can be organised, depending on the experience and ability of the class. Data so collected can be represented in tables and/or graphs. The following questions are useful guides to collecting data.

Looking at newspapers/magazines:

(i) What proportion of your newspaper/magazine is devoted to what broad topics – i.e. local news, international news, sport and so on? You might want to compare different newspapers and then focus in on one. Use column centimetres or inches to measure the amount of coverage.

(ii) Looking specifically at the sporting sections of the magazine or newspapers: What proportion of the coverage is given to which sports? What proportion is given to men's sports as compared to women's sports; the sports played by cultural minorities in the community; the sports played by different social class groups? Which sports are absent? Which present? Are there differences in the ways different sports are presented?

Looking at the electronic media:

(i) Calculate how much of television coverage in one week is devoted to sport. As far as you are able to tell from a TV guide, which sports receive the most coverage on which channels? What sports seem to be absent?

(ii) Watch a general sports programme such as the *Wide World of Sport* and note which sports receive coverage and calculate how much time is given to different sports. You might consider how much time is given to women's sports, men's sports, mixed sports as well as other categories of sport.

A further step is to look more closely at how social meanings are constructed in the choices of language and of media images such as photographs and camera angles.

Choose one or two print texts and look at these more closely:

(i) If it has a photograph, what images are portrayed? How does it seem to have been taken? What camera angles have been used? Is it live or staged? How does it relate to the text? Is it an action shot taken during the game? Who else is in the photograph and what are they doing? What does the caption say? To what aspects of the player(s) does it draw our attention?

(ii) How does the headline fit with the text (and/or accompanying photographs)? What metaphors or other language devices are employed to catch your eye? What does it promise?

(iii) In the article(s) itself, who or what are the main protagonists? What words or phrases are used to describe them? What words are used to describe what they do and how they do it? Try to collect all the words and phrases for each of the major participants, e.g. 'The Russian (Kournikova) looked lovely but played like a dog . . . ' (SMH 28 August 2002: 38).

Interpretation

Having collected this information and organised it in ways which make patterns visible, the next step is to make sense of the data in terms of the implications for how we understand sport and the people who are associated with it (including spectators, officials, parents and so on). It is useful to ask:

(i)   What interpretations can you give to the data you have collected? What do the patterns in the data suggest about the place of sports and particular sports in (insert relevant country) society? How are sports, players, athletes, and other major participants in the texts represented? Do male and female athletes warrant the same amount of coverage? Are male and female players? represented in the same or in different ways? Are teams from (insert home country) represented in the same way as teams or team members from other countries and so on? Why might this be the case?

(ii) How is the article written? What is assumed about the reader (in terms of prior knowledge, values, interests, understanding of technical language)? How does this serve to include or exclude certain groups of people?

And for the electronic media:

(iii) For what viewers does it seem intended? How do you know this? Look, for example, at the scheduled time, the advertisements. What viewers are excluded by the language, choice of sport, type of coverage, etc.?

Explanation

For both print and electronic media, broader questions can then be asked. To more fully address the social implications of their data, students may need to read about and discuss issues associated with gender, race, ethnicity, nationalism and sport.

(i)   How do you explain what you have found? What point of view does it (do they) take about the sport, about the participants in the article, their performance, behaviour, relationships, appearance, etc?

(ii) Relate what you have found from your analysis of the text(s) to what you understand as the dominant discourses or sets of values and beliefs associated with social class, race, ethnicity, age, gender, nationalism and sport in your society.

(iii) How are these dominant discourses (re)produced or challenged by these texts?

(iv) What might TV or videos look like which challenge dominant ideological positions? Why has the coverage that you have analysed been produced in this way and not in a different way?

A final possible step is to support students in creating and producing their own media messages. In doing so they should consider what sets of meanings and values they wish to incorporate into their representations of sport and to examine the likely effects on those who would watch their product.

A media analysis in practice: the 2002 US Tennis Open

The following is an example from a task drawing on the questions above and used with a tertiary subject on sociocultural perspectives of sport and physical activity. The idea to examine the 2002 US Tennis Open coverage came from one group of students who took a qualitative approach to compare the nature of the coverage of female players as compared to male players across a tabloid and a broadsheet newspaper for the duration of the event. I have not reproduced their analysis exactly, but for convenience chose instead to focus on one newspaper, the *Sydney Morning Herald*, a broadsheet newspaper widely read across the state of New South Wales in Australia. Initially I intended to use quantitative and qualitative forms of data collection to provide the basis for an analysis of the ways in which the female and male players were represented. However, as often happens in the close analysis of texts, other themes emerged.

Quantitative analysis

To illustrate the quantitative component of the activities described above, I asked a student to collect all of the coverage from the *Sydney Morning Herald* (*SMH*) for the duration of the 2002 Open and to calculate the amount of coverage in column centimetres across the following categories.

 (i)   articles covering female players only;
 (ii) articles covering male players only;
(iii) articles which mentioned both female and male players;
(iv) the size of photographs for male as compared to female players.

The following figures provide an indication of the coverage of the 2002 US Tennis Open in the *SMH* for the period of 28 August to 10 September. In terms of the size of the articles (that is, the amount of space devoted within the articles), 44 per cent of coverage was devoted to male players, 33 per cent to female players and 22 per cent to both. There was only one article difference in the number of articles devoted to male (twelve) players as compared to female players (eleven). In both amount of space and number of articles this compares very favourably with print coverage of women's sport in general which ranges from around 2 to 10 per cent (Phillips 1997).

When the amount of space devoted to photographs of male and female players was calculated, 51 per cent of the total space given to photographs was devoted to photographs of male players and 44 per cent to female players, 5 per cent of the photographs contained images of female and male players. Thirteen of these photographs were of male players, seven of female players and one of both.

Qualitative analysis

As demonstrated above, media coverage of tennis is an interesting choice for analysis, because it terms of quantity of coverage, particularly in the print media, it can often challenge the typical pattern of much smaller amounts of women's coverage compared to that of men. This raises questions about why this is the case. How is tennis different from, and the same as, other sports? Does it challenge the dominant discourses, the ways of thinking about the world, nations, sport, gender, race and so on which have been documented as being produced and reproduced in coverage of other sports? The amount of coverage suggests, for instance, that tennis is quantitatively different in its coverage of men and women from that of most other elite professional sports. Does this carry through to the qualitative aspects of the coverage – to the content of the articles and photographs? What clues can be found in the nature of the coverage?

The headlines in the *Sydney Morning Herald* during the Open provide the first clue. This list of headlines suggests some of themes taken up in the coverage and the rather different focus on the female players as compared to the male players:

Cat woman pounces but beaten prey is still a winner
Capriati swears she's due respect
Injury and insult: dodgy knee scuttles Scud, while Hewitt brands ATP liars
Women win the skin game [Haas asked to change a sleeveless shirt]
Frankly my games to blame, declares stoic Dokic
Hewitt happy to forgive and forget [Hewitt accused of racist comments in previous
    game]
Stalker arrested as police flush out Serena pest
This kid is all fight [referring to Hewitt]
Now the players have made their fashion statements when will charges be laid?
    [photos of 10 women players in different attire]
Pistol Pete says Hewitt, Agassi will produce a baseline classic
Defeated Hewitt proud of his efforts as the grand masters take centre stage

A closer look at the articles in the *SMH* during the period of the Open suggest other themes, such as nationalism and age, intersecting with those associated with gender. For instance, the majority of the articles in the *SMH* on male players, certainly until his defeat by Andre Agassi in a semi-final were either partially or totally about the Australian player, Leyton Hewitt. In the lead up to the semi-final the relationship between Hewitt and Agassi is constructed as one between a much 'younger man', currently number one, with his future before him, and the experienced veteran and family man. An article titled and subtitled, 'The kid is all fight: an aging Andre Agassi's lost it and wants it back but Leyton Hewitt won't let the title slip without a struggle', begins with the sentence:

> The first time Andre Agassi played Leyton Hewitt, the Australian was 16, wearing oversized shorts with a safety pin to hold them up, and 'looking like he had a couple of strings in his shoes'.
>
> (Overington 2002c: 31)

The words used in the article to describe Agassi include 'swifter and leaner', as 'being in great shape' (no matter what his age); he is quoted talking about his family and his responsibilities to his son and wife on the days before the match. Hewitt is described as having few responsibilities, he can 'relax a bit, have something to eat, and try to sleep before the match'. He is also described in terms of the pressure on him as current world number one, particularly when he has achieved this level at such 'a young age'. Hewitt (and Agassi) are written about in ways which allow for them to lose, at least from the perspective of the writers in the *SMH*, without disgrace. Both stories are acceptable – the older man who has years of successes behind him defeated by the young man who will replace him or the young man defeated this time by the veteran, but who has many years more to make his mark.

This construction of the situation is confirmed by the headlines the day after Hewitt's defeat by Agassi: 'Defeated Hewitt proud of his efforts as the grand masters take centre stage: Andre Agassi's experience overcame Leyton Hewitt's youth'. The nationalistic theme continues as Caroline Overington writes about Hewitt's ordeal as he played under difficult circumstances with an American crowd against him and against an experienced player (who is also described as having Hewitt's ex coach in his box). All of these themes are taken up in the following quote:

> Hewitt was beaten by Andre Agassi in Saturday's semi-final. There is no shame in that. After all it took some courage just to walk on court, where 23,000 foot-stomping, flag-waving fans had gathered to pray for his demise.
>
> Hewitt has few friends in New York. The stadium at Flushing Meadows was titled firmly against him. Enormous stars-and-stripes banners were swirling through the heat. The crowd was not so much cheering for Agassi as braying for the downfall of the world's No. 1. One particularly offensive man in a large orange shirt kept screaming: 'Finish off the kang-a-roo!'
>
> (Overington 2002d: 19)

Those sections of the article that are not about Hewitt's management of his defeat and his reactions to the American crowd are primarily a breakdown of the statistics of the match and a brief section on Agassi's feelings about the match and his preparation for the match with Sampras. The final two sentences point to a continuation of a theme which has been evident throughout the Hewitt/Agassi and now Sampras coverage: 'The final will be the first fought out between two men in their 30s. Wheelchairs are ready.' In terms of the wider world of sport, this sentence supports an assumption that sport is for young people, that is, people under

30, and not for the middle aged or elderly. Like any discourse, if oft repeated and if it fits with existing assumptions or beliefs, it becomes part of what is taken for granted. A point of view that sport is only for the young serves to marginalise those who are not young, it leads them and others to assume that they cannot be active in the kinds of ways a vigorous sport demands.

As demonstrated above the amount of coverage dedicated to the female participants in the 2002 Tennis Open is not much less than that of the men. Indeed the largest photographs, often taking up half a page, are of women and these are mostly action shots. As suggested above the headlines that accompany the photographs and the choices of angles in the photograph suggest that the coverage does little to challenge both racial and gender stereotypes. The other major participant in the Open coverage besides Leyton Hewitt was Serena Williams. She was written about in relation to three main themes: her choice of clothing, the contest with her sister, and the man who was stalking her. There are two large action photographs of Williams. The first is a three-quarter shot to the upper thigh, taken from the side, her back arched as she prepares to serve. The angle of the first photograph is one very common in the coverage of Serena Williams, emphasising as it does the angle of her breast and buttocks. In this photograph the intention seems to emphasise the 'sexiness' of her 'oily blackbody suit [which] she called . . . a catsuit' (Overington 2002a: 38). Williams herself is quoted as describing the suit as 'sexy', but adds that it also makes her 'run faster and jump higher'. The headline that accompanies this article is 'Cat woman pounces but beaten prey is still a winner'. The headline is a play on the 'catsuit' that captured much of the attention of the press during the Open. The article is about 'poor Corina Morariu' who drew Serena Williams in the first round. The first four paragraphs are taken up with a description of the effects of her fight against leukemia on Morariu. She is described as 'blushing and holding up her racquet as the crowd gave her warm applause' and later in the article, as having now returned to the women's tour with 'a full head of soft curls and a pretty determined look on her face'. In contrast to the fragility of Morariu, Williams is constructed here and elsewhere as tough, strong and forbidding. The author of the article uses Williams own words to write: 'She agreed it was "unfortunate" that she had to play Morariu but, hey, this is a grand slam, "and we're like animals out there"' (Overington 2002a: 38). This reference to 'animals' seems to be consistent with the way in which both Williams sisters are constructed as aggressively sexual rather than 'feminine', as voluptuous women who exhibit what are traditionally the character-istics in white western society associated with men.

The second photograph supports this interpretation. It is a full front shot, again to the lower thigh, where she is making ready to hit a backhand shot. The photograph is taken from below, a position that is generally associated with increasing the 'power' of the person photographed (Kress and Van Leeuwen 1990). Williams' mouth is wide open and her whole body tensed ready for a powerful backhand. It is a photograph which makes her look like a warrior, ready for battle; it emphasises her power, muscularity and toughness. The caption, however, for this photograph is 'A screamer: Serena Williams puts her all into a backhand return during the US Open final' (Overington 2002e: 19). Through the use of the word 'screamer' to sum up the image, it serves to minimise the power evident in the camera angles and choice of shot. There is something of a theme of describing female tennis players derogatively in terms of the noises they make: Monica Seles as a 'grunter' and Serena Williams as a 'screamer'. Such references serve to trivialise the power and effort behind their play. The article that accompanied this photograph is primarily about the relationship between the two sisters, particularly with Serena's defeat of Venus Williams in the Open.

The nature of the coverage of the other female tennis players in the Open is fairly predictable. One of the remaining large photographs (no accompanying article) is a mirror image of Hantuchova and Mauresmo with arms raised in a winning salute (*SMH*, 4 September 2002: 40). The caption is 'Light and power: they may use different methods but Daniela Hantuchova, left, and Amelie Mauresmo share a similar taste for fashion and winning at the US Open'. An article on Jelena Dokic explores her 'poor performance' in relation to her 'troubled relationship with her father', despite quoting Dokic as saying that 'it wasn't a factor' (Overington 2002b: 29). The photograph accompanying the article has Dokic slumped in a chair eyes closed. A third extended article, reproduced from the *Los Angeles Times*, discusses the fairness of Haas being asked to remove his sleeveless shirt in the context of the 'revealing' clothing the women are permitted to wear. This again is accompanied by a side-on photograph of Serena Williams back arched and breasts and buttocks accentuated. The photograph of Haas has him sitting in a chair, taking another shirt out of his bag while an official looks on.

These examples of the coverage from a mainstream broadsheet newspaper point to a number of sets of beliefs and values which are being drawn on to make the texts interesting by connecting with what are anticipated to be readers' beliefs, values and points of view. So what beliefs, values and points of view are being both constructed and drawn on to produce these texts? The first is the most obvious one and that is the ways in which what it means to be female and male in western society are constituted by the differences in coverage of the female and male tennis players. For tennis, unlike other sports such as soccer, rugby league, gridiron, rugby union, baseball and so on, there is very little difference in the amount of coverage. Tennis therefore seems to be a sport in which both men and women's forms of the game are judged to be equally of interest to readers. A closer analysis of the nature of the coverage, however, suggests a set of themes that do little to challenge dominant discourses or mainstream points of view associated with nationalism, gender, race and sport. It could be argued on the other hand that the Williams sisters, through the ways in which they choose to represent themselves as strong and sexy, do challenge stereotypical notions of white femininity, and further that the media is challenged in the way in which they deal with this. However, other research (Davis and Harris 1998, cited in Denham *et al*. 2002) suggests that black athletes, in general, are often described in terms of their physicality and their 'natural ability' rather than their strategic capacity or their intellect. The level of analysis here does not allow for these themes to be explored in detail, but they certainly provide further possibilities for investigation.

Conclusion

This chapter has endeavoured to provide an argument and a method for a critical analysis of media coverage of sport and physical activity. The example provided is only one way of working with media texts. Sports coverage is an obvious target for investigation, but media analysis in the context of physical education should go beyond a focus on sport. Physical education, as is often pointed out, is the only area in the school curriculum particularly concerned with the body. This should not be limited to the sporting body either in the physical components of physical education or in the more theoretical components. A media analysis then should also look at the many different ways the media takes the active (or inactive) body as its focus, including the meanings constructed about health, fitness and body shapes, the representations of different kinds of physical activity and the people who engage in them, the ways in which the body is constructed in and through the advertising of the fitness industry and so on. The advantage of the media is that students are avid consumers and much more than we often imagine quite critical consumers; these talents and interests can be drawn on and extended to help produce students who can engage critically with the barrage of information and entertainment in the 'information age'.

References

Bassett, G. (1990) 'Masculinity and the representation of sport on television', a paper presented at the Commonwealth Conference on Sport, Physical Education and Leisure, Auckland, New Zealand.

Brown, P. (1998) 'Representations of place: imaging Newcastle through media coverage of the 1997 Australia Rugby League Grand Final', *ACHPER Healthy Lifestyles Journal* 45(4): 5–9.

Burroughs, A., Ashburn, L. and Seebohm, L. (1995) '"Add sex and stir": homophobic coverage of women's cricket in Australia', *Journal of Sport and Social Issues* 19(3): 266–84.

Denham, B.E., Billings, A.C. and Halone, K.K. (2002) 'Differential accounts of race in broadcast commentary of the 2000 NCAA men's and women's final four basketball tournaments', *Sociology of Sport Journal* 19: 315–32.

Fairclough, N. (1992) *Discourse and Social Change*, Cambridge: Polity Press.

Fairclough, N. (1995) *Media Discourse*, London: Edward Arnold.

Kane, M.J. (1996) 'Media coverage of the post title IX athlete: a feminist analysis of sport, gender and power', *Duke Journal of Gender Law and Policy* 3(95): 95–127.

Kinnick, N.K. (1998) 'Gender bias in newspaper profiles of 1996 Olympic athletes: five contemporary major dailies', *Women's Studies in Communication* 21: 212.

Kirk, D. (1997) 'Schooling bodies for new times: the reform of school physical education high modernity', in J.-M. Fernandez-Balboa (ed.) *Critical Aspects in Human Movement*, Albany: SUNY Press.

Kress, G. and Van Leeuwen, T. (1990) *Reading Images*, Geelong: Deakin University Press.

Lenskyj, H. J. (1998) '"Inside Sport" or "On the Margins"? Australian women and the sport media', *International Review for the Sociology of Sport* 33(1): 19–32.

Luke, A., O'Brien, J. and Comber, B. (1994) 'Making community texts objects of study', *Australian Journal of Language and Literacy* 17(2): 139–149.

McKay, J. (1995) '"Just do it": corporate sports slogans and the political economy of enlightened racism', *Discourse: Studies in the Cultural Politics of Education* 16: 191–201.

MacNeill, M. (1998) 'Sex, lies and videotape: the political and cultural economies of celebrity fitness videos', in G. Rail (ed.) *Sport in Postmodern Times*, New York: SUNY Press.

Markula, P. (2001) 'Beyond the perfect body: women's body image distortion in fitness magazine discourse', *Journal of Sport and Social Issues* 25(2): 158–79.

Media Awareness Network (2003) 'What is media literacy?' http://www.media-awareness.ca/eng/med/bigpict/mlwhat.htm (24 January 2003).

Mikosza, J. M. and Phillips, M. G. (1999) 'Gender, sport and the body politics: framing femininity in the "Golden Girls of Sport" Calendar and the "Atlanta Dream"', *International Review for the Sociology of Sport* 34(1): 5–16.

Overington, C. (2002a) 'Cat woman pounces but beaten prey still a winner', *Sydney Morning Herald*, Aug 28: 38.

—— (2002b) 'Frankly games to blame, declares stoic Dokic', *Sydney Morning Herald*, Aug 30: 29.

—— (2002c) 'The kid is all fight', *Sydney Morning Herald*, Sept 6: 31.

—— (2002d) 'Defeated Hewitt proud of his efforts as the grand masters take centre stage', *Sydney Morning Herald*, Sept 9: 19.

—— (2002e) 'Serena's streak leaves Venus waning', *Sydney Morning Herald*, Sept 9: 19

Pirinen, R. (1997) 'Catching up with men? Finnish Newspaper coverage of women's entry into traditionally male sports', *International Review for the Sociology of Sport* 32(3): 239–49.

Phillips, M. (1997) 'An illusory image: a report on the media coverage and portrayal of womens sport in Australia 1996', Canberra: Australian Sports Commission.

Special Broadcasting Service (SBS) (2002) 'SBS Triennial Funding Submission 2003–2006' http://www.sbs.com.au/sbscorporate (23 March 2003).

Tinning, R. (2002) 'Toward a "modest pedagogy": reflections on the problematics of a critical pedagogy', *Quest* 54(3): 224–40.

Wilson, B. (1997) '"Good Blacks" and "Bad Blacks": media constructions of African-American athletes in Canadian basketball', *International Review for the Sociology of Sport* 32(2): 177–89.

Wright, J. and Clarke, G. (1999) 'Sport, the media and the construction of compulsory heterosexuality: a case study of women's rugby union', *International Review for the Sociology of Sport* 34(3): 227–43.

Part IV

The challenges of critical inquiry in physical education

Chapter 15

New practices, new subjects and critical inquiry

Possibility and progress

David Kirk

Introduction

The notion of a critical pedagogy was introduced to the sport and physical education community in the early to mid-1980s (e.g. Kirk 1986; Lawson 1984; McKay and Pearson 1984). This early work challenged some conventional assumptions, ideas and practices in physical education teacher education and sports science degree courses, and was intended mainly for the consumption of teacher educators and prospective teachers. While the notion attracted some interest in the latter half of the 1980s, it was also roundly criticised for being long on critique and short on constructive alternatives (e.g. O'Sullivan *et al.* 1992). At the time, much of the writing on critical pedagogy was concerned with advocacy rather than action, and this critical response was perhaps justified.

The chapters in this volume show the extent of the progress that has been made in shifting from advocacy to action in the intervening period. Wright and Macdonald in Chapters 1 and 2 set out some of the theoretical premises of their interest in critical inquiry and problem-solving, while the remaining chapters provide research evidence of how these notions might be implemented with students in school programmes. The notions of problem-solving and critical inquiry embrace a range of practices, as well as theoretical perspectives on student learning, from concerns for the technical and personal through to the ideological and social, respectively. Macdonald's overview of learning theories requires the identification of behaviourism, information-processing and social constructivism to capture the range of the authors' concerns and, indeed, the continuum of teacher-directed to student-centred learning.

At one end of the continuum of practices are Sanders', Mallet's, and Griffin and Sheehy's chapters, which are concerned primarily with problem-solving in relation to the technical and tactical challenges presented by physical activities, such as games and sports. Griffin and Sheehy provide excellent examples of how to modify tasks in order to offer graded challenges to players of different levels of ability. A little further along this continuum is Hastie's chapter, concerned with problem-solving in relation to team administration, team preparation and game play challenges that can be met during a season of sport education. Hastie's focus is broadened further through his idea of establishing a sports board and allied committees for sport education in order to provide young people with opportunities to practice participatory democracy, at least with respect to local concerns.

New Zealand's attempts to recognise aspects of Maori culture in physical education recounted by Burrows, and Macdonald's report of the implementation of a rich task centred on the organisation of a sports festival, each contains elements of problem-solving in relation to actual physical activities. Their principle concern, however, is with issues that go beyond physical activity, in Burrows' case to ethnicity and Macdonald's to an integrated learning experience. Fitzgerald and Jobling's chapter focuses on student-lead research with young disabled people, while Wright's chapter shows how a range of analytical techniques can be used to examine the media and sport. Neither of these examples involves actual participation in physical activity and might be located at the critical inquiry end of the continuum, since they are each concerned with ideology critique.

Gard's chapter on movement, art and culture alone attempts to show how it might be possible to move across the entire continuum of technical and personal through to ideological and social and do this through physical activity experiences. Indeed, Gard addresses explicitly the relationship between the notions of problem-solving and critical inquiry and suggests that each addresses issues at a different level and of a different order. He uses dance as movement education, dance as art and dance as culture to provide examples of how problem-solving and critical inquiry can be centred on the experience of embodiment. His work presents a radical challenge to physical education, for reasons I will elaborate shortly.

This range of concerns represented by the continuum of problem-solving and critical inquiry is in my view highly appropriate. Each chapter presents important, significant and constructive criticisms of current practices in physical education, and each provides evidence of new possibilities for physical education in schools. At the same time, the authors are quick to point to potential barriers to change, and to other challenges facing any education system, researcher, school or teacher who may wish to take up these challenges. In order to understand the scale of the challenges facing the approaches to physical education proposed by the authors, I will map out in the next section some of the historical forces that construct the context in which their proposals are being made. I will then note some of the contemporary forces the authors identify as part of their rationale for the shift towards forms of critical inquiry. In light of this analysis, I conclude by assessing the prospects for problem-solving and critical inquiry approaches and their potential to provide a guide to new forms of physical education.

Schooling for docility–utility: sketching the historical context of current school practices

The authors are quick to emphasise that notions of critical inquiry and problem-solving are not new, either in education more generally or in physical education in particular. They point by way of example to the work of John Dewey and to the movement of educationists, respectively. But despite these examples, in the historical context of the practice of mass compulsory schooling in late modernity, these are indeed new ideas with radical implications.

Contemporary schools first appeared in their current form between the 1860s and 1880s in countries such as Britain, Australia and the USA, when laws were passed requiring all children between the ages of approximately 5 to 13 years to attend school. Schools developed two key institutional imperatives at this time. The first was the social regulation of the cadre of children by working on the bodies of the children. Faced with large groups of students who came from families where there was no tradition of attending school on a regular basis, schools developed a range of what Foucault (1979) called 'little practices', many of which were concerned with the movement of children's bodies in time and space. For instance, the timetable was invented in this context to provide regularity and predictability to the school day. Children were required to sit in rows, often in an order that showed explicitly their rank as scholars within the class. Children were subjected to drilling and exercising that used military notions of rank and file to make the observation of their behaviour easy to see and correct when necessary. But if this first imperative was for (in Foucault's terms) 'docility', for obedience, the second was for 'utility', for productivity. Mass compulsory schooling was paid for from public funds. Consequently, the second imperative was to produce productive bodies, children who would become healthy, robust adults, able to contribute to national and domestic economies. These roles were of course strongly gendered at this time, with the expectation that men would be bread-winners and women child-bearers and child-rearers.

Arguably, contemporary schools have retained these two key institutional imperatives in scarcely altered form (Kirk 1999). Practices of regulating bodies may be less severe that they were in Victorian England, for example, but they nonetheless remain central to the operation of schools for the masses. Attempts to subvert these key features of schooling provide evidence of their longevity and immutability. For instance, A.S. Neill's so-called free-school at Summerhill, established in the 1920s, developed a certain notoriety precisely because Neill attempted to change the power relationships between pupils and teachers and to remove compulsion in terms of how students spent their time (Neill 1968). Another example is the de-schooling movement and its notable contributors such as Everett Reimer (1971) and John Holt (1977). A further example within the more conventional school system was the movement to open plan classrooms in primary schools. In Britain during the 1970s, schools were built to a new design that dispensed with classroom walls in order to facilitate the implementation of an integrated curriculum. As Hamilton (1977) noted, however, this experiment failed, at least in its original form, as teachers began to use partitions to re-assert their own classroom spaces and the conventional institutional imperatives of schooling.

Within this institutional context, where the dual imperatives of schooling for docility–utility have remained more or less intact for more than a century, school learning has regularly been characterised as abstracted from real life. Lave (1997) refers to this view of learning as the 'culture of acquisition', in which it is assumed that it is the task of the school to transmit to children the valued accumulated factual knowledge of a society, and it is children's task to acquire and reproduce this knowledge. She claims it is further assumed that:

> Cognitive benefits follow only when the process of learning is removed from the fields in which what is learned is to be applied. This belief underlies standard distinctions between formal and informal learning, so-called context-free and context-embedded learning, or logical and intuitive understanding. Schooling is viewed as the institutional site for decontextualizing knowledge so that, abstracted, it may become general and hence generalizable, and therefore transferable to situations of use in the 'real' world.
>
> (Lave 1997: 18)

Building on Lave's work, Walkerdine (1997) argues that the culture of acquisition remains valued and dominant in schools because it forms part of a larger set of discourses concerned with civilised rationality and governmentality. She points out that the ways of thinking required by school versions of mathematics, for example, as rational, logical and unemotional, are deeply sexist, racist, class-based and ethnocentric. Walkerdine (1997) argues that it is important to more fully develop Lave's notion of practice. She suggests that practices produce 'subjects', which are in the Foucauldian sense discursive constructs rather than actual individuals. For example, during the history of the modern school, the practices of developmental psychology produced 'the child' as a subject of schooling, a norm against which actual children could be measured in terms of their capacities to 'get it' within the culture of acquisition. The production of a subject also describes the delimited range of positions a particular individual might be able to occupy in relation to other individuals, and the ways in which they can relate to other positions. In other words, the notion of a subject position not only establishes a measure for normalcy within a practice, but it also inscribes relations of power between subjects. If, as Walkerdine suggests, practices produce subjects, then the practice of school learning will inevitably produce particular relations of power among learners and between learners and other members of the school community.

There is a striking parallel between Lave's and Walkerdine's critiques of school learning in subjects such as mathematics and critiques of traditional forms of sport-based physical education. For example, Siedentop (1994) argues that the teaching of sport in physical education has been decontextualised and abstracted in a similar way to mathematics.

> Skills are taught in isolation rather than as part of the natural context of executing strategy in game-like situations. The rituals, values and traditions of a sport that give it meaning are seldom even mentioned, let alone taught

in ways that students can experience them. The affiliation with a team or group that provides the context for personal growth and responsibility in sport is noticeably absent in physical education. The ebb and flow of a sport season is seldom captured in a short-term sport instruction unit . . . physical education teaches only isolated sport skills and less-than-meaningful games.

(Siedentop 1994: 7–8)

This decontextualisation of learning is made possible by what Ennis (1999) calls the multi-activity curriculum model that is a dominant and widespread approach to organising school physical education. This model is characterised by short units of activity (six to ten lessons), minimal opportunities for sustained instruction, little accountability for learning, weak or non-existent transfer of learning across lessons, units and year levels, few policies to equalise participation between boys and girls (in co-ed) and high–low skilled players, and a student social system that undermines teacher authority. It might be argued that Ennis' and Siedentop's criticisms are most pertinent to the context of the USA. However, as Curtner-Smith (1999), Penney and Chandler (2000), Green (1998), Jones and Cheetam (2001) and Williams and Bedward (2001) each show, the emergence and consolidation of the national curriculum physical education since the early 1990s has done little to dislodge this or a similar form of the sport-based, multi-activity curriculum as the centre-point of physical education practices in schools in England and Wales.

Like the critique of school mathematics, there is a large body of evidence to suggest that this decontextualised approach to physical education disadvantages girls (Williams and Bedward 2001; Wright 1996), particular ethnic groups (Benn 1996; Vescio et al. 1999), and alienates motorically less gifted (Carlson 1995) and disabled young people (Kosma et al. 2002), while reproducing and celebrating hegemonic masculinity (Nilges 1998; Wright 1997). Moreover, a ubiquitous and leading goal of many multi-activity physical education programmes is to promote lifelong participation in physical activity. This aspiration is based on the assumption that, presented with an introduction to a wide range of activities, young people will find one or two that will sustain their interest and participation. Yet all of the available research evidence collected since the late 1960s shows that only a small proportion of adults elect to participate in the competitive sport activities that dominate secondary school programmes (Deem and Gilroy 1998; Kirk 1996; Kirk et al. 1996).

This is the context in which the authors in this volume are writing about critical inquiry and problem-solving. There can be no question that, even if the notions are not necessarily novel, they are radical in their implications nevertheless. If practices produce subjects in the sense that Walkerdine (1997) outlines, then the pedagogies of critical inquiry and problem-solving may produce young people who challenge and possibly subvert the institutional imperatives for docility–utility. At the very least, such pedagogical practices may alter this dual goal of docility–utility to an extent that it is barely recognisable compared with its current form. This,

I believe, is indeed the authors' intent in this volume, and so it is not unreasonable to describe this purpose as radical in its implications for schooling in general and for physical education more particularly.

From primary to recontextualising fields

As Wright (Chapter 1 in this volume), Macdonald (Chapter 2), and Burrows (Chapter 8), each note, there has been a trend within syllabuses and policy documents, especially in Australia and New Zealand, to propose that students engage in forms of critical inquiry. There would appear to be at least four reasons for this shift, identified by Wright, Macdonald, Glasby and Macdonald, and Burrows:

- A shift on a global scale to knowledge-based economies, signaling important changes to workplace practices.
- The ongoing development and everyday use of information and communication technologies.
- Shifts in physical culture, such as the ongoing development of media sport, and increasing professionalisation, commercialisation and commodification of a range of physical activity practices, including leisure activities.
- Increasing recognition of the cultures of ethnic minorities in the context of ongoing migration and the occurrence of ethically and socially diverse communities.

None of these developments is directly related to the practices of physical education, nor even the practices of schooling. They are developments that have occurred in what Basil Bernstein (1990) calls the primary field of knowledge production. In this field, knowledge enters the public domain through the work of a range of knowledge-producing agencies, such as universities and other research organisations, government policy-makers, and commercial agencies, such as multinational companies.

The contributions to this book provide an excellent example of the possibilities for the reconstruction of school knowledge when agents in another of Bernstein's fields, the recontextualising field, are able to access knowledge produced in the primary field and rework it into a pedagogical form in the course of constructing school subject syllabuses.

Agents in this recontextualising field include seconded teachers, academics, specialist curriculum writers and education bureaucrats. They have an explicit remit to write curricula for use in Bernstein's secondary field, where schools, teachers and students are located. But they do not always necessarily access the primary field in the process of constructing new syllabuses. Indeed, evidence from a number of studies of curriculum development using Bernstein's framework shows that more often curriculum writers' main point of reference when producing new syllabuses is practices within the secondary field of educational institutions

(Glasby *et al.* 2001). The consequence of so doing is that writers tend to merely reproduce previous forms of the subject, resulting in innovation without change. And the real risk of merely reproducing former versions of a subject, as in the case of Harold Benjamin's cautionary tale of the sabre-tooth curriculum, is cultural obsolescence (Peddiwell 1939).

What makes this collection of papers important is it shows that genuinely new forms of physical education are possible when agents in the recontextualising field attend to social, cultural and economic developments at large. Burrows' chapter provides an excellent example of how a growing recognition of Maori cultures in New Zealand has resulted in the reconstruction of physical education to incorporate traditional Maori forms of physical activity. Wright's chapter on media demonstrates in a very explicit way how students themselves can be provided with analytical tools that enable them to access and critique the knowledge production process of various media in relation to physical culture. Glasby and Macdonald's chapter likewise builds on an analysis of shifts in workplace practices predicated on the development of information technologies to suggest that nego-tiation of content and of assessment practices will inevitably become part of school practices.

Producing new subjects through new practices: future prospects for critical inquiry

Each of these papers also shows that the movement of knowledge from the recontextualising to secondary fields is fraught with difficulties. Macdonald's chapter reporting on her experiences of attempting to implement in Spender High School rich tasks built on the principle of curriculum integration shows what can happen when an innovation based on constructivist learning theories and aimed at critical inquiry meet head on with the institutional imperatives of docility–utility. It is important that we do not dismiss Macdonald's study as merely another example of the failure of an innovation to take hold in the 'real world' of school. I want to suggest instead another reading built on Lave's analysis of the culture of acquisition and Walkerdine's notion that practices produce subjects.

I want to suggest the reasons why the teachers in English, Art and HPE were so apparently busy and unable to accommodate Macdonald's and her teacher colleague's requests for assistance, and for the students' apparent scepticism, are directly concerned with the disruption the rich task threatened to the institutional practices that produce docility–utility. To make this point another way, the rich task did not merely call for a reorganisation and redeployment of teacher time, classroom space and resources. It also projected a different subject to the conventional student identity based on docility–utility.

Michael Gard's chapter brings these issues into stark relief. To do embodied critical inquiry through dance, to 'think their way into the movement' and to 'move as a way of imagining' has the potential to create a new subject position, but one that is currently quite inconsistent with and potentially subversive for current and dominant forms of school practice. This is why Gard, quite properly, has serious concerns about the location of dance within a physical education context, and why at the same moment he sees the massive potential to locate dance as a regular aspect of physical education.

The key issue that Gard makes explicit and that the other contributions to this book also identify and tackle in various ways is the relationship of school practices to the construction of what Bourdieu calls the habitus (see Shilling 1993). The habitus for Bourdieu is the embodiment of an individual's experiences over time, an accumulation of ways of being that have been learned to fit the range of social situations in which a person acts and is acted upon. In short, the habitus is the material embodiment of social values, dispositions and tastes. To promote problem-solving and critical inquiry through the forms of physical education described in this book is to attempt to interrupt the habitus of students and their years of socialisation into particular ways of being embodied. For some, conventional forms of physical education match closely with the values, dispositions and tastes they have already encountered and accommodated in their lives. These young people are the sporty, active and enthusiastic students. For others, school physical education is foreign and alienating, most clearly illustrated by Fitzgerald and Jobling in the case of young disabled people and Burrows in the case of the Maori in New Zealand.

What this collection of papers does, in the face of what is a frankly enormous task, a task that challenges the defining institutional imperatives of contemporary schooling, is to show that such radical change is possible. The chapters by Griffin and Sheehy, Mallet, Sanders and Hastie show that young people can become more physically capable in relation to a range of physical activities. More than this, through pedagogical models such as tactical games and sport education, they can come to see these dominant forms of sporting activity differently. The chapters by Glasby and Macdonald and Fitzgerald and Jobling provide a persuasive case for the educational benefits that can flow from giving young people the ability and responsibility for generating their own knowledge and determining how they wish their competence to be judged. Despite Macdonald's apparent failure to successfully implement a rich task at Spender High and despite the challenges Burrows describes to new syllabuses incorporating Maori ways of knowing, both chapters present ideas that are worth thinking and working with further.

In all of this, the authors are correct to argue that their ideas and proposals are responding to advocacy in society broadly for new notions of citizens and workers. If school is to have any relevance in this process, radical solutions are indeed required. The kinds of subjects currently produced by the practices of schooling cannot hope to produce the citizens and workers that it has been argued are required for the future. But for these problem-solving and critical inquiry practices to work in schools, all educational workers including teachers, administrators and teacher educators need to understand that the practices that produce the subjectivity of docility–utility, however appropriate these may have been to the late nineteenth and early twentieth centuries, have now surpassed their usefulness. In this respect, this book can perhaps provide a guide to its readers as to where the future of physical education in schools must lie if it is to retain its cultural relevance in new times.

References

Benn, T. (1996) 'Muslim women and physical education in initial teacher training', *Sport, Education and Society* 1(1): 5–22.

Bernstein, B. (1990) *The Structuring of Pedagogic Discourse*, London: Routledge.

Carlson, T.B. (1995) 'We hate gym: student alienation from physical education', *Journal of Teaching in Physical Education* 14: 467–77.

Curtner-Smith, M.D. (1999) 'The more things change, the more they stay the same: factors influencing teachers' interpretations and delivery of the National Curriculum Physical Education', *Sport, Education and Society* 4(1): 75–98.

Deem, R. and Gilroy, S. (1998) 'Physical activity, life-long learning and empowerment – situating sport in women's leisure', *Sport, Education and Society* 3(1): 89–104.

Ennis, C.D. (1999) 'Creating a culturally relevant curriculum for disengaged girls', *Sport, Education and Society* 4(1): 31–50.

Foucault, M. (1979) *Discipline and Punish: The Birth of the Prison*, London: Penguin

Glasby, T., Glover, S., Kirk, D., Macdonald, D. and MacPhail, A. (2001) 'Constructing pedagogic discourse in health and physical education: understanding curriculum change through the work of Basil Bernstein', roundtable presentation to the American Educational Research Association Annual Meeting, Seattle, April.

Green, K. (1998) 'Philosophies, ideologies and the practice of physical education', *Sport, Education and Society* 3(2): 125–43.

Hamilton, D. (1977) *In Search of Structure: A Case Study of a New Scottish Open-plan Primary School*, London: Hodder and Stoughton.

Holt, J. (1977) *Instead of Education*, Harmondsworth: Penguin.

Jones, R. and Cheetam, R. (2001) 'Physical education in the National Curriculum: its purpose and meaning for final year secondary school students', *European Journal of Physical Education* 6: 81–100.

Kirk, D. (1986) 'A critical pedagogy for teacher education: towards an inquiry-oriented approach', *Journal of Teaching in Physical Education* 5(4): 230–46.

—— (1996) 'The crisis in school physical education: an argument against the tide', *The ACHPER Healthy Lifestyles Journal* 43(4): 25–7.

—— (1999) 'Embodying the school/schooling bodies: physical education as disciplinary technology', in C. Symes and D. Meadmore (eds) *The Extra-Ordinary School: Parergonality and Pedagogy*, New York: Peter Lang.

Kirk, D., Nauright, J., Hanrahan, S., Macdonald, D. and Jobling, I. (1996) *The Sociocultural Foundations of Human Movement*, Melbourne: Macmillan.

Kosma, M., Cardinal, B.J. and Rintala, P. (2002) 'Motivating individuals with disabilities to be physically active', *Quest* 54(2): 116–32.

Lave, J. (1997) 'The culture of acquisition and the practice of understanding', in D. Kirshner and J.A. Whitson (eds) *Situated Cognition: Social, Semiotic and Psychological Perspectives*, New Jersey: Erlbaum.

Lawson, H.A. (1984) 'Problem-setting for physical education and sport', *Quest* 36: 48–60.

208 David Kirk

McKay, J. and Pearson, K. (1984) 'Objectives, strategies and ethics in teaching introductory courses in sociology of sport', *Quest* 36: 261–72.

Neill, A.S. (1968) *Summerhill*, Harmondsworth: Penguin.

Nilges, L.M. (1998) 'I thought only fairy tales had supernatural power: a radical feminist analysis of Title IX in physical education', *Journal of Teaching in Physical Education* 17(2): 172–94.

O'Sullivan, M., Siedentop, D. and Locke, L. (1992) 'Toward collegiality: competing viewpoints among teacher educators', *Quest* 44: 266–80.

Peddiwell, J.A. (1939) *The Sabre-Tooth Curriculum*, New York: McGraw-Hill.

Penney, D. and Chandler, T. (2000) 'Physical education – what future(s)?', *Sport, Education and Society* 5(1): 71–88.

Reimer, E. (1971) *School is Dead*, Harmondsworth: Penguin.

Shilling, C. (1993) *The Body and Social Theory*, London: Sage.

Siedentop, D. (1994) 'The sport education model', in D. Siedentop (ed.) *Sport Education: Quality PE through Positive Sport Experiences*, Champaign, IL: Human Kinetics.

Vescio, J., Taylor, T. and Toohey, K. (1999) 'An exploration of sports participation by girls from non-English speaking backgrounds', *ACHPER Healthy Lifestyles Journal* 46(2/3): 14–19.

Walkerdine, V. (1997) 'Redefining the subject in situated cognition theory', in D. Kirshner and J.A. Whitson (eds) *Situated Cognition: Social, Semiotic and Psychological Perspectives*, New Jersey: Erlbaum.

Williams, A. and Bedward, J. (2001) 'Gender, culture and the generation gap: student and teacher perceptions of aspects of the national curriculum physical education', *Sport, Education and Society* 6(1): 53–66.

Wright, J. (1996) 'The construction of complementarity in physical education', *Gender and Education* 8(1): 61–80.

Wright, J. (1997) 'The construction of gendered contexts in single-sex and co-educational physical education classes', *Sport, Education and Society* 2(1): 55–72.

Index